The Rise of the Indonesian Financial Service Authority

Chandra Kusuma

The Rise of the Indonesian Financial Service Authority

Domestic Implementation Gaps in Portfolio Investment Liberalization

palgrave
macmillan

Chandra Kusuma
Fiscal Policy Agency
Ministry of Finance of the Republic
of Indonesia
Jakarta, Indonesia

ISBN 978-981-19-3849-8 ISBN 978-981-19-3850-4 (eBook)
https://doi.org/10.1007/978-981-19-3850-4

This Palgrave Macmillan imprint is published by the registered company Springer Nature Singapore Pte Ltd.
The registered company address is: 152 Beach Road, #21-01/04 Gateway East, Singapore 189721, Singapore

Preface

The pursuance of more open and liberal international portfolio investment flows by Association of South East Asia Nations (ASEAN) has created observable gaps in domestic policy implementation between the regional commitments to financial liberalization and domestic implementation in Indonesia. In order to explain these gaps, in this book, I focus on a newly established authority within Indonesian financial services institutions that has emerged as the ultimate decision-maker for portfolio investment liberalization, the Indonesian Financial Services Authority (FSA). My main argument in this book is that, in the area of portfolio investment liberalization, the emergence of the Indonesian FSA has resulted in implementation gaps in Indonesia. I reveal that the endowment of an 'independent and free' status, as well as the FSA's power over the Indonesian financial sector, has allowed agents in the FSA to provide different positions or responses to the already agreed ASEAN financial liberalization initiatives.

Contrary to the expectations of most neoliberalism writers that the independent status of an institution would advance financial liberalization, I unfold that the 'independent and free' status of the Indonesian FSA has actually stymied financial liberalization. In doing so, I employed a modified account of the historical institutionalism approach, or 'the agents-in-context' approach, examining how and why the Indonesian FSA has emerged as an independent authority. The insight drawn from applying a modified historical institutionalism approach to the case study of Indonesian portfolio investment liberalization is the original contribution to knowledge, to critique and complement existing works in the regionalism literature in general, and ASEAN financial integration particularly.

Further, in this book, I also explain how agents within the Indonesian FSA operate within their institution to stymie the ASEAN liberalization of portfolio investments process. I expose that these agents were further attempting to harness other international standards, such as the Basel Standards or the International Organization of Securities Commissions (IOSCO) Principles, towards the 'national interest'. The agents appear to only consider the standards as one of the tools to develop their own domestic market, and still seem reluctant to commit to the international financial regulatory standards if the standards particularly resulted in opening up further financial services liberalization. I further disclose that the enactment of the new Indonesia Trading Law creates another domestic stumbling block for ASEAN's portfolio investments liberalization agenda. Post-2015, the ratification of an international liberalization agreement is required to go through higher scrutiny by escalating the process for the approval to the House of Representative. Thus, Indonesian FSA agents are using this as an opportunity to resist ASEAN portfolio investments liberalization initiatives. I expect to contribute to the body of knowledge on Indonesia, specifically the relationship between regional governance policy initiatives on portfolio investment liberalization, and the domestic political/bureaucratic context in Indonesia. I also hope to contribute to the analysis of implementation gaps in the ASEAN Community more generally by focusing on a prominent topic in a major ASEAN state.

Jakarta, Indonesia

Chandra Kusuma

Acknowledgements

"*Then which of the favours of your Lord will you deny?*" (Surah 55 of the Quran)

Alhamdulillah (Praise be to Allah)

I dedicate this book to my parents, my wife and my two children. I am always indebted to my mother, Erlina Yusni, and my late father, Damojo, who never had the opportunity to attend a university only for me to get the highest education possible. I am grateful to my wife, Renata Sadjad, for her continuous support and inspirations in accompanying me during the process of publishing this book. Thank you for continuously being on my side. My daughter, Aqila Shafiqah Chandra, you are the source of my intelligence and my inspiration for not giving up. My son, Akram Sirath Chandra, you are one of Allah's countless blessings to the family.

My sincere gratitude and highest appreciation to my mentors and colleagues at the School of Political Science and International Studies, The University of Queensland in Brisbane, Australia—Prof. Shahar Hameiri, Dr. Melissa Curley and Prof. Stephen Bell. Thank you for your patience, support, guidance and advice for me to finally produce this book. Allow me to also lengthen the acknowledgement here to my only brother, Muhammad Agung Darlianto, as well as my Parents-in-Law for their continued support and prayers, Dr. Rhiza and Erna Sadjad. Thank you for adding colour to my life and reminding me to be continuously humble and modest. Thank you for believing in and keep praying for me.

I wish to acknowledge that the empirical research carried out as parts of most contents in this book were financially supported by the Australia Awards Scholarship of the Department of Foreign Affairs and Trade (DFAT), Australia.

I also wish to acknowledge the two anonymous reviewers for the proposal stage, and the two anonymous reviewers for the manuscript stage, as facilitated by the Palgrave Macmillan. Last, but not least, I would like to thank all members of the team at the Palgrave Macmillan providing an end-to-end support for publishing this book.

Contents

1	**Introduction**	1
	The Indonesian Financial Services Authority (FSA)	2
	Operational Definitions	3
	The Domestic Implementation Gaps	7
	Scope and Limitation	14
	Contribution to Literature	15
	Research Design	16
	Structure of the Book	17
	References	19
2	**Modified Historical Institutionalism**	21
	Early Literature on Regionalism	22
	Approaches That Explain Domestic Policy Implementation	23
	Institutionalism and Modified Historical Institutionalism Approach	36
	Sociological Institutionalism	37
	Rational-Choice Institutionalism	39
	Historical Institutionalism	40
	Modified Historical Institutionalism	43
	"Agents-in-Context" Approach	46
	References	50

3 **The Emergence of the Indonesian FSA** 55
Indonesia and the Early Financial Liberalization (1980s–1996) 57
Indonesia and the 1997–1998 Asian Financial Crisis 64
The Early Proposal for a Single Financial Services Authority (1999–2003) 66
Delays in the Establishment of the Indonesian FSA (2004–2010) 72
The Transition Period (2011–2013) 79
Conclusion 85
References 86

4 **The Indonesian FSA and Stymied Portfolio Investments Liberalization** 89
The Indonesian FSA Power and Authorities 91
Asean Trading Link 97
Asean Framework for Cross Border Offering of CIS 104
ASEAN Disclosure Standards 109
ASEAN Banking Integration Framework 113
Other Related Flows 118
International Financial Standards And Regional Financial Integration 119
Basel Committee on Banking Supervision Standards 122
IOSCO Objectives and Principles of Securities Regulation 124
IAIS Insurance Core Principles 127
The Roles of the Indonesian MOF and Bank Indonesia in Portfolio Investment Liberalization Post the Establishment of the Indonesian FSA 132
The Financial Sector Stability Committee (FSSC) 140
Conclusion 145
References 147

5 **Emerging Challenges to Domestic Implementation of Portfolio Investments Liberalization** 149
The Enactment of the New Trading Law 151
Domestic Legal Ratification Process in Indonesia 154
The Case of Ratification of the AFAS Protocol and SOC 161
Conclusion 170
References 171

6 Conclusion 173
The Agents-in-Contexts 173
The Domestic Implementation Gap 176
References 178

Index 179

List of Charts

Chart 3.1	Crude oil price (1975–1987) (*Source* World Bank DataBank)	59
Chart 3.2	GDP growth (annual %)—world (1975–1987) (*Source* World Bank DataBank)	60
Chart 3.3	GDP growth (annual %)—Indonesia (1975–1987) (*Source* World Bank DataBank)	61
Chart 3.4	Indonesia portfolio equity, net inflows (balance of payments, current US$) (*Source* World Bank DataBank)	65
Chart 3.5	The Indonesian FSA transition period (*Source* Indonesian FSA Internal Document)	81
Chart 4.1	The Indonesian FSA organizational structure (*Source* Indonesian FSA Internal Document)	92
Chart 4.2	ASEAN Trading Link Illustration (*Source* Securities Exchange of Thailand [SET])	98
Chart 4.3	Asset Composition of the Indonesian Financial Services Sector * (*Source* Indonesian Financial Services Sector Master Plan 2015–2019; *Data as of 2014)	117
Chart 4.4	Indonesia financial system safety net framework: coordination mechanism (*Source* Adapted from Law Number 9 of 2016 & Indonesian MOF Internal Document)	142

Chart 4.5 FSCC Coverage (*Source* Indonesian MOF Internal Document) 144
Chart 5.1 Illustration of the domestic ratification process in Indonesia (post-2015) (*Source* Adapted from Indonesian MOF Internal Document) 159

List of Tables

Table 1.1	Summary of observable implementation gaps	10
Table 3.1	Jakarta composite index performance (1996–1998)	65
Table 4.1	Position of approval from "Home Jurisdiction" and "Host Jurisdiction"	106
Table 4.2	Indonesia observance status to the IAIS insurance core principles	130
Table 4.3	Financial Stability Committees (FSCs) in the world	145
Table 5.1	Ratification of AFAS protocol and SOC—Indonesia	162

CHAPTER 1

Introduction

The ASEAN Economic Community (AEC) Blueprint 2015 has provided an overall guideline for each nation to "transform ASEAN into a region with free movement of goods, services, investment, skilled labour, and freer flow of capital" (ASEAN, 2008). The more recent AEC Blueprint 2025 also provides details about how to achieve more open and liberal Association of Southeast Asia Nations (ASEAN) international portfolio investment flows (ASEAN, 2015, 2016). However, the response from Indonesia is puzzling in the sense that Indonesian political elites express their best intentions and commitment to adhere to the regional standards being commissioned by ASEAN; that is, to facilitate more open and liberal ASEAN international portfolio investments flows. Meanwhile, domestic policies do not reflect this conformity with the regional standards, or policy steps to achieve it partially or incrementally. Thus, while Indonesian political elites keep agreeing on ASEAN initiatives for a more open and liberal international portfolio investment regime, as is evident within the top ASEAN leadership, at the bureaucratic level domestic authorities in Indonesia evidently show different responses to maintain the existing regime. Therefore, I aim to unfold why are there gaps in the domestic implementation of a more liberal international portfolio investment regime in Indonesia?

C. Kusuma, *The Rise of the Indonesian Financial Service Authority*,
https://doi.org/10.1007/978-981-19-3850-4_1

The Indonesian Financial Services Authority (FSA)

I focus on a newly established authority within Indonesian financial services institutions that has emerged as the ultimate decision-maker for portfolio investments liberalization, the Otoritas Jasa Keuangan (OJK), hereinafter referred to the Indonesian Financial Services Authority (FSA). This emergence itself is a result of the legal enactment of Law Number 11 Year 2011 on the Indonesian FSA, providing the legal basis for its status as the sole authority for financial sector supervision in Indonesia. I argue that, using the case of portfolio investment liberalization, the emergence of the Indonesian FSA has resulted in domestic implementation gaps in Indonesia. The endowment of an "independent and free" status as well as the FSA's full power over the Indonesian financial sector has allowed FSA bureaucrats to provide different positions to the already agreed ASEAN financial liberalization initiatives. Thus, in contrary to the expectations of most writers (such as the works of Gill, 1995; Overbeek, 2005; Pijl, 1998) on institutional independence in the context of neoliberalism, FSA agents have actually stymied liberalization, rather than advance it. Furthermore, and also in contention with prevailing wisdom, these bureaucrats are further attempting to harness international standards, such as the Basel Standards or the International Organization of Securities Commissions (IOSCO) Principles, not towards advancing liberalization, but towards advancing what they see as Indonesia's "national interest", thus constraining the domestic implementation of the already committed regional integration initiatives. While the ultimate goal of the international standards is regulatory convergence leading to closer financial integration, the Indonesian FSA seems to only consider the standards as one tool to develop Indonesia's own domestic market. Placing the national interest first, the FSA seems reluctant to commit to the international financial regulatory standards, if those standards result in further financial services liberalization.

I then also unveil another emerging challenge to portfolio investments liberalization in Indonesia with the enactment of the new Indonesian Trading Law, Law of the Republic of Indonesia Number 7 Year 2014 on Trading. The enactment has shifted the policymaking process related to portfolio investment liberalization by involving the Parliament and providing the possibility of wider public involvement. Thus, as revealed in this book, this law creates another domestic stumbling block for ASEAN's portfolio investment liberalization agenda. It is an additional challenge for further domestic implementation of regional portfolio investments. Later I reveal that increasing trade protectionism policies, as well as the enhancement of a checks and balances system on liberalization efforts, were the central background to the enactment of the new Indonesia Trading Law. Although, on the flip side, the law emerged initially as a response to the old and outdated Dutch colonial law related to trading. The enactment of this law marks the instigation of Indonesian trade-related laws and regulations, over the use of Dutch colonial law. In addition, the law also emerged as an effort to synchronize all other related laws and regulations related to trading.

To explain the domestic implementation gaps, I examine how and why the Indonesian FSA has emerged as an independent authority. Further, I also aim to explain how agents within the FSA use the "independent and free" status to stymie the liberalization process of portfolio investments. In order to achieve these related goals, I deploy an approach that is able to fully comprehend the existence of domestic implementation gaps in portfolio investments liberalization. Most importantly, the approach accounts for interactions between institutions and agents. The emergence and operationalization of the FSA derived from neoliberal ideas. Over time, the interaction between agents in Indonesia and these ideas produced the contemporary FSA. Instead of promoting neoliberal ideas as initially intended by adopting portfolio investments liberalization, the Indonesian FSA seems to stymie liberalization. This is to say that the interactions here are not only limited to the account of how ideas affect the conduct of agents, but also the account of agents' interplay in shaping the institutions. In addition, I also need to consider the structural context surrounding agents and implementation, as institutional transformation is also a result of interactions between agents and structural constraints. To that extent, I adopt a modified account of the historical institutionalism approach, as employed in Bell and Feng (2013) and Bell and Hindmoor (2015), or "the agents-in-context" approach. The deployment of this approach covers the historical emergence of the FSA.

Operational Definitions

The following definitions are provided to clarify key terms utilized throughout the book. By ASEAN top leaders, I mean the highest ranks in the ASEAN governance structure. At the ultimate level, ASEAN's governance structure consists of the heads of states that meet biannually. The highest reporting line in the ASEAN governance structure is the ASEAN Summit. It "shall comprise the Heads of State or Government of the Member States" (ASEAN, 2007, p. 10), and oversee the three-Councils, namely the ASEAN Political-Security Community (APSC) Council, the ASEAN Economic Community (AEC) Council, and the ASEAN Socio-Cultural Community (ASC) Council. Initiatives related to portfolio investment liberalization are under the reporting line of the AEC Council. At the implementation level, there are the sectoral ministerial bodies. Portfolio investment liberalization initiatives fall under the purview of one of these sectoral ministerial bodies, namely the ASEAN Finance Ministers' Meeting (AFMM), along with the Technical Committees and Forums under its reporting line, such as the ASEAN Capital Market Forum (ACMF), the Working Committee on Financial Services Liberalization (WC-FSL) and the Working Committee on Capital Account Liberalization (WC-CAL). For instance, the initiatives for portfolio investment liberalization are usually provided and endorsed by ASEAN top leaders (mostly at the Ministerial or Central Bank Governor level, later escalated for endorsement at the Summit). The next governance structure directly under the head of states is the ministerial level as represented by the Ministers of the related sectors. The discussions of portfolio investment liberalization in ASEAN is currently under the financial services liberalization and the purview of ministers for the financial services sector.

Further down are the three Technical Committees and Forums mentioned above, the ACMF, the WC-FSL and the WC-CAL. Under the ACMF, AMS aims to facilitate a closer integration and liberalization of member's capital markets. For instance, the ASEAN Trading Link and the ASEAN Framework for Cross Border offering of CIS, that I discuss in more detail later, are under the coverage of the ACMF. The WC-FSL covers the other financial services liberalization initiatives, including insurance, pension funds and other financial services institutions. Since its establishment, regulation and supervision of these other financial services are under the sole authority of the Indonesian FSA. WC-CAL discusses more integrated and liberalized capital account flows among AMS in the region. Overall, all these three Technical Committees and Fora focus their work on achieving closer financial integration and liberalization in ASEAN. Indeed, the Indonesian MOF is the focal point for these three Technical Committees and Fora because ASEAN's institutional framework recognizes only the MOF in its structure. However, the ACMF and the WC-FSL scope of works fall under the authority of the FSA.

In addition, the works of the WC-CAL also fall under the authority of Bank Indonesia. As for the term "different responses", I mean that Indonesian bureaucratic officials pursue different domestic policy from the agreed ASEAN initiatives. Officials clearly exhibit a more conservative approach to portfolio investment liberalization. Thus, there is an implementation gap between the high-level commitments and the implementation of policy at the domestic level. The central focus of this book is to examine the existence of the implementation gap and explain its emergence, particularly in the area of portfolio investments liberalization.

In order to clearly define the boundaries of instruments classified as "portfolio investments", they are defined here as provided for by the International Monetary Fund (IMF) below:

> ...cross border transactions and positions involving debt or equity securities, other than those included in direct investment or reserve assets...covers, but is not limited to, securities traded on organized or other financial markets...usually involves financial infrastructure, such as a suitable legal, regulatory, and settlement framework, along with market-making dealers, and a sufficient volume of buyers and sellers.... (IMF, 2009, Balance of Payments and International Investment Position Manual, p. 110)

In addition, stemming from several Free Trade Agreements (FTAs) and Bilateral Investment Treaties (BITs) that Indonesia is a party to, the coverage of portfolio investments in this book includes "shares, stocks, bonds and debentures and any other forms of participation in a juridical person and rights or interest derived therefrom" (ASEAN Comprehensive Investment Agreement, 2009, p. 7). Further, I exclude the classification of foreign direct investments (FDI) from the discussions due to its different nature from the portfolio investments.

Meanwhile, the term "political elites", for the purpose of this book, refers to the leaders and sub-leaders of the state. This definition captures the division of elites as suggested by Dahl (1989). This definition is open to debate, for instance as suggested by Blondel and Müller-Rommel (2007). Pakulski and Tranter (2015) argue that the practical definition of political elites includes "the incumbents of the most powerful positions of power and authority in the largest, most influential and most resource-rich national organisations, primarily the state itself" (p. 19). Consistent with the operational definition of the high-level governance structure in

ASEAN as mentioned in the preceding paragraph, these leaders constitute the ASEAN Summit and the ministerial level elites, depending on the sectors, constitute the ministerial level structure under the ASEAN Summit. Meanwhile, the bureaucratic level refers to the bureaucrats in the Indonesian FSA as well as the surrounding institutions, in this case the Indonesian MOF and the Bank of Indonesia. As the Indonesian FSA has emerged in a central role in portfolio investment liberalization, its bureaucrats have exercised their authority in the public policy process to provide different positions on how portfolio investment liberalization should proceed.

As mentioned in the earlier section, FSA bureaucrats are also utilizing their institutional status to harness the international standards towards the "national interest" and elude the domestic implementation of the regional integration initiatives already committed to. Thus, international standards within this book means the most recognized international standards related to portfolio investment liberalization with worldwide assessments and applications. In practice, some notable ASEAN financial integration initiatives operate under the full compliance of all or most parts of international financial standards. Regional integration requires that states adhere to the most recognized international standards. For instance, a regional integration initiative under the ASEAN Capital Market Forum (ACMF) requires compliance with most parts of the International Organization of Securities Commissions (IOSCO) Objectives and Principles of Securities Regulation. Meanwhile, I see "national interest" as one of the major public policy principles in Indonesia that prioritizes the Indonesian public interests over other interests. The interpretation of the term "national interest" itself is often associated with the weighing of the benefits and detriments of a policy for the general public in Indonesia. Although in practice, this interpretation may diverge among domestic institutions. For instance, the FSA seems to weigh the detriment of the volatile portfolio investment flow and the protection of domestic financial industry in implementing portfolio investment liberalization policies.

Lastly, as an important part of the approach employed throughout this book, the term "agents" refers to high-level officials (Chief Executive Officer/CEO level) as well as all the bureaucratic level under the leadership of those high-level officials. Throughout, this book will show that the Indonesian FSA's high-level officials (Chief Executive Officer/CEO level) as well as all the bureaucratic level are utilizing their wider structural contexts to stymie domestic portfolio investment liberalization. To this extent, "agents" here are mutually shaping the institution, the Indonesian FSA. Thus, the "agents-in-context" approach that operationalized throughout empirical chapters in this book. The features of "mutually shaping" relationships between agents and institutions, as well as the account on wider structural contexts to that relationships, are central to the operationalization steps of the approach. For instance, the operationalization of "agents-in-context" approach in Chapter 3 in this book is to identify the backgrounds to the emergence of the Indonesian FSA. In doing so, this identification allows the identification of primary agents as well as the isolation of related institutions along the five different time periods. The identification of backgrounds here, as commonly found in a traditional historical institutionalism, is also to determine the "critical juncture" and "path dependence" that highly correlate with institutional changes.

The Domestic Implementation Gaps

It is important to initially describe the nature of the gaps in domestic implementation in Indonesia itself to provide the existing context for the progress of portfolio investment liberalization. In one instance, to further liberalize the ASEAN equity and debt market, ASEAN elites have agreed to implement the ASEAN Trading Link that connects exchanges among ASEAN states using an electronic platform (ASEAN, 2017; ASEAN Capital Market Forum, 2016). Through the establishment of this link, ASEAN expects that there will be one centralized access point in the region to give investors the ease of access to ASEAN capital markets. Agreeing to this ASEAN Trading Link means Indonesia needs to adopt a business model that, firstly, allows the overseas capital market broker to trade capital market products directly on the Indonesia Stock Exchange (IDX). Secondly, adoption of the business model also requires Indonesia to deregulate its overseas clearing and payment system to settle capital market products cross-border trading. However, Indonesian officials still maintain the regime of restricting capital market products trading solely through the domestic capital market broker and using the domestic clearing and payment system for settlement. As to date, the regulatory framework and policies in Indonesia prohibit cross-border trading using an overseas capital market broker or overseas clearing and payment system. In addition to equity and debt markets, there are also discussions in ASEAN on moving forward for more "flavored"[1] products, such as for Real Estate Investment Trusts (REITs) or Exchange-Traded Funds (ETFs). However, bureaucrats in the Indonesian FSA have expressed reluctance to move forward as they are even being conservative with the plain products.

In another instance, ASEAN elites have also agreed to implement the ASEAN Disclosure Standards that aim to facilitate the offering of equity and debt products across multiple states in the region. ASEAN expects that this will provide ease of facility towards issuers, since there will be only one set of prospectuses disclosure standards to prepare for products offering in the region (ASEAN, 2017; ASEAN Capital Market Forum, 2016). A single set of disclosure standards means Indonesia needs to deregulate its disclosure standards by, firstly, allowing the use of an overseas trustee in the capital market product cross-border offering. Secondly, Indonesia needs to allow the use of overseas capital market professionals to do their business in Indonesia cross-border without a physical presence. Finally, Indonesia is required to adopt a one-approval regime for disclosure. This means that if a capital market product has been offered and approved for trading in one state, it can also be automatically traded in another state without further registration and approval by local authorities. However, the current regulatory framework and policy in Indonesia still maintains the compulsory domestic trustee in any capital market product offering, both domestic and cross-border. The same policy of "only domestic allowed" also applies to the engagement of capital market professionals. As for a one-approval regime for disclosure, bureaucrats in the Indonesian FSA still maintain the policy of registration and approval by local authorities to any capital market product offered within Indonesian jurisdiction.

Meanwhile, for other related flows, such as external borrowings and lending in the banking sector, ASEAN elites have agreed to a further liberalization of the remaining restrictions (ASEAN, 2016, 2017). This means that elites committed to open all of Indonesia's banking sector transactions, including in trade credits, loans, currency, deposits and other assets

[1] The term "flavored" here refers to the inversion of the plain-type investment products. While the plain-type investments products point to basic or simple products (such as bonds, or futures, or options), "flavored" products mean that there are modifications made to the plain-type investment products, making them more of complex securities (such as REITs and ETFs).

and liabilities. In general, Indonesia has allowed the external lending and borrowing in trade credits. However, the gaps in domestic implementation are mostly in transactions other than trade credit. For instance, bureaucrats in the FSA still maintain the limitation on banks' foreign loans of up to 30% of reserve. There is also a restriction to place the Indonesian Rupiah deposit from Indonesian Rupiah foreign exchange purchasing. Another instance are restrictions on loans to non-residents for consumer credit and domestic use purposes. All these restrictions are expected to be liberalized under the commitment made by ASEAN elites, thus leaving domestic implementation gaps in Indonesia. Regardless, in all the abovementioned implementation gaps, bureaucrats in the FSA clearly exhibit a more conservative approach to portfolio investment liberalization than that deliberately committed to in ASEAN.

Details of the observable implementation gaps are mostly as summarized in the following Table 1.1. Table 1.1 also shows the pursuit by ASEAN of a more open and liberal regime of portfolio investments to achieve overall regional financial integration. Thomas (2007), in his work on early ASEAN financial regionalism, also has previously explained this pursuit by concluding that:

> there is a vision of the region, an AEC, which places a high value on deeper economic and financial integration as the engine of future regionalisation. Indeed, across all policy dialogues is the clear recognition that economic and financial integration is the keystone for any future regionalisation. (p. 153)

However, as also revealed in Table 1.1, there are still detailed domestic implementation gaps in ASEAN portfolio investment liberalization in Indonesia. Some scholars in ASEAN have noticed, in general, the existence of such domestic implementation gaps. For instance, Nesadurai (2014), as she explored the political economic reality of the ASEAN states, suggested that:

> Although policy-makers appear to recognize the growth and employment benefits of liberalization and regional integration, they also embrace varying degrees of state intervention in the domestic economy in order to meet those domestic distributive and non-economic goals that they believe cannot be effectively achieved through economic liberalization and the market mechanism. (p. 413)

Table 1.1 Summary of observable implementation gaps

Nature of transactions	*Transactions to be liberalized*	*Related ASEAN strategic initiatives for liberalization*[a]	*Indonesia existing implementation (Gap)*
Portfolio inflows			
Equities and debt	• Domestic purchases by non-residents • Domestic companies raising funds abroad • Issues by residents abroad	• *ASEAN Trading Link* The ASEAN Trading Link connects exchanges among ASEAN states using an electronic platform. Through the establishment of this link, investors will have one centralized access point in the region to give investors the ease of access to ASEAN capital markets • *ASEAN Exchange Connectivity* The Connectivity aims to integrate the Central Counter Party (CCP) and Clearing system, and the Custodian Central Depository (CSD) and Settlement system • ***ASEAN Banking Integration Framework*** (ABIF) ABIF allows Qualified ASEAN Banks (QABs) to integrate fully and to be given market access within ASEAN. The end goal of this integration would be to facilitate intra-ASEAN trade and investment	• Officials wish to still maintain the current regime of exchanges and to decline in committing to the initiatives of ASEAN Trading Link and ASEAN Exchange Connectivity • Specifically, to integration plan of CCP and Clearing system as well as CSD and Settlement System, officials also wish to decline such integration • Officials still wish to halt the development of ABIF in terms of fully integrating the banking system. However, they are open partially to the idea of QABs. As of current, officials prefer to opt for bilateral banking system cooperation. ASEAN views that such bilateral agreements may eventually lead to full integration

Nature of transactions	*Transactions to be liberalized*	*Related ASEAN strategic initiatives for liberalization*[a]	*Indonesia existing implementation (Gap)*
Other related inflows[b]			
External borrowings (Banks)	• Trade credits • Loans • Currency • Deposits • Other assets and liabilities	• *Further liberalization of the remaining restrictions subject to* ***domestic conditions and appropriate safeguards***	• External borrowing in trade credit transactions is generally allowed • Officials wish to still maintain the limitation on bank's foreign loan up to 30% of reserve • Officials wish to still maintain the right to examine incoming Indonesian Rupiah and Foreign Currency that exceeds Rp. 100 million or $10,000[c] • Officials wish to maintain the restriction to place Indonesian Rupiah deposits from Indonesian Rupiah foreign exchange purchasing[c] • Officials wish to still maintain the requirement of minimum 1-week derivative tenor and the obligation to submit underlying[c]

(continued)

Table 1.1 (continued)

Nature of transactions	*Transactions to be liberalized*	*Related ASEAN strategic initiatives for liberalization*[a]	*Indonesia existing implementation (Gap)*
Portfolio outflows			
Repatriation of funds			Repatriation of funds is generally allowed in Indonesia
Equities and debt	• Non-residents Raising Funds Domestically • Purchases Abroad by Domestic Residents	• *ASEAN Framework for Cross Border Offering of Collective Investment Scheme* (CIS) The Framework introduces a streamlined authorization process for mutual fund managers to make cross-border offerings to retail investors in the ASEAN region • *ASEAN Disclosure Standards* The Standards aim to facilitate the offering of equity and debt products across multiple states in the region. This provides will provide ease of facility towards issuers, since there will be only one set of prospectuses disclosure standards to prepare for products offering in the region • *Streamlined Review Framework for ASEAN Common Prospectus (Framework)* The Streamlined Review Framework for the ASEAN Common Prospectus was initiated to streamline the reviewing process of prospectuses if issuers want to list or offer equity and plain debt products	• Overall, regulatory framework in Indonesia is already aligned with the standards set in ASEAN Framework for Cross Border Offering of CIS. However, officials still wish to decline to commit to the framework due to unresolved issues, such as Assets under Management (AUM) limitation • Overall, regulatory framework in Indonesia is unable to follow the standards as set in ASEAN Disclosure Standards and the Streamlined Review Framework. Officials still wish to decline to commit to the framework to maintain the current restrictions in place • Foreign Banks (non-residents) are basically allowed to raise funds domestically. However, officials wish to maintain the policy that the funds raised shall be for domestic use only • Officials wish to maintain a prohibition for Banks to purchase equities abroad • Officials wish to maintain a prohibition for domestic Pension Funds and Insurance companies to purchase equities abroad

Nature of transactions	*Transactions to be liberalized*	*Related ASEAN strategic initiatives for liberalization*[a]	*Indonesia existing implementation (Gap)*
Other related outflows[b]			
External lending (banks)	• Trade credits • Loans • Currency • Deposits • Other assets and liabilities	***Further liberalization of the remaining restrictions subject to domestic conditions and appropriate safeguards***	• External lending in trade credit transactions is generally allowed • Banks are basically allowed to give loan to non-residents. However, such loan is restricted only for for consumer credit and domestic use purposes[c] • Officials wish to still maintain the right to examine outflows of Indonesian Rupiah and Foreign Currency that exceeding Rp. 100 million or $10,000[c] • Officials wish to still maintain the requirement of minimum 1-week derivative tenor and the obligation to submit underlying[c]

[a]The strategic initiatives for liberalization as set out in the column refers to initiatives that have been endorsed by ASEAN elites (mostly at the ministerial level, later escalated for endorsement at the Summit). These initiatives have also been formally documented in ASEAN documents

[b]The inclusion of other related inflows and outflows to this summary mostly with regard to the close connection of banking lending and borrowing activities with portfolio investment in the form of, for instance, real estate investment. In addition, there are also discussions on specific products, such as Real Estate Investment Trusts (REITs) or Exchange-Traded Funds (ETFs)

[c]This position is based on data collected prior to 2015

Source Author's Analysis

Overall, in responding to more open and liberal portfolio investment liberalization, officials either still decline to join a related ASEAN strategic initiative or to maintain the existing regulatory regime.

Scope and Limitation

In this book, I do not examine the reasons for the Indonesian political elites' decisions to agree to ASEAN's financial liberalization initiatives in the first place. My focus is on showing that there are domestic implementation gaps relative to already agreed initiatives, and explaining these gaps. I also only cover the extent of the contemporary historical emergence of the Indonesian FSA as an independent authority in the Indonesian financial sector. Thus, for instance, the Law Number 23 Year 1999 on Bank Indonesia mostly regulates the independent status of the Indonesian central bank. However, the focus of this book is on the content of the law that directly correlates to the rise of the Indonesian FSA. This book also limits the focus of the ASEAN regional integration initiatives only to portfolio investment liberalization initiatives due to methodological constraints and the vast coverage of ASEAN regional integration initiatives. There are undoubtedly other substantial regional integration initiatives in the financial sector alone, such as in the areas of customs or money laundering or taxation issues. However, these other initiatives are beyond the scope of discussion in this book.

The scope of this book is largely on portfolio investment liberalization due to the importance of the portfolio investment flows within the context of Indonesian political economy. For instance, later, I associate volatile Indonesian economic conditions before the Asian Financial Crisis in 1997–1998 to portfolio investment flows liberalization in the 1990s. That condition was ultimately one of the major factors that brought down President Soeharto after thirty-two years in power. Thus, portfolio investments have played an important role in Indonesian history, and is an important part of the story of the rise of the powerful Indonesian FSA in financial services supervision. The impact of international portfolio investment inflows and financial liberalization has long been the subject of scholarly debate. Some scholars argue that overflows of portfolios in the case of financial integration might not be apparent or positively correlated with the economic development of emerging countries (Hwang & Sitorus, 2014; Rhee & Yang, 2014). However, prominent literature on the subject still suggests that financial liberalization, especially in the form of more relaxed regulatory framework and/or unrestricted capital controls, would encourage more international portfolio investment flowing into states, or "hot money" flows, demanding more appropriate policy measures domestically in each state and regionally (such as the works of Agénor, 2003; Kabigting & Hapitan, 2012; Mendoza, et al., 2009; Rethel, 2012; Rodrik & Velasco, 1999; Xaypanya et al., 2015). Thus, states need to be vigilant to financial liberalization efforts that are expected to bring "hot money" flows.

The results of empirical work laid out in this book are findings from the field, with all the limitations provided. These include limitations such as inability to access all the meetings and classified documents. Limitation of access here affects the scope of the discussions in the book. For instance, in order to continuously update the works of financial liberalization, one may need to attend series of meetings. In doing so, one can get full background picture behind an official's decisions in an international forum. There may also be internal policy or background papers behind an official's decisions that cannot be retrieved during the field. Thus, this book relies on the formal positions of the Indonesian FSA agents delivered during meetings, as well as formal position of the Indonesian FSA as transcribed in the unpublished internal documents. Another major limitation is the reluctance of the interviewees to provide more detailed information due to the status of the interviewer as a senior official in Indonesian MOF. For instance, a market player or an association member in the financial sector may hold back and talk normative when they knew that the interviewer affiliates with the government or a former regulator.

Contribution to Literature

I expect to contribute to existing literature in the following ways. Firstly, the insight drawn from applying a modified historical institutionalism approach to the case study of Indonesian portfolio investment flow liberalization will form part of the book's original contribution to knowledge, to critique and complement existing works in the regionalism literature in general and ASEAN financial integration in particular. Secondly, I expect to contribute to the body of knowledge on Indonesia, specifically the relationship between the regional governance policy initiatives on portfolio investment flow liberalization, and the domestic political/bureaucratic context in Indonesia. In this sense, it will also add to the literature of

Indonesian domestic politics as well as regional debates about ASEAN and its sustainable and utility. Thirdly, I will also contribute to wider debates about ASEAN Centrality, particularly those focusing on the limitations of operationalizing regional agreements for ASEAN into the future. Fourthly, from a practical point of view, I expect to contribute to the analysis of Indonesian domestic policies on portfolio investment flow liberalization. Thus, related parties in Indonesia may refer to this book in formulating future strategy to deal with the gaps in responding to ASEAN initiatives. Finally, I will also add to the analysis of the implementation gaps in the ASEAN community more generally by focusing on a prominent topic in a major ASEAN state.

Research Design

The book is primarily a qualitative study, using descriptive and evaluative methods. I choose to use the single case study of Indonesia because of the consideration that the research aims to provide a deep-explorative and context-specific description of the issues. The research utilizes semi-structured qualitative interviews with officials and experts from Indonesia, as well as market players or associations in the region. Officials from the Indonesian MOF, Bank Indonesia and the Indonesian FSA. In addition, I also extend the qualitative interviews to ASEAN officials leading the Working Groups and Task Forces under the ASEAN cooperation framework, as well as ASEAN Secretariat officials, where possible. The aim of these semi-structured qualitative interviews was to gather as much information as possible in exploring the existing implementation gaps with those committed to in ASEAN. This also enabled the capture of underlying rationales, unambiguously or obliquely, behind the implementation gaps.

Another method I employed is an extensive review of primary and secondary material including relevant existing documents, memos, annual reports and minutes of meetings attended. In order to analyse these various documents and transcripts, I use content analysis along with other methods. The aim of using content analysis is mainly to outline and review the corresponding ASEAN official documents against formal positions adopted by corresponding domestic authorities. Other than those methods mentioned earlier, this research also utilized participant observation methods when attending selected ASEAN meetings, where access is possible. In order to gain access to such meetings, I utilized the networking available from my experience as a public official working in the area of financial liberalization in Indonesia. This direct observation method was useful in identifying discussions during negotiations among AMS that may link up with identified implementation gaps. This method was also important in observing the nuance of negotiations among AMS.

During these direct observations, I acted as an observer. The observer status associates with the representatives from Indonesian domestic authorities to the meeting. For instance, in attending the ASEAN Capital Market Forum (ACMF) meeting, I identified myself as one of the representatives from the Indonesian MOF. However, I acted only as an observer, without any active involvement of any kind. Lastly, I also draw upon available secondary and tertiary quantitative data to contextualize and analyse the material, such as the Gross Domestic Product (GDP) annual growth, the Indonesia portfolio equity net inflows and the historical Jakarta Composite Index (JCI). I collect these available quantitative data from publicly available information, for instance, that provided by the World Bank or the Indonesia Stock Exchange (IDX). In addition, this research also gathered quantitative data from corresponding domestic authorities in Indonesia, such as from the Indonesian MOF, Bank Indonesia and the Indonesian FSA.

Structure of the Book

The organization of the book subsequent to this introduction chapter is as follows. In Chapter 2, I survey the existing literature that has considered and observed the existence of implementation gaps between regional and domestic levels. The survey includes literature that examine the wider applicable context surrounding implementation. The survey particularly looks at approaches that are able to account for bi-directional relations between institutions and agents. I build on the literature review to develop the theoretical and conceptual framework for the rest of the book. The next three chapters after the survey on literature are the empirical analysis chapters based on data collected during fieldwork. In Chapter 3, I outline the contemporary historical emergence of the Indonesian FSA as an independent authority in the financial sector. Central to this chapter is the period where Indonesia had to resort to the IMF as a result of the Asian Financial Crisis. One of the IMF recommendations was to strengthen financial sector supervision through the establishment of an independent financial sector authority. This chapter also accounts for the period where Bank Indonesia emerged as the independent central bank, later also providing backgrounds for the establishment of the Indonesian FSA. This chapter ends at the transitional period of the Indonesian FSA, accounting for the first two years of operations as well as early challenges the institution faced.

Moving to Chapter 4, I seek to explain how agents within the Indonesian FSA operate and what they do. Particularly, this chapter attempts to provide explanations for how the agents use the "independent and free" status of the FSA to stymie the domestic portfolio investment liberalization process. This chapter provides an overview of some of the major initiatives in ASEAN portfolio investment liberalization to describe the way agents reject, halt or substantially delay initiatives. In addition, this chapter deals with the way agents harness international standards towards the "national interest" and avoid the implementation of the regional integration initiatives Indonesia has committed to. As the last empirical chapter of this book, Chapter 5 captures the enactment of the new Indonesian Trading Law as an emerging challenge to further domestic portfolio investment liberalization in Indonesia. This latest development on the enactment of the law is consistent with the FSA agents' efforts to stymie portfolio investment liberalization. The law now requires a domestic ratification process of a portfolio investment liberalization agreement through the House of Representative, rather than enactment by Presidential Decree. Thus, as revealed in the chapter, the law creates another domestic stumbling block for ASEAN's portfolio investment liberalization agenda. To this extent, FSA agents are using one of the main features of the new law, the involvement of the House of Representative in the domestic ratification process, to halt or delay implementation of ASEAN portfolio investment liberalization. Thus, the chapter aims not only to explain the current domestic ratification process of an international financial liberalization agreement, but also to account for the possibility of FSA officials using the process to further stymie portfolio investment liberalization. This chapter also highlights a particular case of ASEAN financial services liberalization to better illustrate the challenges related to the domestic ratification process.

In the concluding chapter, I summarize the overall discussion and how it answered the research questions set out at the beginning. The concluding chapter also puts forward potential areas for further research, as well as practical policy implications, particularly to AMS other than Indonesia.

References

Agénor, P. R. (2003). Benefits and costs of international financial integration: Theory and facts. *World Economy, 26*(8), 1089–1118.

ASEAN (2007). *The ASEAN charter.*

ASEAN. (2008). ASEAN economic community blueprint.

ASEAN. (2009). *ASEAN comprehensive investment agreement.*

ASEAN. (2015). *ASEAN economic community blueprint 2025.*

ASEAN. (2016). *Turning vision into reality for a dynamic ASEAN Community. Annual report 2015–2016.*

ASEAN. (2017). *ASEAN economic community 2025 consolidated strategic action plan.*

ASEAN Capital Market Forum. (2016). *ACMF action plan 2016–2020.*

Bell, S., & Feng, H. (2013). *The rise of the People's Bank of China: The politics of institutional change.* Harvard University.

Bell, S., & Hindmoor, A. (2015). *Masters of the universe, slaves of the market.* Harvard University.

Blondel, J., & Müller-Rommel, F. (2007). Political elites. In *The Oxford handbook of political behavior.* Oxford University Press

Dahl, R. A. (1989). *Who governs? Democracy and power in an American city.* Yale.

Gill, S. (1995). Globalisation, market civilisation, and disciplinary neoliberalism. *Millennium—Journal of International Studies, 24*(3), 399–423.

Hwang, P., & Sitorus, R. E. (2014). A study of financial integration and optimal diversification strategy in ASEAN equity markets. *Journal of Economic Integration, 29*(3), 496–519.

International Monetary Fund (IMF). (2009). *Balance of payments and international investment position manual* (Vol. 6). International Monetary Fund.

Kabigting, L. C., & Hapitan, R. B. (2012). Revisiting financial integration of interest rates of ASEAN5+3, 2000–2011. *Journal of International Business Research, 11*(S3), 1.

Mendoza, E. G., Quadrini, V., & Ríos-Rull, J. V. (2009). Financial integration, financial development, and global imbalances. *Journal of Political Economy, 117*(3), 371–416.

Nesadurai, H. (2014). The political economy of Southeast Asia's foreign economic policies and relations. In R. Foot, S. Pekkanen, & J. Ravenhill (Eds.), *The Oxford handbook of the international relations of Asia.* Oxford University Press.

Overbeek, H. (2005). Global governance, class, hegemony: A Historical materialist perspective. In A. Ba & M. J. Hoffmann (Eds.), *Contending perspectives on global governance: Coherence, contestation, and world order* (pp. 39–56). Routledge.

Pakulski, J., & Tranter, B. (2015). Political elites, elite quality and elite recruitment. *The decline of political leadership in Australia? Changing recruitment and careers of federal politicians* (pp. 17–34). Palgrave Macmillan US.
Pijl, K. v. d. (1998). *Transnational classes and international relations*. Routledge.
Rethel, L. (2012). Each time is different! The shifting boundaries of emerging market debt. *Global Society, 26*(1), 123–143.
Rhee, D., & Yang, D. Y. (2014). Asymmetric effects of global liquidity expansion on foreign portfolio inflows, exchange rates, and stock prices. *Journal of East Asian Economic Integration, 18*(2), 143–161.
Rodrik, D., & Velasco, A. (1999). *Short-term capital flows* (National Bureau of Economic Research Working Paper Series. Working Paper 7364).
Thomas, N. (2007). Developing a regional economic community in East Asia. In M. G. Curley & N. Thomas (Eds.), *Advancing East Asian regionalism*. Routledge.
Xaypanya, P., Rangkakulnuwat, P., & Paweenawat, S. W. (2015). The determinants of foreign direct investment in ASEAN. *International Journal of Social Economics, 42*(3), 239–250.

CHAPTER 2

Modified Historical Institutionalism

I employ a modified version of the historical institutionalism approach, or the "agents-in-context" approach, to explain the policy gaps between Indonesia's commitments in ASEAN in the area of portfolio investments liberalization and domestic implementation of those commitments. The modification of the historical institutionalism approach here is mainly to account for bidirectional interactions between institutions and agents in shaping the overall governance outcome. In addition, the modification is also to account for the inclusion of other structural factors into the context of the agents and institutions "mutually shaping" interactions. Central in this book is the contemporary historical emergence of the Indonesian FSA as an "independent and free" unified financial sector authority and the operationalization of this institution by its agents to stymie the implementation of ASEAN portfolio investment liberalization. The emergence of the Indonesian FSA is the story of an institutional change resulting from the interplay of processes between relevant agents and institutions, within a wider structural context. To that extent, I choose to employ an approach that is able to explain the institutional changes leading to the rise of the Indonesian FSA.

In the immediate section below, I start the survey by discussing early literature on regionalism. In this first part, approaches that do not consider the existence of the domestic implementation gaps is covered. Secondly, survey approaches that do consider the existence of

C. Kusuma, *The Rise of the Indonesian Financial Service Authority*, https://doi.org/10.1007/978-981-19-3850-4_2

the domestic implementation gaps are considered. Included in this survey are neo-Gramscian approaches that put emphasis on the influence of disciplinary neoliberalism, and the contrasting post-structuralist approach that puts emphasis on regulators' governmentality. The discussion on these contrasting approaches leads to a state transformation approach that address the weaknesses of both the neo-Gramscian and post-structuralist perspectives. The state transformation approach puts emphasis on how regional dynamics are internalized and contested within the state. Thirdly, the discussion then looks at regulatory regionalism as a form of regionalism that operates through state transformation. Further on, as the regulatory regionalism and state transformation approach emphasizes the importance of domestic politics in shaping regional governance outcomes, the "oligarchy" thesis on Indonesia and work on "mock compliance" will be examined. The last part of this chapter discusses the institutional theory that I argue providing the most useful perspective on the implementation gaps and the rise of the Indonesian FSA.

Early Literature on Regionalism

This section discusses briefly three prominent early theories on regionalism, namely neo-functionalism, liberal inter-governmentalism and realist theory. This section further concludes that the early literature may be unable to capture existing policy variation across countries. For instance, neo-functionalism focuses on the existence of supranational institutions above domestic regulatory systems (Haas, 1961). According to neo-functionalism, the regionalization process should derive from the willingness of states to submit to large-scale and superior supranational institutions. Thus, neo-functionalism focuses on how the emergence of supranationalism in some areas of policy flows on to others. For instance, neo-functionalism has explained European integration and, predominantly, the creation of the European Central Bank. However, neo-functionalism is not concerned with domestic implementation. As such, the reality of a domestic policy implementation gap does not exist in the assumptions of neo-functionalism. The most important part of neo-functionalism that perhaps relates to the analysis in this book is the point that domestic political actors have roles in the process of integration. For instance, Haas (1961) suggested that the degree of global or regional integration depends on the level of submission of states' political actors to the supranational institution. However, in contemporary regional integration, such as in the case of ASEAN, a state's political actors may not be committed to submit to a supranational institution as is the case in European integration.

Meanwhile, liberal inter-governmentalism acknowledges that there are domestic preferences, but these preferences are consolidated as further reflected at the inter-government level (Moravcsik, 1993; Pollack, 1994). According to liberal inter-governmentalism, the regionalization process should be a result of internationally harmonized domestic government policies. For instance, Moravcsik (1993) explained that the European Community was a result of the orchestration of different states' interests. Like neo-functionalism, liberal inter-governmentalism assumes that there will be no implementation gaps between a regional platform and the domestic level. According to Moravcsik (1993) and Moravcsik and Schimmelfennig (2009), in liberal inter-governmentalism, there is an assumption of a "two-step" process. In the first step process, domestic preferences are formed, and then, in the second step process, appear as a unified position at the international level. Thus, liberal inter-governmentalism may advocate that a policy taken at the regional level has considered domestic preferences. Again, to this end, liberal inter-governmentalism should assume the reality of policy implementation gaps. According to inter-governmentalists, domestic interests must already want a particular regional governance agenda for it to emerge. Realists (such as Drezner, 2007) also suffer the same problem of underplaying domestic contestation in implementation and instead focus heavily on the dominant state actors. For instance, particularly in the area of international finance, Drezner (2007) suggested that Inter-Governmental Organizations (IGOs) basically follow the wishes of the great powers, and if they are unable to follow, they are considered ineffectual. To this end, I look at other explanations that study and consider the existence of domestic policy implementation.

Approaches That Explain Domestic Policy Implementation

This survey starts with the theory of international policy diffusion that partially captures the existence of altered responses provided by domestic authorities in response to the international regulatory framework. "International policy diffusion occurs when government policy decisions in a given country are systematically conditioned by prior policy choices made in other countries (sometimes mediated by the behaviour of international organizations or even private actors or organizations)" (Simmons et al., 2006, pp. 787). In other words, a country may produce policies in reference to the policies taken by other particular countries, or as endorsed by international organizations: for instance, international policy diffusions associated the convergence of financial account openness in East Asia in reference to the completion of financial openness in North America and Western Europe. According to Simmons et al. (2006), the diffusion process itself may take various forms, such as through "coercion", "competition", "learning", and "emulation". Thus, according to the theory of international policy diffusion, domestic implementation gaps are mostly attributable to a state's international interactions and seems to be the result of one or more forms of the diffusion process above.

Simmons et al. (2006) further explained that in "coercion", the stronger states attempt to influence weaker states' policies by "manipulating the opportunities and constraints encountered by target countries, either directly or through the international and nongovernmental organizations" (p.790). Meanwhile, they suggested that "competition" influences other countries' policies to attract investors and buyers. By providing the same regulatory requirements to investors and buyers, for instance, countries are competing for investments. As for "learning", Simmons et al. mentioned that countries adopted policies because there was "a change in beliefs or change in one's confidence in existing beliefs, which can result from exposure to new evidence, theories, or behavioural repertoires" (p. 795). In addition, "emulation" assumed that "policy professionals, academics, international nongovernmental organizations (INGOs), and NGOs can influence governments to adopt new policies simply by making arguments for them" (p. 800). However, from this explanation of the diffusion process, it seems that international diffusion theory still underplays the domestic interactions and institutional context. In the case of Indonesia, the adoption of international standards as domestic regulations implicates complex interactions among domestic authorities and the political process. Thus, although international policy diffusion can partially capture the existence of implementation gaps, the theory suggests that implementation gaps are rather the result of state's international interactions and the diffusion process than domestic contestations.

The survey now turns to other approaches that may better explain the domestic implementation gaps in Indonesia, starting with neo-Gramscian and post-structuralist (governmentality) literature. Both approaches acknowledge that contestation does happen in domestic policy implementation. Hameiri and Jones (2015) describe that both are "more sensitive to how social contestation shapes the formation and operation of governance institutions and the different interests and ideologies privileged by particular regimes and scales" (p. 16). Neo-Gramscian approaches however, overemphasize the solidity of global governance structure as dominant forces behind shifting in domestic governance. In the setting of portfolio investment liberalization, for instance, the dominant forces could be international financial institutions (IFIs), or other international finance standard setters, or transnational organizations imposing the globalization of neoliberalism on states (see Gill, 1995; Overbeek, 2005; Pijl, 1998). Neo-Gramscian approaches thus understand the existence of domestic implementation gaps by reference to the nature of the political project that embed international disciplines in the interests of a transnational capitalist class. Overall, neo-Gramscian approaches put an emphasis on the influence of disciplinary neoliberalism.

Gill (1995) suggested that policies that favour the free-market while preserving the welfare of the higher economic status groups facilitate this embedment. He plainly mentioned that "these policies are cast within a neoliberal discourse of governance that stresses the efficiency, welfare, and freedom of the market, and self-actualisation through the process of consumption" (p. 401). According to him, the imposition of neoliberalism might then take the form of global economic surveillance systems, or international financial standards (such as those of the IMF, World Bank, Bank of International Settlement/BIS or other dominant IFIs), or even through a sovereign bond grade issued by dominant international bond rating agencies (such as those of the "Big Three": Moody's Investors Service, Standard & Poor's and Fitch Ratings). This argument was particularly factual in the case of portfolio investment liberalization in Indonesia. After the Asian Financial Crisis and the fall of the Soeharto regime, one of the ways the IMF had imposed a free-market economy was through the liberalization of the domestic portfolio investment regime. As Gill (1995) also revealed, this imposition from the dominant forces would likely happen in a weak or transitional state. Thus, he expected domestic contestations to arise once the imposed neoliberal discourse is incompatible with the domestic policy implementation.

Overbeek (2005) mentioned that the dominant international forces, such as the IMF or World Bank, are mostly unequipped with the authority to compel states to implement neoliberal ideas. However, he added that the impact and reputation of these dominant forces are so appealing that most states would voluntarily comply with the policy recommendations or restructuring programmes issued by them. He showed that "a wide variety of non-business institutions become subject to a discipline primarily designed for capitalist enterprise" (p. 161), including states, governments or other semi-public institutions. This condition was partly, other than as described in Gill (1995), facilitated by "removing many areas of domestic policy debate from the political arena, and to undermine radical intellectual elites, as a new form of intellectual orthodoxy becomes the dominant framework in which policy issues are cast" (Sinclair, 1994, p. 153). The way neo-Gramscian approach views the domestic implementation gap through the embedding of the "interests of a transnational capitalist class" is perhaps the most relevant point in this discussion on Indonesian implementation gaps. In addition, particularly for Indonesia, the neo-Gramscian view is validated somewhat by the fact that the Indonesian FSA came from a recommendation of the IMF. A key point arising out of the neo-Gramscian perspective is that the Indonesian FSA mirrors the kind of policymaking that neo-Gramscians anticipate, but instead of pursuing further liberalization, the FSA has stymied it. A neo-Gramscian perspective sees resistance to the dominant forces as resistance to neoliberalism, whereas in reality, resistance can involve attempts to harness aspects of international agendas in a fight over power between different domestic coalitions.

In contrast, post-structuralist approaches put the emphasis on regulators' governmentality. Such approaches view the likely unpredictability of governance as a result of dynamics in structural forces. The term "governmentality" itself can be traced back to the concept coined by Michael Foucault in around 1978–1979 during his speech at the Collége de France when he focused on the "genealogy of the modern state" (Foucault, 2007). Lemke (2007) described Foucault's governmentality as:

> First of all, the concept of governmentality demonstrates Foucault's working hypothesis concerning the reciprocal constitution of power techniques and forms of knowledge and of regimes of representation and modes of intervention... Second: rather than presenting an analysis of the development and transformation of political-administrative structures, Foucault concentrates on the multiple and diverse relations between the institutionalization of a state apparatus and historical forms of subjectivation. (p. 44)

After Foucault coined the term "governmentality", there are a number of studies and scholars deploying the governmentality approach (such as Burchell et al., 1991; Barry et al., 1996; Dean & Hindess, 1998).

According to most recent governmentality scholars (Valverde & Mopas, 2004), a range of actors are shaping the overall governance outcome rather than states or other global dominant forces. Thus, the outcome of the governance depends on the degree of power among various actors. Although their work was mainly focusing on security issues, they showed that security governance is currently unbound from the previously dominant domain of states. This is to say that other actors, international or local, have started to increase their roles in security related-issues and de-centred the role of the government. Governmentality, therefore, understands domestic implementation gaps with reference to the interests of these other actors in shaping the overall governance outcome. Another more recent take on governmentality and well within the scope of financial services is the work of Heng and McDonagh (2008). Focusing on work related to curbing terrorist financing, they argued that a "governmentality approach reorients the focus away from a single sovereign "centre" node/source/hegemon, and instead explores more complex forms of governance that operate beyond, above and below conventional assumptions of sovereign authority" (p. 560). This is consistent with Valverde and Mopas (2004) in the sense that international actors, as opposed dominant forces, attempted to shape overall governance outcomes. In another work, Aitken (2010) preferred to employ governmentality to microfinance, which he sees as an "assemblage". According to him, this assemblage is "consisting of two intersecting conceptions of incorporation; on one hand an attempt to incorporate poor populations without access to credit more fully into formal financial practices and, on the other hand, an experiment in enmeshing microfinance itself more fully into global capital markets as an 'investable' asset" (p. 225).

Although governmentality might explain domestic implementation gaps due to various domestic actors' interests, there is less reference on how these various interests interact and influence each other, nor to how these interests deal with structural limitations. This is particularly pertinent in the financial sector, which is characterized by a higher level of state involvement as well as the global governance. In the case of Indonesia, governmentality may be unable to consider the interactions between state actors within the Indonesian MOF and the Indonesian FSA as an independent financial regulator. A particular key point of governmentality that is perhaps relevant to this focus is the idea that actors like the Indonesian FSA come to fully internalize the governmentality rationality of global or regional financial regulation. Although governmentality may put the focus on whether or not regulators have internalized international governmentality, there is still a need for the clarification of the context that shapes agents' behaviour. Up to this point, this survey on both neo-Gramscian and governmentality perspectives concludes that each approach represents alternative positions on how to look at existing domestic implementation gaps.

Hameiri and Jones (2015) have pointed to these contrasting extreme positions as a weakness of both approaches in explaining domestic implementation gaps. They argued that "neo-Gramscians often overstating the unity, coherence and efficacy of global governance as an expression of dominant transnational class interests, and poststructuralists tending to overstate fragmentation, fluidity and haphazardness of governance outcomes because of their neglect of structural constraints and material power-relations" (p. 50). Further, and to address those weaknesses explained above, Hameiri and Jones (2015) then build on a framework of state transformation to bridge both neo-Gramscian and governmentality approaches. State transformation put emphasis on how regional or global dynamics are internalized and contested within the state. Hameiri and Jones argued that state transformation reflects "rescaling" the governance from domestic affairs to regional or global scale. In particular, they wrote:

> Crucially, this does not necessarily mean shifting the locus of authority to pre-existing supranational institutions at the regional or global levels, but rather the rescaling of parts of the national, or in some cases subnational, state, so that these are removed from a purely domestic context and are integrated into regulatory regimes operating on a regional or global scale. (pp. 51–52)

According to Hameiri and Jones, the process of "rescaling" itself affects the interests of domestic social groups surrounding the issue, in turn creating contestation in the domestic socio-political context involving coalitions that may transcend the domestic-international divide.

Their state transformation approach asserts that parts of the state apparatus are reoriented towards embedding international agendas in the local context. But this is always contested, so depending on the coalitions that emerge around particular issues, outcomes may range from no rescaling to full adoption of international agendas and everything in-between.

The state transformation approach itself largely draws on the theory from Poulantzas and Jessop to argue that the state is inherently an expression of social power, reflecting social relations and conflicts rooted in processes of capitalist development (Hameiri & Jones, 2015). Accordingly, it has a "strategic selectivity" that it systematically privileges certain groups and interests in society, their ideologies and strategies, more than others. There may be a structural context that directs policymakers in a particular direction even without state power being instrumentalized by social groups. In Indonesia specifically, the state has been shown by many to operate in the interests of an oligarchy that also dominates politics. Jones (2016) particularly utilized the state transformation approach to explain AEC-related domestic implementation gaps. He argued that the future development of "regional economic integration is fundamentally shaped by socio-political contestation over the distribution of economic power and resources" and revealed that "the entrenched nature of dominant oligarchic interests across most of the region has precluded any embrace of full liberalisation and regional-scale economic governance" (pp. 665-666). As surveyed in the preceding section, scholars of the "oligarchy" thesis suggested that contemporary Indonesian politics is still significantly dominated by the interests of a few oligarchs.

The state transformation approach is basically the flipside of regulatory regionalism, or the "global governance as state transformation". In their next work on the state transformation approach, Hameiri and Jones (2016) argued that modern global governance is "creating and transforming domestic state apparatuses to serve internationally determined priorities and impose international disciplines on other parts of their states and societies" (p. 794) rather than, for instance, establishing a supranational institution to which states may shift some or the majority of their authority. Therefore, the state transformation approach understands domestic implementation gaps in reference to local contestation of the creation and transformation process. Further, Hameiri and Jones (2016) also argued that in the case where there is a state authority shift, it is rather to domestic institutions "that are more accountable to international than domestic actors" (p. 794). They observed that the "global governance as state transformation" here can transpire in the following modes: "(1)

the transboundary networking of states; (2) the acquisition by powerful state agencies of governance functions beyond their borders; and (3) the production of "meta-governance" by international institutions" (p.798). These three modes, in implementation, can happen at the same time.

They explained that in the first mode, as also observed by Gill (1992), that there was a change in preference to utilize more the "quasi-autonomous structure of global finance" or other self-governing type of institutions than democratic institutions such parliament or the elites. This utilization ultimately led to increased transnational networking, both in formal or informal institutional structures, away from local power relations. As Gill (1992) argued "a shift in the predominant forms of state economy relations away from the welfare-nationalist forms of state towards disciplinary neo-liberalism" is inevitable. In the case of Indonesia, an independent institution like Bank Indonesia has its own transnational network, like the BIS Central Bank Governance Network or ASEAN Central Bank Forum with, it is assumed, less interference from other state actors. Although the ASEAN Central Bank Forum and the central banks are still excluded from a formal ASEAN governance structure, as financial services-related issues are currently the dominant domain of the Ministry of Finance. Yet, these "quasi-autonomous structures of global finance" or other self-governing type of institutions are indeed emerging in Indonesia and have changed the governance of state policymaking.

Meanwhile, in the second mode, global governance proceeds as the cross-border practices of domestic institutions take up an enhanced international regulatory role. This enhanced international role includes a certain degree of autonomy vested into a domestic institution to cooperate with other corresponding institutions transnationally to tackle particular problems affecting the institutions involved. This cooperation includes not only the normal exchange of information or consultancies but also includes real build-ups in the field, funding resources and infrastructures. Further, in the third mode, global governance happens "through the use of international organisations as instruments of 'meta-governance'" (Hameiri & Jones, 2016, p. 800). In this mode, international organizations' scope of works includes the synchronization and alignment of rules and regulations for cross-border purposes. Through sets of regional or international standards, these international organizations also have the task to make sure that states adhere to the standards, including actions like regular supervision and evaluation of the standards' implementation. For instance, global securities regulators recognize the

International Organizations of Securities Commissions (IOSCO) as the global securities' standard setters and leader of cross-border cooperation for securities regulation capacity building.

Overall, the state transformation approach helps to explain implementation gaps by looking at the institutional transformation process. This approach understands institutions as located within power relations shaped by the dynamics of capitalism—the social forces, their relative power relations, conflicts and coalitions. It explains the existence of domestic implementation gaps by reference to the existence of domestic socio-political contestation. Later, I will discuss the Indonesian oligarchy in order to understand domestic socio-political contestation. The transformation approach arguably locates institutional dynamics within the wider applicable context surrounding implementation. In addition, this approach also serves as the starting point for identifying the existence of domestic quasi-autonomous or self-governing institutions. To this extent, the emergence of the Indonesian FSA can be classified as one of these domestic quasi-autonomous or self-governing type of institutions.

The preceding discussion on state transformation leads this discussion to regulatory regionalism as a form of regionalism that operates through state transformation. Regulatory regionalism views the "region" as potentially internalized within the ostensibly domestic institutions and governance processes of states. According to regulatory regionalism, a concomitant absorption of change into the domestic regulatory framework can take the form of a shared regional regulatory framework, though the result of change depends on domestic contestations over the form and outputs of modes of governance. Increasingly, regional governance takes the form of regulatory networks embedding governance practices, policies and standards at the national, or sometimes subnational, level. Nevertheless, that implementation occurs at the domestic level and is, therefore, subject to contestation at that level, shaping the actual outputs of the regional governance agenda. To this end, regulatory regionalism further strengthens the case for the inclusion of regional standards in domestic regulatory mechanisms. Some scholars engaging with the concept of regulatory regionalism (Fernández-i-Marín & Jordana, 2015; Hameiri & Jones, 2015; Jayasuriya, 2015) have argued that regional governance will be transferred into domestic regulatory frameworks resulting in domestic contestations. Jones and Hameiri (2019) also particularly argued that the AEC operates via regulatory regionalism. According to them, domestic contestation appears within the ASEAN integration because the regional agendas need to be implemented by the AMS, despite the fact that these agendas are non-binding to the AMS. Thus, within the context of this book, the concept of regulatory regionalism that assumes regionalization takes place through the embedding of regional regulations within the domestic governance processes and structures of states would serve as an initial point to understand the existence of policy implementation gaps. Consequently, it is important to understand the contours of domestic politics in Indonesia.

Many scholars of Indonesian politics emphasize the dominant role of a small politico-business "oligarchy". Hadiz and Robison (2013, p. 37) define oligarchy "as a system of power relations that enables the concentration of wealth and authority and its collective defence". Thus, the foundation of the oligarchs, as in many cases including Indonesia, lies on the "material power resources" or their wealth. Winters (2011) wrote that:

> Oligarchs are actors who command and control massive concentrations of material resources that can be deployed to defend or enhance their personal wealth and exclusive social position. (p. 6)

In other words, oligarchs consist of a small group of people with a large amount of wealth resources and they are utilizing those resources to protect their wealth and societal exclusiveness through, among other means, dominating the political system. Winters (2011) argues that:

> Oligarchy refers to the politics of wealth defense by materially endowed actors. The defense of riches by oligarchs involves specific challenges and capacities not shared by other forms of minority domination or exclusion. Oligarchy describes how that defense is pursued – a process that is highly variable across political contexts and historical periods. (p. 7)

In reference to Indonesia, Winters (2013) then wrote that "the power of oligarchs is formidable and that their influence over the country's politics is deep and distorting", and that "for the present oligarchs and oligarchy rightfully hold a central place in the analysis of Indonesian politics" (Winters, 2013, p. 12).

Most of latest literature on the Indonesian "oligarchy" thesis (such as the works of Fukuoka, 2013; Hadiz & Robison, 2004, 2013; Winters, 2011, 2013) argued that the rise of the "oligarchy" in Indonesia was nurtured under President Soeharto and, up until now, that a few oligarchs still continue to dominate Indonesian political economy despite the democratic transition. For instance, Hadiz and Robison (2013) note that recent institutional changes occurring in Indonesia, such as financial sector reform or improvements in good corporate governance practices, were unable to break the dominant power of a few oligarchs. They also suggest that not only do these few oligarchs have strong political connections and use these connections to embed their interests in institutions, but also a lot of them are even actually political actors themselves. Hadiz and Robison (2004) made the case of the central bank's liquidity fund (Bantuan Likuiditas Bank Indonesia/BLBI) and the Indonesian Bank Recapitulation Agency (Badan Penyehatan Perbankan Nasional/BPPN), as examples to show Indonesia's failure to deal with the small oligarchy. They argue that conglomerates used the scheme of BLBI and the emergence of the government agency BPPN to fulfil their financial interests in the banking sector. The continuation of oligarchy in Indonesia and its network throughout the country undoubtedly influenced the public policymaking process. Thus, the Indonesian oligarchy uses policy implementation processes to preserve their power.

Winters (2013) also argued that in line with the development of democracy in Indonesia, a few oligarchs still continue to enjoy domination over Indonesian policymaking processes. He mentioned that a small oligarchy uses the political apparatus and infiltrates domestic institutions. He provided a list containing prominent political figures in Indonesia and their oligarchic details, with former President Susilo Bambang Yudhoyono, former President Megawati Soekarnoputri and Vice President Jusuf Kalla are among those in the list. The list also mentioned prominent Indonesian tycoons, such as Aburizal Bakrie or Chairul Tanjung, who were also once involved in politics. In another work, Fukuoka (2013) also implied the same argument suggesting that the oligarchy in Indonesia continues to survive despite democratic development in the country called the "democratic oligarchy". He argues that Indonesian leaders, under the administration of the former President Susilo Bambang Yudhoyono, avoided implementing reforms that are in contention with a few oligarchs' interests to accumulate wealth. As a result, consistent with Hadiz and Robison (2013), he concluded that a few oligarchs still retain a dominant role in aspects of Indonesia's policymaking process. Thus, again, the proponents of the "oligarchy" thesis suggest that domestic policy implementation in Indonesia is subject to a few oligarchs' interests.

However, there are also some notable "optimistic" works on Indonesia's efforts to deal with a small oligarchy. For instance, although Aspinall (2013, 2014) accepts the argument on the continuity of a small oligarchy even in contemporary Indonesia, he advocated the increasing role of societal power and other actors within the Indonesian political framework. For instance, Aspinall (2014) showed that despite acknowledging significant improvements in Indonesian healthcare provision, there are still prominent challenges in the way if a few oligarchs' interests in the healthcare sector are to be overridden. Aspinall and Berenschot (2019) seem to be more pessimistic in arguing the apparent existence of the informal politics of "clientelism" in Indonesia. They are particular:

> To be sure, formal institutions such as laws, policies, and official procedures do affect the functioning of state institutions. But the actual impact of regulations depends on the capacity of individuals and groups to use informal, personal exchange relationships to manipulate their implementation. Analysis of Indonesian politics should thus endeavour to understand the interplay between formal and informal dimensions of politics and view informal politics as a constituent element of state power. (p. 13)

In another work, for instance, Tapsell (2015) also provided the case of the increasing role of non-oligarchic media to the popular rise of the current President Joko Widodo. On the "optimistic" view, he concluded that Widodo's rise was greatly attributable to societal power and the use of informal media by the voting public. This is consistent with the conclusion of Mietzner (2014) on "the influence of non-oligarchic or counter-oligarchic actors and groups" in the analysis of the "oligarchy" thesis of the Indonesian politics. A "non-oligarchic" thesis can refer to the more recent accounts discussing the development of intra-elite struggle that has shaped more recent and bitterly fought contests, such as the case with the latest election campaign in Indonesia. Hadiz (2018) argued that:

> Indonesian Islamic populism…has come to play a bigger role in political competition because of the way that intra-elite conflict has evolved in democratic Indonesia. Specifically, they have the capacity to mobilise people in such events as mass rallies and demonstrations in ways that benefit certain contending elites, largely by making appeals to religious sentiment (p. 568)

Overall, despite their "optimistic" works, the findings on "non-oligarchy" are somehow still consistent with the "oligarchy" thesis suggesting that domestic policy implementation is unlikely to escape a few oligarchs' interests. The debate on Indonesian oligarchy outlined above is perhaps one of the most relevant and useful debates in providing a major background to the analysis in this book, explaining the domestic political economy that may contribute to domestic implementation gaps. It may help to explain and contextualize how Indonesia as a state function. However, the works on Indonesian oligarchy need further analysis and elaboration, particularly in the case here related to portfolio investment liberalization. Having reviewed the "oligarchy"" thesis, portfolio investments liberalization may not be in the best interests of the few oligarchs as it may take over the domestic markets and lead to their wealth being distributed to others. For instance, liberalizing the domestic market to be more open and freer would expose the oligarchy the risk that foreign businesses may take over their clients. If this is the case, then political elites should not have committed to the liberalization initiatives in the first instance. Thus, I look for another way to look at the implementation gaps.

Particularly in the case of finance, the most obvious way in which the oligarchy thesis has been applied is to argue for "mock compliance" with international agendas. The work of Andrew Walter (2008) is relevant in this regard. He argues that in response to international financial standards, states are confronted with both external and domestic pressure. "Governments caught in between these contradictory pressures often opt for a strategy of mock compliance" (Walter, 2008, p. 5). In his theory of compliance, he argues that states effect perfunctory implementation to bridge between the condition of non-compliance to international standards with pressures from International Financial Institutions (IFIs), and domestic supporters for full substantive compliance to international standards. For example, in the case of Indonesian banking supervision, he highlighted that the government decided to formally agree to the IMF banking reform plan in response to IFIs and the pressure from domestic agents of reform. He further argued that, in Indonesia's case, the compliance gap resulted from "high and concentrated private sector compliance costs and continuing obstacles to third party monitoring of compliance, combined with a government apparatus in which private sector influence remained embedded" (p. 76). Thus, according to the theory of compliance, private actors strongly influence how the states act. In other words, the outcome of domestic implementation greatly depends on how strong the influence of the private sector is in the public policymaking process.

The theories of "mock compliance" and "oligarchy" as elaborated above have relevance for the analysis in this book, as they highlight aspects of the contemporary Indonesian political landscape and consider domestic contestations. Domestic implementation gaps are visible within the frameworks of both the "mock compliance" and "oligarchy" theses. In the case of the "oligarchy" thesis however, leaders' attempts to further liberalize the domestic portfolio investment regime may not match the interests of the oligarchs in defence of their domestic wealth. The claim of needing protection from foreign players in the market is a classic oligarchy tool that secures their interests. Oligarchs further argue that even when foreign actors are allowed, it should be via joint ventures with the local players. To this end, although acknowledging the contribution of the literature on Indonesian "oligarchy" and "mock compliance" to our understanding of domestic contestations, I will still look at other ways to explain the existence of domestic implementation gaps in portfolio investments liberalization. The oligarchy thesis here needs to be supplemented by another approach because while oligarchy explains the extent to which the state works in Indonesia, it is not sufficiently able to explain FSA agents' efforts to stymie portfolio investment liberalization. I need to examine the institutions where the agents are located and explore how they and other institutions interact to eventually stymie t portfolio investment liberalization. Thus, in the section below, I look at how institutionalism explains domestic implementation gaps.

Institutionalism and Modified Historical Institutionalism Approach

The final part of this chapter discusses the institutional theory that this book considers provides the most useful insight into implementation gaps and the rise of the Indonesian FSA within the area of portfolio investments liberalization. The emergence of the Indonesian FSA is a story about institutional change and institutional relations. As the state transformation approach may refer the rise of the Indonesian FSA to a domestic quasi-autonomous or self-governing type of institution, engagement with institutional theory here enhances the explanations on how and why that particular institution has risen to power. As Peters (2012) argues:

> If the institutionalist perspective is to provide a useful alternative to more individualistic and purposive explanations of political life, then it must be able to say how the institutions that are so central to the theory come into being in the first instance. Further, once the institutions are created there needs to be a clear logic for change. (p. 37)

As there are different variations of institutional theory, each of these also deliver different approaches to institutions. In addition, institutional theory discussions here also complement the institutional relations account of the Indonesian FSA with other related domestic institutions in Indonesia.

Institutional theory, which attempts to explain institutions as a variable in social and political issues, is particularly relevant to help this book explain the implementation gap. Institutions which, briefly, consist of organizations' rules and norms, affect how agents act. Those rules and norms are the guidelines that bind the behaviour of agents. Thus, institutional theory argues that agents are expected to follow the pre-arranged rules and norms of an organization. There are variants of institutional theory, such as those approaches that have emerged from new institutionalism, namely historical institutionalism, rational-choice institutionalism, sociological institutionalism (Hall & Taylor, 1996; Pollack, 1996), as well as the more recent discursive institutionalism (Blyth, 2002; Hay, 2008; Schmidt, 2008). All of these institutionalist approaches converge on the assumption that agents should act in accordance with an organization's rules and norms. Thus, the main problem with all these variants of institutional theory is that they underemphasize the bidirectional, or "mutually shaping" relationships between institutions and agents. The sub-sections below explain each of these variants of institutional theory, ultimately lead to the adoption of a modified historical institutionalism approach used in this book.

Sociological Institutionalism

According to sociological institutionalism, organizations' rules and norms "include, not just formal rules, procedures or norms, but the symbol systems, cognitive scripts, and moral template" (Hall & Taylor, 1996, p. 947). One of the most important features of sociological institutionalism is the inclusion of these informal rules and norms in the definition of institutions (Campbell, 1998). Sociological institutionalists modify a society's cultural practices, leading to a formal form of institutionalization of those cultural practices (Hall & Taylor, 1996). These cultural practices may derive from informal practices performed within the organization, are later institutionalized and diffused throughout the organization. These cultural practices, along with an organization's formal rules and norms, shape the behaviour of agents. Another feature of sociological institutionalism is the "cultural approach" to the relationships between institutions and agents. Sociological institutionalists argue that agents act based on an organizations' formal and informal rules and norms that are disseminated to them. Accordingly, change in institutions happens "because it enhances the social legitimacy of the organization or its participants" (Hall & Taylor, 1996, p. 949). Sociological institutionalists might suggest that the rise of the Indonesian FSA should be a product of cultural practices in the way Indonesia governs the financial sector and, further, agents should abide by these cultural practices.

According to sociological institutionalism, institutional changes should happen because most of the agents accept them as prescribed rather than the agents themselves making institutional changes. However, Hall and Taylor (1996) also suggested that the identification of cultural authority can be problematic. In other words, there should be an analysis of the actors advocating particular cultural practices and subsequently disseminating these practices to the organization agents. Even more problematic is the possibility that in some cases, the acceptance of these cultural practices may hinder the achievement of an institution's formal objectives. That is to say, that there might be formal rules and norms that are positioned below particular cultural practices. To use a more well-known term, this condition refers to what is called the "logic of appropriateness". March and Olsen (1989), among the first to coin the term, say of the "logic of appropriateness" that "action stems from the conception of necessity, rather than preference" (p. 160). As to explaining domestic implementation gaps, sociological institutionalism may be problematic mainly due to the assumption of agents' acceptance to cultural practices. The story of domestic implementation gaps here is the story of the emergence of a newly established institution that may differ from the embedded cultural practices of financial supervision. In addition, the fact that different Indonesian agents behave differently may suggest the non-existence of overarching cultural norms.

Rational-Choice Institutionalism

Meanwhile, rational-choice institutionalists assume that "political actors are rational and will act to maximize their self-interest" (Steinmo et al., 1992). This assumption means that, given that an organization's rules and norms are fixed variables that may be unable to be straightforwardly transformed, agents will accordingly adjust their strategies to get the most benefit from the organization (Hall & Taylor, 1996). For example, rational-choice institutionalists explain that political actors use certain political strategies due to limitations in the existing rules and regulations. Thus, as a result of their strategies, political actors can still act in accordance with rules and regulations while maximizing their political interests. In addition, rational-choice institutionalists can also explain company managers' cost minimization strategies. As managers are bound to a company's rules, they have the responsibility to maximize the companies' profits through minimizing the costs of production. According to rational-choice institutionalists, managers need to take rational decisions that not only fully minimize the costs of production but also to fit within their company's rules. One of the distinguishing features of the rational-choice institutionalism is the assumption that agents have already set their targets and try to maximize their self-interest in achieving the targets within the boundaries of rules and regulations. As a result, according to rational-choice institutionalists, changes to institutions occur in reference agents' attempts to get the best out of organizational rules and norms.

This explanation is also consistent with earlier scholars of rational-choice institutionalism. For instance, Williamson (1975) argued that changes to the structure of companies depend on the way managers carry out the "transaction cost economics" within their companies. The most important contribution of rational-choice institutionalism, and also the most relevant point in the context of this book, is that the way it looks at the creation of an institution. Institutional creation is a product of interactions and intended compromises among relevant actors to achieve their self-interest maximization (Hall & Taylor, 1996). Thus, rational-choice institutionalists would have explained the institutional rise of the Indonesian FSA with reference to the interests of the relevant actors surrounding its establishment. Each of these relevant actors assumingly implemented particular strategies to maximize their interest and which ultimately brought changes to the institution. As to explaining domestic implementation gaps, an over-emphasis on actors' contributions to changes may seem problematic. The emergence of the Indonesian FSA is also a story of institutional ideas stemming from Bank Indonesia's independence and the mandate of IFIs' neoliberalism during structural adjustment programmes in 1998.

Historical Institutionalism

The term historical institutionalism was first brought into the literature of new institutionalism in the field of political science in the early 1990s. The literature shows that the term was first used extensively in a 1992 publication in which comparison was drawn to earlier versions of new institutionalism (1992). Steinmo et al. argued that historical institutionalism considers "policy continuities over time within countries and policy variation across countries" (p. 11). In general, the core concepts of historical institutionalism lie on what scholars' term "critical juncture" and "path dependence" that highly correlate with institutional changes. Path dependence is often considered as the later stages or consequences of the critical juncture (Capoccia & Kelemen, 2007; Fioretos et al., 2016). While some scholars (such as Capoccia & Kelemen, 2007; Collier & Collier, 1991) have provided variations in the definition of critical juncture, there was an agreement that critical juncture corresponds to a "turning point". This refers to a point that triggered changes in institutions (critical juncture), eventually leading to long-term normalized conditions (path dependence) until the next critical juncture. To this extent, historical institutionalism is particularly useful to analyse the historical emergence of the Indonesian FSA by identifying the timeline of institutional changes.

Rixen and Viola (2016) refer to the concepts of critical juncture and path dependence in the international relations field as "change" and "stability". However, they also introduce a third concept, "event sequencing". This concept basically states that there are sequential relationships between one to another critical juncture affecting the existence of path dependence. This means that the existing critical juncture may as well be the result of past events or earlier critical junctures. Moschella and Vetterlein (2016) offer instances of "event sequencing" in the development of IMF as an international institution of financial sector surveillance. They argue that there were a series of financial crises that had shaped IMF roles as today's financial sector surveillance. The concepts of critical juncture, path dependence and event sequencing refer to a variant of historical institutionalism that sees institutions as "sticky". In other words, historical institutionalists still see institutions as a limitation on actors, rather than both interacting. To this extent, the next development of historical institutionalism put more emphasis on institutional changes, at least starting from the introduction of the so-called "institutional dynamism". This is the second main variant of historical institutionalism which sees institutions as evolving, rather than restraining or being "sticky".

According to Thelen and Steinmo (1992), as part of the second main variant of historical institutionalism, institutions change over time through the effect of different variables. They argued that "institutional dynamism" can occur either through existing institutions or through the formation of new institutions. They explained that dynamism through existing institutions is more likely to happen with fewer changes in the institution itself. Meanwhile, dynamism can also occur through the formation of new institutions. However, in dynamism through existing institutions, the parties or actors, related to the institutions will apparently be unchanged. The parties or actors expect themselves to adjust to the transformation happening within an institution. The dynamism, in this case, occurs as a result of parties' or actors' responses to particular interests within the institution. According to Thelen and Steinmo (1992), the variables for this dynamism were ranging from institutions' interaction with socio-economic and political conditions, or institutions' ability to adapt to changes in goals and strategies. As a result of interaction and adaptation, institutions can either rise to become a major institution from being previously under-developed, or replace the older version entirely. To this extent, the concept of "institutional dynamism" up to this point helps this book by providing explanatory possibilities for the emergence of the Indonesian FSA.

Thelen and Steinmo (1992) further argue that dynamism also happens when there are extraordinary pressures on institutions, both internally and externally. Unlike dynamism that happens through the existing institutions, the dynamism here occurs "when political actors adjust their strategies to accommodate changes" (p. 17). They took the case as provided by Thelen (1991) in explaining the dynamism that happened in Germany's labour politics. She explained the successful case of the "dual system" that:

> ...refers to the juxtaposition in Germany of centralized collective bargaining through multi-industrial unions and a statutory system for plant labor representation through autonomous works councils that are formally separate from the unions. (p. 2)

She, thus, concluded that internally the pressures may come from the political behaviour of parties or actors within the institution. Meanwhile, she also suggested that externally the pressures may come as a result of an event outside the institution yet affecting the responses of parties or actors within the institution.

For historical institutionalists, "when ideas become accepted and are embodied into a structural form then the institution has been created" (Peters, 2012, p. 76). However, actors or agents are the ones who implement ideas. Institutional changes thus require not only the institution but also agents creating the change. Peters (2012) described agency question in historical institutionalism as the following:

> There is an important question of agency involved in the formation of institutions in the historical institutionalist perspective. The formative moment crucial in this approach, and the logic of path dependency follows from that formative moment. It is clear that ideas are important elements in the formation of the institution, but ideas do not act on their own but require policy entrepreneurs or some analogous actor to use the idea to create policy and to create institution. (p. 76)

This question of agency came from observations that "historical institutionalist are not particularly concerned with how individuals relate to the institutions within which they function" (p. 83). Peters further added that "[t]here appears to be an implicit assumption of the approach that when individuals choose to participate in an institution, they will accept the constraints imposed by that institution" (p. 83).

Historical institutionalists emphasize that agents follow an organization's defined rules and norms (Thelen & Steinmo, 1992). Thus, the assumption that agents are behaving to maximize their own benefit or self-interest is unproblematic for historical institutionalist. "That is to say, without denying that human behaviour is rational or purposive, it emphasizes the extent to which individuals turn to established routines or familiar patterns of behaviour to attain their purposes" (Hall & Taylor, 1996, p. 939). Historical institutionalists broadly engage with a definition of institutions that include guidance for the agents to produce outcomes.

Institutions include "formal organizations and informal rules and procedures that structure conduct" (Thelen & Steinmo, 1992, p. 2). Peter Hall's commonly established definition of the institution, for instance, also offers a similar interpretation that states that an institution comprises "the formal rules, compliance procedures, and standard operating practice that structure the relationship between individuals in various units of the polity and economy" (Hall, 1986, p. 19). Other key scholars, such as North (1990), also included the sub-argument that institutions comprise of formal and informal limitations to agents' relations.

In sum, "historical institutionalists associate institutions with organizations and the rules or conventions promulgated by formal organization" (Hall & Taylor, 1996, p. 938). According to historical institutionalists, an institutional creation is derived from the acceptance of ideas and the embodiment of those ideas into a set of rules and norms. Within the context of this book, historical institutionalism serves as one of major theoretical anchors to comprehend the institutional creation of the Indonesian FSA. However, historical institutionalism alone may be unable to explain the question of institutional change. Thus, for instance, in the case of the emergence of the Indonesian FSA as the focus of this book, historical institutionalism might have difficulties in explaining the progressive development of the institution from its first establishment until its current form. In addition, relevant agents and other structural factors surrounding institutions also shape institutional change. As Peters (2012) suggested, historical institutionalism perhaps "appears much better suited to explain the persistence of patterns than to explain how those patterns might change" (p. 77). Further, on the point of relevant agents, he also mentioned the assumption of historical institutionalists that "when individuals choose to participate in an institution they will accept the constraints imposed by that institution, but that linkage is not explored" (p. 83).

Modified Historical Institutionalism

To this point, this section has provided an overview of the three major variants of institutional theory, namely the sociological, rational-choice and historical. However, these accounts fundamentally assume that agents act in accordance with an organization's rules and norms. Thus, the main problem with these variants of institutional theory is that they underemphasize bidirectional, or "mutually shaping" relationships between institutions and agents. Bidirectional means that agents play an active role in reshaping institutions to create. Agents are the ones who implement ideas and change institutions. Many scholars (such as Bell, 2011; Bell & Feng, 2013; Bell & Hindmoor, 2015; Campbell, 2004; Crouch, 2005; Thelen & Steinmo, 1992) have also criticized the unidirectional relations of institutions and agents, implying that the interactions between institutions and agents are bidirectional or "mutually shaping". This bidirectional relationship shows that agents are not merely governed by the rules and norms of an organization. Yet, institutions could also enable agents to eventually transform the organization. Unidirectional theorization may be problematic in explaining the emergence of the Indonesian FSA because during their historical and contemporary emergence, agents actively form the shape of institutions. In addition, there are also compromises between agents to, for instance, determine the extent of separation between macro- and micro-banking supervision. More of these stories are in the next chapter.

Some scholars (such as Blyth, 2002; Hay, 2008; Schmidt, 2006) later postulated so-called discursive institutionalism. The idea of discursive institutionalism generally assumes that agents have their own ideas and interpretation of organizations' rules and norms. Discursive institutionalists believe that agents' ideas and interpretations can also shape institutions. The interactions between these ideas and interpretations with institutions can explain institutional change. For instance, Schmidt (2008) argued that discursive institutionalism "puts agency back into institutional change by explaining the dynamics of change in structures through constructive discourse about ideas" (p. 316). The way discursive institutionalism treats agents facilitates the institutional changes. Thus, discursive institutionalists treat agency:

> rather than serving as external structures for rule-following, are simultaneously structures and constructs internal to the agents themselves. Agents' background ideational abilities enable them to act in any given meaning context to create and maintain institutions while their foreground discursive abilities enable them to communicate critically about those institutions and so to change or maintain them. Institutional change in DI [discursive institutionalism], therefore, as opposed to in HI [historical institutionalism], is dynamic and explainable across time through agents' ideas and discourse, rather than largely static because of path-dependent structures and unexplainable critical moments. (p. 322)

In another instance, more specific to financial market integration, Hay (2008) showed that policymakers may act based on their own ideas and interpretations in response to international pressure for financial market liberalization. In particular, he argued the following:

> pointing to the pervasiveness in the existing literature of a significant tension between globalization and public policy—such that the extent of globalization is seen as a simple index of the degree of the loss of autonomy of (domestic) public policy makers...For as I have sought to demonstrate, the challenges that public policy makers face from, say, processes of economic integration are specific to the contexts in which those policy makers are located. Overly aggregated and general accounts of globalization can only fail to capture and reflect that specificity; as such, they distort significantly the constraints faced by public policy makers today. (pp. 13–14)

To the extent explaining implementation gaps, discursive institutionalism is relevant because it confirms the existence of agents' ideas and interpretations in their own institutions. In order to explain an institutional change, a discursive approach to institutions would explain that there are changes to those ideas and interpretations. While it is outside the scope of this book, discursive institutionalism may also help explaining the sustainability of ASEAN as a regional organization that lasted for more than fifty years now. For instance, as summarized in the work of Davies (2018), the existence of ceremonial and representation are preserved by ASEAN officials over the substance of the cooperation itself.

However, as Peters (2012) also revealed, a discursive approach to institutions has less focus on how institutions affect agents. Changes to agents' ideas and interpretations can "inevitably be influenced to some extent by their involvement with the institutions, and more particularly by their involvement with the other members of the institution" (p. 122). For instance, it is not merely agents' ideas and interpretations that contribute to the rise of the contemporary Indonesian FSA. These ideas and interpretations also interact with the institution itself and other institutions surrounding it. In the context of this book, other institutions here may include Bank Indonesia or the Indonesian MOF. This also means that members of these institutions, interact with agents' ideas and interpretations. Above all, the discussion of discursive institutionalism is important within the context of this book because it is an agent-centred approach (Hay, 2008; Schmidt, 2006). Considered to be the next generation of historical institutionalism, a discursive approach to institutions puts more emphasis on agents' ideas and interpretations as compared to other variants of institutional theory.

Consistent with the above-mentioned critics, Bell (2011) has argued that agents' ideas and interpretations are also shaped by their interactions with structural contexts other than their own institutions. Thus, discursive institutionalism, or using Bell's term "new constructivist", is still unable to consider agents' interaction with this wider structural context. For instance, Indonesian officials' decision to hold on to the existing portfolio investment regime is strongly associated with their interactions with other domestic authorities and the condition of domestic politics. Agents are bound to not only their own institution but also other institutional settings. Thus, in approaching the emergence of the Indonesian FSA and to ultimately explain the rationale for the implementation gap, this book is interested in how agents also form (or impact upon) the institution in "mutually shaping" relationships. Furthermore, the construction of the surrounding structural context also interacts with agents' behaviour, and ultimately this interaction then forms the overall governance outcome.

"Agents-in-Context" Approach

From the discussion on the variants of institutional theory above, thus far the book concludes that historical institutionalism serves as one of the major theoretical anchors to comprehend the institutional creation of the Indonesian FSA as the rationale for the existing domestic implementation gaps. Consequently, this book uses an approach that expands the account of historical institutionalism. This expansion includes features that can incorporate both the bidirectional relationship and the surrounding structural context. This is the approach that Bell and Feng (2013) termed as the "agents-in-context" approach. In particular, they explained:

> the approach used here gives greater scope to agency, accepting that agents and institutions are mutually shaping over time and that agents are the ultimate propellant of change. We argue that agents have a degree of discretion in institutional environments, more than established theory suggests. We also argue that institutional environments are not only constraining but also potentially empowering. The main problem with established institutional theory, such as sticky HI [historical institutionalism], is that it begins

> analysis by considering the impact of institutions on agents, largely a top-down, constraining view. Agents are seen as enmeshed and constrained by institutions, leaving consideration of agency almost as a secondary issue. We utilize a somewhat different ontology, which starts with agents and their behavior. Our approach works outward from agents and examines how they build and shape institutions and negotiate institutional constraints and opportunities. Also, agents not only operate in institutions but are also influenced by wider contexts. (pp. 29–30)

The expanded version of historical institutionalism that can help explaining the implementation gap is the account of interactions between agents with their broader contexts, or the "wider structural context". This is because agents are not only interacting with their own institutions, but also with a broader structural context. If institutions can be defined briefly as "the rules and norms (formal and informal) that shape actor behaviour" (Bell & Hindmoor, 2015, p. 21), "structural" can be perceived as other factors that affect behaviour. Bell and Feng (2013) argue that "agents interact not only with the proximate institutions in which they are embedded but with wider meta-institutional contexts that also shape behaviour and opportunities" (p. 27). Bell and Hindmoor (2015) suggest that "structural" is better defined as within a broader context than solely institutions. Hay's (2002) definition of "structural", for instance, "means context and refers to the setting within which social, political and economic events occur and acquire meaning" (p. 94). Further, the notion of the "structural" itself can basically include any significant aspects that might affect responses of the agents (Hay, 2002; Jessop, 2007). Structural factors, thus, can also include background as a result of events happening in the past. For instance, this book traced back the structural factors in the emergence of the Indonesian FSA from the very first point this institution was proposed by the IMF until the contemporary development. This structural factor is also notably one of the important parts of financial regulatory reform in Indonesia. As institutions and agents are largely bidirectional, or "mutually shaping", this is also the case with agents and the broader structural context.

Earlier studies on institutionalism (such as Pontusson, 1995; Thelen, 1999, 2010; Thelen & Steinmo, 1992) actually have already considered the construction of wider structural contexts. However, most of these studies do not put forward this account of the wider structural contexts and instead focus largely on parts of an institution. This book adopts the structural context as employed in Bell and Feng (2013) and Bell and Hindmoor (2015). In particular, the incorporation of wider structural contexts works as described by Bell and Feng (2013) below.

> The approach here is to treat the impact of wider meta-institutional contexts more systematically and to do so through a more unified theoretical approach that posits an active role for "situated agents" within institutional and wider settings who respond to the constraints and opportunities presented to them. The account being developed here thus analyzes agents who are dialectically engaged in shaping and being shaped by their relevant institutions and wider contexts over time. (p. 32)

To that extent, "the essential insight of institutional theory is confirmed but broadened beyond the institutional domain" (Bell & Hindmoor, 2015, p. 24). Thus, this book uses the "agents-in-context" approach to explain the emergence of the Indonesian FSA due to the features of "mutually shaping" relationships between agents and institutions, as well as the incorporation of the account on wider structural contexts to that relationships.

The work of Bell and Feng (2013) particularly explains the institutional transformation of the People's Bank of China (PBC) in the form of expanded authorities. Their work also notably emphasized on the identification of related parties, or actors, in the context of banking and monetary reform in China. In doing so, they expanded the analysis of different variables affecting the transformation. This expansion allows the analysis of key agents' responses to the context of causes on institutional changes. Thus, they believed that the analysis is not primarily focusing on, for instance, the financial crises as the external pressures to PBC institutional change, but also how agents are interacting with such external pressures. Thus, "agents-in-context" approach is basically an alternative to the more traditional historical institutionalism concept.

The work of Bell and Feng (2013) was particularly looking at the PBC as the key party or actor behind China rapid economic and financial development. They argued that the institutional changes in the case of the expanded authorities of PBS are attributable to domestic politics condition among China's party elites. "Our answer is that the rise of the PBC has been based on a relationship of growing mutual dependency with the party leadership" (Bell & Feng, 2013, pp. 5). This conclusion was based on the analysis using HI with "agents-in-context" approach as previously explained in preceding paragraphs. The approach involves identification of parties or actors playing a central role in institutional change settings. Bell and Feng (2013) further argued that there was an interaction between parties or actors in PBC with China's party elites bringing the result of institutional changes. However, they considered that such interaction is happening due to the occurrences of external pressures to China's overall economic and financial development.

As an approach that expands the account of historical institutionalism, "agents-in-context" is fit to be the theoretical overarching in explaining the emergence of the Indonesian FSA. The features of "mutually shaping" relationships between agents and institutions, as well as the account on wider structural contexts to that relationships, have been operationalized in the PBC case. This book uses the same approach to a particular case study in Indonesia. This book therefore proceeds with the following theoretical steps. Firstly, drawing on historical institutional theory, this book identifies the agents and their nature, as well as isolating institutions that are central to the establishment of the Indonesian FSA. Secondly, this book traces the bidirectional relationships between agents and their institutions, as well as the broader structural contexts surrounding these relationships. For instance, this tracing of bidirectional relationships extends to the contexts within the postponement of the Indonesian FSA establishment and the transitional periods.

In conclusion, this chapter has reviewed some of the early literature in regionalism, literature that studies domestic implementation, as well as literature that incorporated wider structural contexts. This book finally settles on the employment of the "agents-in-context" approach as outlined above. This chapter argued that as institutions and agents are largely bidirectional, or "mutually shaping", this is also the case with agents and the broader structural context. Both features of the approach, the "mutually shaping" relationships between agents and institutions and the ability to incorporate wider structural contexts to that relationships, are well-suited to the objective of explaining how and why the Indonesian FSA emerged. In the next chapter, we start unveiling key empirical findings to explain the rise of the Indonesian FSA.

References

Aitken, R. (2010). Ambiguous incorporations: Microfinance and global governmentality. *Global Networks, 10*(2), 223–243.

Aspinall, E. (2013). Popular agency and interests in Indonesia's democratic transition and consolidation. *Indonesia, 96*, 101–121, 219.

Aspinall, E. (2014). Health care and democratization in Indonesia. *Democratization, 21*, 1–21.

Aspinall, E., & Berenschot, W. (2019). *Democracy for sale: Elections, clientelism, and the state in Indonesia*. Cornell University Press.

Barry, A., Osborne, T., & Rose, N. (1996). *Foucault and political reason: Liberalism, neo-liberalism, and rationalities of government*. University of Chicago Press.

Bell, S. (2011). Do we really need a new 'constructivist institutionalism' to explain institutional change? *British Journal of Political Science, 41*(4), 883–906.

Bell, S., & Feng, H. (2013). *The rise of the people's Bank of China: The politics of institutional change*. Harvard University.

Bell, S., & Hindmoor, A. (2015). *Masters of the universe, slaves of the market*. Harvard University.

Blyth, M. (2002). *Great transformations: Economic ideas and institutional change in the twentieth century*. Cambridge.

Burchell, G., Gordon, C., & Miller, P. (1991). *The Foucault effect: Studies in governmentality: With two lectures by and an interview with Michel Foucault*. University of Chicago Press.

Campbell, J. (1998). Institutional analysis and the role of ideas in political economy. *Theory and Society, 27*(3), 377–409.

Campbell, J. L. (2004). *Institutional change and globalization*. Princeton University Press.

Capoccia, G., & Kelemen, R. D. (2007). The study of critical junctures: Theory, narrative, and counterfactuals in historical institutionalism. *World Politics, 59*(3): 341–369.

Collier, R. B., & Collier, D. (1991). *Shaping the political arena: Critical junctures, the labor movement, and regime dynamics in Latin America*. Princeton University Press.

Crouch, C. (2005). *Capitalist diversity and change recombinant governance and institutional entrepreneurs*. Oxford University Press.

Davies, M. (2018). *Ritual and religion: The invention of ASEAN*. Cambridge University Press.

Dean, M., & Hindess, B. (1998). *Governing Australia: Studies in contemporary rationalities of government (Reshaping Australian Institutions)*. Cambridge University Press.

Drezner, D. W. (2007). *All politics is global: Explaining international regulatory regimes*. Princeton.

Fernández-i-Marín, X., & Jordana, J. (2015). The emergence of regulatory regionalism: Transnational networks and the diffusion of regulatory agencies within regions. *Contemporary Politics, 21*(4), 417–434.

Foucault, M. (2007). *Security, territory, population lectures at the college De France, 1977–78*. Palgrave.

Fukuoka, Y. (2013). Oligarchy and democracy in Post-Suharto Indonesia. *Political Studies Review, 11*(1), 52–64.

Gill, S. (1992). Economic globalization and the internationalization of authority: Limits and contradictions. *Geoforum, 23*(3), 269–283.

Gill, S. (1995). Globalisation, market civilisation, and disciplinary neoliberalism. *Millennium—Journal of International Studies, 24*(3), 399–423.

Haas, E. B. (1961). International integration: The European and the universal process. *International Organization, 15*(3), 366–392.

Hadiz, V. R. (2018). Imagine all the people? Mobilising Islamic populism for right-wing politics in Indonesia. *Journal of Contemporary Asia, 48*(4), 566–583.

Hadiz, V., & Robison, R. (2004). *Reorganising power in Indonesia: The politics of oligarchy in an age of markets (Routledge Curzon/City University of Hong Kong South East Asian Studies; 3)*. Routledge.

Hadiz, V., & Robison, R. (2013). The political economy of oligarchy and the reorganization of power in Indonesia. *Indonesia, 96*(35–57), 219–220.

Hall, P. A. (1986). *Governing the economy: The politics of state intervention in Britain and France*. Oxford University Press.

Hall, P. A., & Taylor, R. C. R. (1996). Political science and the three new institutionalisms. *Political Studies, 44*(5), 936–957.

Hameiri, S., & Jones, L. (2015). *Governing borderless threats: Non-traditional security and the politics of state transformation*. Cambridge.

Hameiri, S., & Jones, L. (2016). Global governance as state transformation. *Political Studies, 64*(4), 793–810.

Hay, C. (2002). *Political analysis*. Palgrave.

Hay, C. (2008). Globalisation and public policy. In M. Rein, M. Moran, & R. E. Godin (Eds.), *Oxford handbook of public policy*. Oxford University Press.

Heng, Y., & McDonagh, K. (2008). The other War on Terror revealed: Global governmentality and the Financial Action Task Force's campaign against terrorist financing. *Review of International Studies, 34*(3), 553–573.

Jayasuriya, K. (2015). Regulatory regionalism, political projects, and state transformation in the Asia-Pacific. *Asian Politics & Policy, 7*, 517–529.

Jessop, R. D. (2007). *State power: A strategic-relational approach*. Polity.

Jones, D. M. (2016). ASEAN's imitation economic community: The primacy of domestic political economy. In B. Jetin, & M. Mikic (Eds.), *ASEAN economic community*. Palgrave Macmillan.

Jones, L., & Hameiri, S. (2019). Southeast Asian region governance: Political economy, regulatory regionalism, and ASEAN integration. In T. Carroll, S. Hameiri & L. Jones (Eds.), *The political economy of Southeast Asia, Vol. 4: Politics and uneven development under hyperglobalisation*. Palgrave.

Lemke, T. (2007). An indigestible meal? Foucault, governmentality and state theory. *Distinktion: Scandinavian Journal of Social Theory, 8*(2), 43–64.

March, J. G., & Olsen, J. P. (1989). *Rediscovering institutions: The organizational basis of politics*. Free Press.

Mietzner, M. (2014). Oligarchs, politicians, and activists: Contesting party politics in Post-Suharto Indonesia. In *Beyond oligarchy: Wealth, power, and contemporary Indonesian Politics* (p. 99). Cornell.

Moschella, M., & Vetterlein, A. (2016). Self-reinforcing and reactive path dependence: Tracing the IMF's path of policy change. In T. Rixen, L. A. Viola, & M. Zürn (Eds.), *Historical institutionalism and international relations: Explaining institutional development in world politics* (pp. 143–164). Oxford University Press.

Moravcsik, A. (1993). Preferences and power in The European-Community—A liberal intergovernmentalist approach. *Journal of Common Market Studies, 31*(4), 473–524.

Moravcsik, A., & Schimmelfennig, F. (2009). Liberal intergovernmentalism. In A. Wiener, T. A. Borzel, & T. Risse (Eds.), *European integration theory* (pp. 64–84). Oxford University Press.

North, D. C. (1990). *Institutions, institutional change and economic performance*. Cambridge University Press.

Overbeek, H. (2005). Global governance, class, hegemony: A historical materialist perspective. In A. Ba & M. J. Hoffmann (Eds.), *Contending perspectives on global governance: Coherence, contestation, and world order* (pp. 39–56). Routledge.

Peters, B. (2012). *Institutional theory in political science: The new institutionalism* (3rd ed.). Continuum.

Pijl, K. v. d. (1998). *Transnational classes and international relations*. Routledge.

Pollack, M. A. (1994). Creeping competence: The expanding agenda of the European Community 1. *Journal of Public Policy, 14*(2), 95–145.

Pollack, M. A. (1996). The new institutionalism and EC governance: The promise and limits of institutional analysis. *Governance, 9*(4), 429–458.

Pontusson, J. (1995). From comparative public policy to political economy. *Comparative Political Studies, 28*(1), 117–147.

Rixen, T., & Viola, L. A. (2016). Historical institutionalism and international relations: Towards explaining change and stability in international institutions.

In T. Rixen, L. A. Viola, & M. Zürn (Eds.), *Historical institutionalism and international relations: Explaining institutional development in world politics* (pp. 3–34). Oxford University Press.
Schmidt, V. A. (2006). *Democracy in Europe: The EU and national polities.* Oxford University Press.
Schmidt, V. A. (2008). Discursive institutionalism: The explanatory power of ideas and discourse. *Annual Review of Political Science, 11*(1), 303–326.
Simmons, B. A., Dobbin, F., & Garrett, G. (2006). Introduction: The international diffusion of liberalism. *International Organization, 60*(4), 781–810.
Sinclair, T. (1994). Passing judgement: Credit rating processes as regulatory mechanisms of governance in the emerging world order. *Review of International Political Economy, 1*(1), 133–159.
Tapsell, R. (2015). Indonesia's media oligarchy and the Jokowi Phenomenon. *Indonesia, 99*, 29–50.
Thelen, K. (1991). *Union of parts: Labor politics in post-war Germany.* Cornell University Press.
Thelen, K. (1999). Historical institutionalism in comparative politics. *Annual Review of Political Science, 2*(1), 369–404.
Thelen, K. (2010). Beyond comparative statics: Historical institutional approaches to stability and change in the political economy of labor. In G. Morgan, J. Campbell, C. Crouch, O. Pederson, & R. Whiteley (Eds.), *The Oxford handbook of comparative institutional analysis.* Oxford University Press.
Thelen, K., & Steinmo, S. (1992). Historical institutionalism in comparative politics. In S. Steinmo, K. Thelen, & F. Longstreth (Eds.), *Structuring politics: Historical institutionalism in comparative analysis.* Cambridge University Press.
Valverde, M., & Mopas, M. (2004). Insecurity and the dream of targeted governance. In W. Larner & W. Walters (Eds.), *Global governmentality: Governing international spaces.* Routledge.
Walter, A. (2008). *Governing finance: East Asia's adoption of international standards.* Cornell.
Williamson, O. (1975). *Markets and hierarchies, analysis and antitrust implications: A study in the economics of internal organization.* Free Press.
Winters, J. (2011). *Oligarchy.* Cambridge University Press.
Winters, J. (2013). Oligarchy and democracy in Indonesia. *Indonesia, 96*, 11–33, 220.

CHAPTER 3

The Emergence of the Indonesian FSA

This chapter provides a detailed historical account of the emergence of the Indonesian FSA as an independent authority in the financial sector. This book argues that the rise of the Indonesian FSA is one of the main explanations of the existence of domestic implementation gaps in Indonesia, particularly in the area of portfolio investment liberalization. This chapter shows that the FSA's rise basically relates to the 1997–1998 Asian Financial Crisis that hit Indonesia hard. As a consequence, Indonesia had to deal with the IMF and follow neoliberal structural reform programmes mandated by the IMF. This ultimately resulted in the endowment of "independent and free" status to the Indonesian FSA. This chapter shows that there were important events leading to that endowment of power to a newly established institution. Furthermore, and most importantly, agents were involved in the institutional shaping of the Indonesian FSA. The rise of the FSA was also a result of agents' determination to keep pushing for its establishment. In addition, FSA agents came together to establish the FSA's powers and key ideas, despite the fact that they came mostly from two different institutions, the Indonesian MOF and Bank Indonesia.

A detailed historical account of the emergence of the Indonesian FSA as an independent authority in the financial sector is provided in this chapter. This account is provided by reviewing five different time periods that form the chapter's structure: (1) Early Financial Liberalization (1980s–1996); (2) Asian Financial Crisis (1997–1998); (3)

C. Kusuma, *The Rise of the Indonesian Financial Service Authority*,
https://doi.org/10.1007/978-981-19-3850-4_3

Early Proposal for Single FSA (1999–2003); (4) Delays in Establishment (2004–2010); and (5) Transition Period (2011–2013). The first period between 1980 and 1996 was marked by the global economic recession and a sharp decline in oil prices. As Indonesia went through deteriorating economic conditions in the 1980s, the government took certain measures to liberalize the financial sector. Eventually these measures caused another severe, instead of sustainable, domestic economic condition in the 1990s. The severe economic conditions then led Indonesia to slump during the 1997–1998 Asian Financial Crisis, the second period of focus here. The increased public pressures and anti-Chinese riots that occurred in this period concluded with the fall of the longest-serving President, President Soeharto, who had been previously in power for thirty-two years. As a consequence of the worsening economic conditions, Indonesia had to turn to the IMF in order to escape the damaging impacts of the crisis on the overall economy by requesting the approval of the IMF's Stand-By Credit. The IMF approved a total amount of US$10.14 billion over a three years period. However, these funds came with the introduction of a neoliberal reform agenda, including financial sector restructuring and structural reforms.

As this chapter will unveil, these conditions were the start of the emergence and the embryo of the Indonesian FSA. The third period, therefore, focuses on the early proposal for a single financial authority during the period 1999–2003. This is the period in which the Indonesian FSA was starting to take shape. After that, there is the fourth period when there was postponement to the establishment of the FSA. Despite changes in national priorities causing a delay in the establishment of the FSA, during the period 2004–2010, agents continued to carry out efforts to implement the FSA's ideas. The section covering the postponement period breaks down in detail these efforts. The fifth and last period, 2011–2013, was a transitional period for the FSA. During this transition period, agents continued to shape the institutional form of the Indonesian FSA through transitional works in infrastructure, budget and other areas. Agents also had to deal with internal and external pressures that threatened the existence of the institution. Further on, details of early challenges to the institution in its early operational years close the empirical discussions in this chapter. In the immediate section below, this chapter provides an overview of the early financial liberalization period in Indonesia as a background to look at conditions prior to the onset of the Asian Financial Crisis.

The operationalization of "agents-in-context" approach throughout this chapter is to identify the backgrounds to the emergence of the Indonesian FSA. In doing so, this identification allows the identification of primary agents as well as the isolation of related institutions along the five different time periods. The identification of backgrounds here, as commonly found in a traditional historical institutionalism, is also to determine the "critical juncture" and "path dependence" that highly correlate with institutional changes. The "agents-in-context" approach here uses the determination of "critical juncture" and "path dependence" to identify the agents and institutions that are central to the story of the Indonesian FSA. In doing so, this chapter found that the main agents in the establishment of the Indonesian FSA were coming from the Indonesian MOF and Bank Indonesia, or the main institutional players in the establishment of the FSA. However, it is ultimately the FSA agents that shape the FSA's current level of power and key ideas.

Indonesia and the Early Financial Liberalization (1980s–1996)

The first relevant historical event was the global economic recession in the early 1980s, accompanied by the sharp decline in oil prices. Indonesia went through a worsening economic condition in the 1980s which led to financial liberalization and deregulation soon afterwards. The liberalization and deregulation measures that happened in the 1980s, have their origins in the shift of power in the mid 1960s. President Sukarno, the nationalist first President of the Republic of Indonesia, was replaced by the President Soeharto. According to Hamilton-Hart (2012) and Simpson (2010), the shift of power happened in the mid-1960 was closely related to Indonesia's alliances to the U.S., and the "pro-western countries". Hamilton-Hart (2012) further argued that the fall of President Sukarno also marked the fall of the communist movement that flourished during the regime, particularly after the occurrence of The Thirtieth September Movement.[1] She concluded that the fall of Sukarno and the

[1] The Thirtieth September Movement, or also known as G-30S/PKI, was a movement initiated by the Indonesia Communist Party (Partai Komunis Indonesia or PKI) to depose President Sukarno and replace Indonesian ideology with Communism. The movement involved the kidnapping and brutally killing the Indonesian Armed Forces Generals. President Soeharto, at that time the Commander-in-Chief of the Indonesian

communist movement in Indonesia had paved the way for capitalism to enter into Indonesia. This was also the beginning of a lengthy period of the New Order under President Soeharto regime.

Simpson (2010) argued that the road to capitalism in Indonesia was particularly apparent with the appointment of a group of ministers responsible for economics and finance affairs during the early days of President Soeharto regime. This group of ministers were known as the "Berkeley Mafia", referring that most of its members graduated from University of California, Berkeley. Nitisastro (2011), informally considered as the leader of the "Berkeley Mafia", has summarized all the economic and finance policies during his tenure. The summary suggests the transformation of Indonesian economy from nationalism under President Sukarno to internationalism under President Soeharto. As Hamilton-Hart (2012) and Simpson (2010) also suggest that only under this tenure, Indonesia started to introduce policies to boost economic growth mirroring those in the U.S. and other liberal market economy countries. Most of these policies consisted of measures to liberalize and deregulate the Indonesian domestic market, including in the 1980s that Indonesia had to deal with the impact of the oil price slump. More discussions on these liberalization and deregulation are discussed later in this section. Ultimately, the financial liberalization and deregulation caused another severe domestic economic condition in the 1990s.

This severe condition reflects the vulnerability of the Indonesian economy during that time, which resulted in the damaging impact of the Asian Financial Crisis to Indonesia. The story here begins with Indonesia's heavy dependence on oil by late 1970s. During that time, Indonesia had relished the opportunity of a sharp increase in oil prices. Oil prices had increased significantly from only US$ 12.90/barrel in 1978 to US$ 30.90/barrel in 1979 as illustrated in the graph below. Eventually, oil prices reached a peak of US$ 36.80/barrel in 1980. However, shortly after this peak, the oil market experienced a drastic decline and oil prices recorded their lowest during 1980s at US$ 14.35/barrel in 1986 as captured also by Chart 3.1. With a heavy reliance on oil exports, such conditions hit Indonesia hard with a decline in its state revenue. As a result, the government needed to address financial reform with the main objective initially to reduce the heavy reliance on oil (Cho & Khatkhate,

Armed Forces, was appointed as the person in charge to eliminate the movement and stabilize the domestic situation.

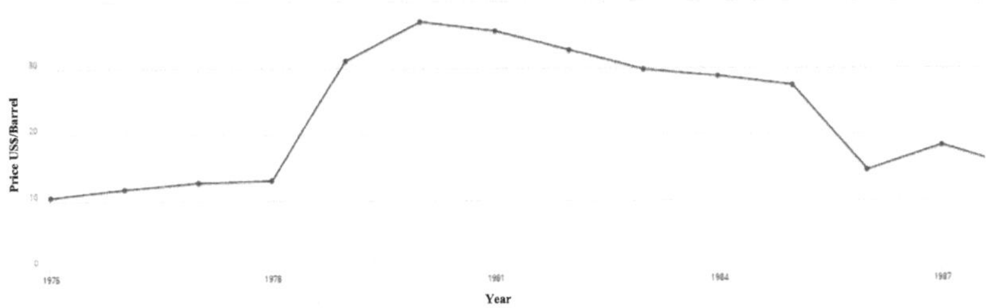

Chart 3.1 Crude oil price (1975–1987) (*Source* World Bank DataBank)

1989; Gultom-Siregar, 1993; Resosudarmo & Kuncoro, 2006). The government, in official Indonesian Budget Memo 1983–1984, also later addressed the need for financial reform (Nota Keuangan dan Rancangan Anggaran Pendapatan dan Belanja Negara Tahun 1983/1984 [Indonesian Budget Memo 1983–1984], 1983).

The official Indonesian Budget Memo 1983–1984 acknowledged that oversupply in the international oil market at that time had forced the Organization of the Petroleum Exporting Countries (OPEC) put limitation on production and restrict the oil prices. As a result, such limitations and restrictions significantly affected Indonesia's state revenue as oil exports were a major source of state revenue. The government predicted only 5.7% increases in oil revenue during that period. This was a massive decline in revenue projection as compared to 22.9% increases in the preceding period (1981–1982). Thus, the Budget Memo further initiated alternative major sources for state revenue streams while reducing reliance on oil exports. The Budget Memo actually stressed the government's main objective to carry out reform, which was to reduce the heavy reliance on oil. Further, the reform was a product of a government response to Indonesia's declining economic condition. This is also to say that there was almost no discernible global or international external pressure to carry out the reform. This is as opposed to, for instance, the pressure from the IMF to reform in late 1990s as part of the response to the Asian Financial Crisis.

The global economic recession in the early 1980s also added to the severity of economic conditions during that time, bearing in mind the impact of a sharp decline in oil prices. In 1982, the world's Gross Domestic Product (GDP) annual growth reached its lowest peak during the period of 1978–1987 (Chart 3.2). The world's GDP at that time recorded less than 0.4% of annual growth. This record was continuing the declining trend of GDP annual growth since the recorded level of 5.3% in 1976. The same trend happened with Indonesia's GDP annual growth (Chart 3.3). By 1982, Indonesia experienced an astounding decline in annual growth to only 2.2% from around 8% in the preceding year. There were fluctuations in annual growth in the following years, yet growth never really recovered. Thus, the impact of the sharp decline in oil prices alone might not have been enough to force the government to carry out reform. Nevertheless, the global economic recession in the early 1980s clearly left the government with little space. In the end, the government had to introduce reform packages starting from 1983 until late 1990s.

Kuntjoro-Jakti (1986) provided a comprehensive explanation on the rationale the Indonesian government used to promote economic reform at this time. He argued that "as global recession begun to be felt in the economy, the non-LNG [Liquefied Natural Gas] and non-refinery manufacturing sector practically stagnated under the combined impact of declining purchasing power and rising costs" (p. 103). Indonesia needed to seek alternatives to the overreliance on oil and gas. However, due to the global economic recession, the government was unable to stimulate other potential sectors to substitute the oil and gas sector. As a result,

Chart 3.2 GDP growth (annual %)—world (1975–1987) (*Source* World Bank DataBank)

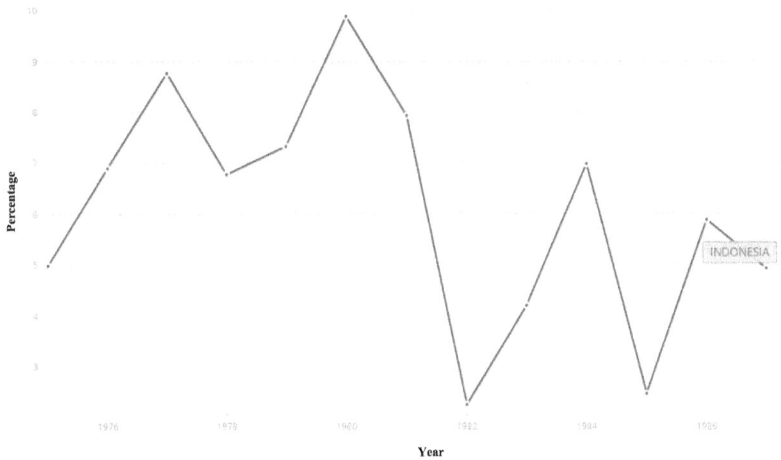

Chart 3.3 GDP growth (annual %)—Indonesia (1975–1987) (*Source* World Bank DataBank)

Indonesia was "in the face of the continuing and growing deficit potentials of the Balance of Trade in particular the Current Account" (p. 105) and had to perform "anti-cyclical" fiscal and monetary measures. These measures engendered significant reductions of government spending, as well as exchange rate policy changes to a managed floating exchange rate system. Consequently, "the government not only imposes tight money policy throughout this period, but also "deregulate" its monetary policy framework" (p. 105). One of the reasons for the introduction of reform packages was to facilitate these actions.

Most of the reform packages until late 1990s, also discussed in the following paragraphs, can directly relate to Indonesia's early efforts at financial liberalization. Through these reform packages, the government carried out financial sector deregulation and capital account liberalization policies all the way until late 1990s. In the end, these reforms had pushed the volatile portfolio investment, or the so-called "hot money" flows coming without restrictions into Indonesia during that period. The "hot money" flows meant that foreign capital flows reached high level by as early as 1993.

Both the global economic recession in the early 1980s and the sharp decline in oil prices during the period 1982–1983 laid the early foundations for Indonesian financial sector liberalization. In 1983, as a response to continuous sharp decline in growth and a significant deficit of the balance of payments, Indonesia issued a reform package called as "PAKJUN 83" or the June 1983 Package. "Prior to June 1, 1983, Indonesia had most of the characteristics of a financially repressed system. The banking sector was heavily regulated and entry was very restricted" (Gultom-Siregar, 1993). Thus, the package intended to relax those restrictions, predominantly on the borrowing and lending of Indonesian national banks. As Cho and Khatkhate (1989, p. ix) note, it consisted of three principal components:

> (a) elimination of ceilings on bank credits; (b) gradual narrowing of loan categories from access to Bank Indonesia (BI) liquidity credits; and (c) deregulation of state banks' interest rates on most categories of deposits and on all loans except a few priority loans.

At that stage, there was barely any specific and clear intent to relax the regulations for capital inflows from overseas. Nevertheless, "PAKJUN 83" marked the earliest of government's efforts to deregulate and liberalize the domestic financial system, especially in the banking sector.

However, the decline of oil prices continued to reach its lowest peak in the period of 1982–1983. As a result, Indonesia needed to deal with another sharp turn of growth and balance of payments in 1986. Indonesia was again prompted to introduce another reform package known as "PAKTO 1988" or the October 1988 Package. While the "PAKJUN 83" intended to relax the restrictions on borrowing and lending of Indonesian national banks, "PAKTO 1988" was intended to not only further deregulate banking but also remove restrictions on trade measures. As it was the case with "PAKJUN 1983", "PAKTO 1988" again marked the further decline of a restrictive banking regime in Indonesia (Haggard & Maxfield, 1996). As Hanna (1994) argues that:

> Having dealt with banking, the next reform package (PAKDES in, December 1988), focused on stimulating the capital market and other non-banking financial institutions. The government issued new regulations covering the establishment of multi-finance companies empowered to engage in leasing, factoring, venture capital, credit-card operations and consumer credit. (p. 11)

"PAKDES 1988" was considered the first milestone for the deregulation of capital market and other financial institutions (Trihayati, 1993). Before the launch of "PAKDES 1988", the government had control over every aspect of the capital market and other financial institutions. The control included not only supervision of the market activities but also the conduct of the market itself. For instance, the government was the institution that conducted stock market trading while at the same time the government also carried out supervision of trading activities. Although there were no regulations to liberalize equities or debts flows, with "PAKDES 1988" the government had started to loosen its role to exclusively supervise equity and debt markets. All the reform packages mentioned in this section form an important part of our story of the emergence of the Indonesian FSA. Most of the measures taken during the period of these reform packages include the financial sector, particularly banking sector, deregulation and liberalization. These reform packages marked the deliberate efforts taken by the government that was still in overall control of the financial sector at that time. The story of the Indonesian FSA is also a story of taking away some of this control from the government and giving it to an "independent and free" institution. This story even followed the one that had come earlier, giving away government control over banks to Bank Indonesia.

Further reform packages were introduced in Indonesia up until the early 1990s. For example, "PAKMAR 1989" or the March 1989 Package opened the capital account liberalization door by generally allowing external lending and borrowing in the domestic banking industry. As a result, by early the 1990s, foreign capital flows had reached such a high level that the government started to introduce tighter prudential requirements in the financial sector, such as the adoption by 1993 of the Basel Agreement as a component of the prudential reform package. One of the causes of this alarming level was the volatile portfolio investment inflows in the domestic financial system because of banking deregulation and capital account liberalization (Sheng, 2009). Meanwhile, at the other end, such deregulation and liberalization were not accompanied by the strengthening of the domestic financial system. For example, a minimum capital requirement was not introduced to Indonesia's financial institutions, and external lending and borrowing activities did not follow sound requirements. Efforts to strengthen the domestic financial system only started as late as 1993 when volatile portfolio investments had already poured into Indonesia. In addition, efforts to stimulate domestic capital markets and other non-banking financial institutions were also failing to develop the domestic market (Akimov & Dollery, 2010). The volatile portfolio investments, accompanied by fragility within the domestic financial system, later contributed to Indonesia's vulnerability during the Asian Financial Crisis (Haggard, 2000; Hamilton-Hart, 2000; Sheng, 2009).

Indonesia and the 1997–1998 Asian Financial Crisis

As mentioned in the last section, the impact of Asian Financial Crisis hit Indonesia hard mainly due to its economic vulnerability. Volatile portfolio investment, because of portfolio investment flow liberalization in the 1990s, was central to this economic vulnerability. Starting in 1997, Indonesian net inflows slumped into its lowest, a minus of almost US$ 5 billion (Chart 3.4). This was a free downfall if compared to the intensely positive preceding years of around US$ 1.5 trillion in 1995, or even the US$ 2 trillion a year before the crisis. Later, these conditions were one of major triggers for the existence of the balance of payments crisis that led Indonesia into dealing with the IMF. After that, it took seven years, until around 2004, for Indonesia to recover its net inflows to around the same level as it was in 1996. Even in contemporary Indonesia, the volatility of portfolio investment flows has continued to affect the Indonesian economy. For example, from 2004 to 2016, there were significant ups and downs indicating just how volatile portfolio investment flows were due to, in part, the liberalization included in the reform packages started in the early 1980s as described in the previous section.

Parallel with the net inflow slump, the annual GDP growth of Indonesia was also free falling. Indonesia's annual GDP growth in 1998 was more than minus 13%. The declining trend of the annual GDP growth had started from the middle of the 1990s. For instance, in 1995, the growth was already steady at a rate of more than 8%. Yet, since then, the growth kept declining until a year before 1998, at only less than 5% in 1997. The historical records of the Jakarta Composite Index (JCI) also give a reflection of the vulnerability of the Indonesian economy during the Asian Financial Crisis. During this period, Indonesia also had one of the worst declining stock market indexes as compared to other AMS and East Asian countries. Table 3.1 shows that Indonesia experienced a decline of almost around 38% within the period December 1996 to December 1998. The same table also shows that Malaysia and Thailand experienced among

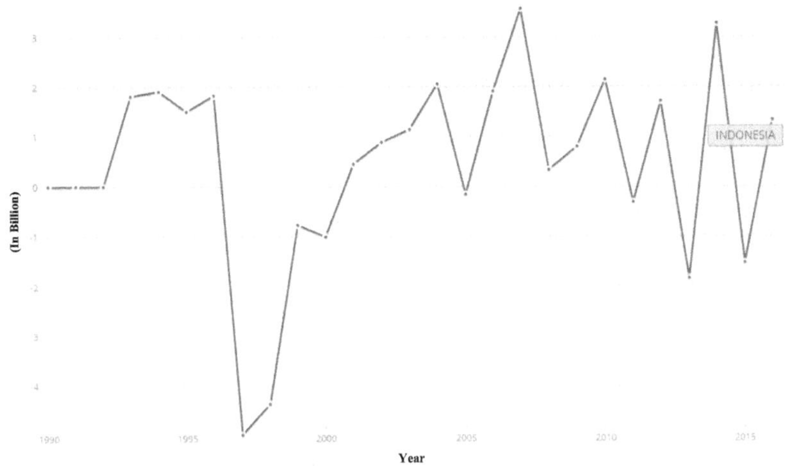

Chart 3.4 Indonesia portfolio equity, net inflows (balance of payments, current US$) (*Source* World Bank DataBank)

Table 3.1 Jakarta composite index performance (1996–1998)

Indonesia	*Malaysia*	*Philippines*	*Thailand*	*China*	*Hong Kong*	*Japan*	*United States*	*UK*
JCI index	FBMKLCI index	PCOMP index	SET index	SHCOMP index	HIS index	NKY index	DJI index	UKI index
−37.56%	−52.65%	−37.90%	−57.21%	25.05%	−25.30%	−28.51%	42.39%	42.83%

Source Indonesia Stock Exchange Market Update (26 April 2018)

the highest declines in AMS with around 53% and 58% respectively. Those numbers were not surprising on their own, as the Asian Financial Crisis originally started from the financial crisis in Thailand, and Malaysia was among the first AMS that experienced the spillover effect. The spillover effect eventually also affected Indonesia. At that time, the condition of the Indonesian economy was already vulnerable due to portfolio investment liberalization and deregulation. Thus, once the spillover came, Indonesia appeared to have less power to stabilize markets and help the economy to bounce back.

As part of the plans to deal with the financial crisis that hit the domestic banking sector, during his last time in the administration, President Soeharto established a new institution, the Indonesian Banking Restructuring Agency (IBRA). This institution had the main task of restructuring all the insolvent banks affected by the Asian Financial Crisis (Presidential Decree No. 27 Year 1998). In order to carry out its task, IBRA closely liaised with the government, through the Indonesian MOF, and Bank Indonesia. If a bank was considered unhealthy based on the assessment of Bank Indonesia, then the bank would be handed over to IBRA for restructuring. To this end, the responsibility of Bank Indonesia was limited to only assess the soundness of all banks. After just around six years of its establishment, the IBRA was wound up in 2004 as it seemed to fail to resolve the insolvent bank problems. Scholars (such as Hadiz & Robison, 2005; Gunawan & Siregar, 2009) have suggested that the failure was mainly attributable to interference from the government as well as financial conglomerates in the restructuring process resulting in the inability of IBRA to sell the majority of bank assets it had acquired. In the next development related to this banking restructuring process post-2004, the Indonesian MOF took over the tasks left from IBRA. This chapter now moves to discussions about critical events after the regional spillover of the Asian Financial Crisis to Indonesia that started the slump of Thai Baht.

The Early Proposal for a Single Financial Services Authority (1999–2003)

As President Soeharto finally handed in his resignation in May 1998 due to increased public pressures and domestic riots, his former Vice President Habibie took his place. Meanwhile, as the Indonesian economy continue to decline, Indonesia then needed to further resort to the IMF for reform plans. This was also a result of pressures from domestic agents for reform (Walter, 2008). This was the first reform plan offered by the IMF to recover the economy (Resosudarmo & Kuncoro, 2006). "Basically, the IMF-supported programme comprised a comprehensive policy package to deal with insolvent and weak banks, and to overcome structural rigidities in the economy" (Djiwandono, 2002, p. 207). As a result, Indonesia signed a series of Letters of Intent (LOI) with the first one being signed in October 1997. The LOI (Indonesia Letter of Intent, 1997) stated that it "outlines the program that Indonesia intends to implement over the next three years to address the fundamental causes of its current financial difficulties, thereby ensuring that the economy is placed on a path of strong and sustainable growth". The introduction of reform plans by IFIs itself is a common practice for countries with financial difficulties or crisis. IFIs, such as the IMF, often confronted governments with the pressure to adopt international regulatory frameworks to achieve more globally accepted regulatory practices (Sheng, 2009). One of those international regulatory frameworks covers adoption of a more liberalized regime of trade and investments, including frameworks related to portfolio investment liberalization.

A senior official at one of the Indonesian domestic authorities confirmed that the series of IMF LOIs was key to a more liberalized regime in the Indonesian financial sector. For instance, capital account deregulation and a freer flow of portfolio investments was at the heart of the IMF structural reform programme. However, the IMF's reform package to deregulate Indonesia's capital account was later proven to be ill-suited (Grenville, 2004; Hamilton-Hart, 2000; Stiglitz, 2001). Meanwhile, pursuing a freer flow of portfolio investments was also proven risky as it encouraged "hot money" flows (see, for instance, Hall, 2012; Reinhart & Calvo, 2000; Rodrik & Velasco, 1999; Rethel, 2012; Walter, 2005). The pursuance of a freer flow of portfolio investment itself was mainly a result of IMF LOIs for Indonesia to develop its non-bank financial institutions industry, including the capital market, insurance and financing companies. The aim was to overcome the over-reliance on the banking system as one of the major sources of the financial crisis. Since then, capital market, insurance and financing companies included as parts of portfolio investments became the focus of liberalization for ASEAN.

More importantly, resorting to the IMF support brought significant changes to the way Indonesia regulates and supervises its financial sector, particularly the banking sector that dominated financial services. The LOI dated 13 November 1998 specifically mentioned that Indonesia was obliged to submit a Central Bank Law to parliament by the end of December 1998 (Indonesia Letter of Intent, 1998). The submission of a Central Bank Law was mainly to give independent status to Bank Indonesia as well as pushing provisions to establish a single financial supervisory authority. Further, in the following year, on 16 March 1999, another LOI reflected a delay in the submission of a Central Bank Law. As the government had submitted the law to parliament, it expected parliament to pass the law by mid-April 1999 (Indonesia Letter of Intent,

1999). Up to this point, as is the case with countries resorting to the IMF, government had no other option than following the IMF's neoliberal reforms accompanying the stand-by credits. Since then, the proposal to establish a single financial supervisory authority has evolved over time and took around thirteen years (back from the original ideas in 1998 to the enactment of the corresponding establishment law in 2011) for Indonesia to finally conclude the establishment of the Indonesian FSA.

Before the Asian Financial Crisis, all financial services regulation and supervision were still under the full, or at least majority, control of the government through the Indonesian MOF. For instance, although banking sector supervision was under the authority of Bank Indonesia, the Indonesian MOF still retained the power to issue banking licences. This also demonstrates that the government was still supporting the operations of Bank Indonesia in banking supervision, including budget and infrastructure. In the next development stage, particularly in the early days of 1998 after the breakout of the Asian Financial Crisis, the government started to reduce its authority over financial services regulation by transferring banking sector regulation. President Habibie enacted the Law No. 10 Year 1998 on Banking. One of the most important features of the law is that the power to issue banking licences was transferred into the hands of Bank Indonesia, marking this as a milestone of full transition of banking sector supervision from the government. In its elucidation part to the general background of the power transfer, the law mentioned the following:

> In order for the banking supervision to work effectively, the authority and the responsibility concerning bank licenses, which formerly under the authority of the Finance Minister shall be transferred to the Chairman of Bank Indonesia. So that Bank Indonesia has a sole authority and responsibility relating to licensing, supervising, and imposing sanctions on a bank which fails to adhere to the prevailing banking regulations. Therefore, Bank Indonesia has the authority and responsibility to evaluate and to decide the feasibility for the establishment of a Bank and/or opening Bank offices. (Law No. 10 Year 1998 on Banking)

However, Bank Indonesia still had the responsibility to support the government during the hard time of the Asian Financial Crisis, particularly to overcome the problems of restructuring insolvent banks as well as strengthening their prudential practices.

The following year after his inauguration, President Habibie then enacted Law Number 23 Year 1999 on Bank Indonesia. This law was basically the exact product as set out in the LOIs as discussed in earlier paragraphs. The enactment of this law itself marked a new era of the central bank as the law endowed independent status to Bank Indonesia. The law specifically mentioned that: "Bank Indonesia is an independent state institution, which is free from any interferences of the Government and or other parties, except for matters explicitly prescribed in this Act" (Article 4). As to the duties and functions of Bank Indonesia, the law mandated that they included: "a. to prescribe and to implement the monetary policy; b. to regulate and to safeguard the smoothness of the payment system; c. to regulate and to supervise banks" (Article 8). As the transformational process of Bank Indonesia continued, the Bank's focus was mainly on monetary policy and payment systems. Meanwhile, regulation and supervision of banks would gradually be handed over to the Indonesian FSA. As the law also inserted a transitional provision in Article 35 stating that "[a]s long as the supervisory entity as referred to in Article 34 has not been established, the banking regulation and supervision task shall be conducted by Bank Indonesia".

Most importantly, the law has set out the proposal for a single financial services authority, the forerunner of the Indonesian FSA, as parts of IMF's financial services reform in Indonesia. In Article 34, the law stipulated the following provision:

> (1) the banking supervision tasks will be conducted by an independent supervisory board of financial services sector which shall be established by an Act. (2) the establishment of such supervisory entity as referred to in paragraph (1) will be taken place not later than December 31, 2002. (Law No. 10 Year 1998 on Banking)

Looking further to the elucidation part of that article, the law stipulated that the supervision coverage of the independent supervisory board of financial services sector covers banking and other financial services companies, including insurance, pension funds, securities, joint venture and financing companies, as well as other institutions that collected and managed public funds. It is through the adoption of a unified financial supervisory system that a single regulator is able to oversee all the domestic financial institutions. One of the main rationales for establishing a unified financial services authority is the need for comprehensive supervision over financial conglomerates (such as Claessens, 2003; Mwenda & Fleming, 2001; Taylor & Fleming, 1999). Although these scholars did not particularly touch on the case of Indonesia, the same rationale was also the major background behind the establishment of the Indonesian FSA. Although their definitions of financial conglomerates in Indonesia may differ from those of these scholars, it is clear that one of the FSA's foci is to oversee financial conglomerates. According to Indonesian FSA Regulation Number 18/POJK.03/2014 on the Implementation of Integrated Governance for Financial Conglomerates, the definition of financial conglomerates includes all financial services institutions that are under the same groups due to ownerships and/or controlling relations.

Further, the elucidation also specified that the new supervisory board is an independent body in carrying out its duties and functions. It only has a reporting obligation to the parliament and has the authority to cooperate with other related institutions, like Bank Indonesia and the Indonesian MOF. The elucidation even required that the independent Bank Indonesia share necessary macroeconomic data with the proposed supervisory board. According to Sitompul (2012), there were two major factors to the amplified discussions of an independent financial services authority in Indonesia, Firstly, he argued that almost all financial crises in the 1990s were the result of political influences. He suggests that ineffective and weak implementation of regulations correlated with the degree of political interference. According to him, the emergence of the Indonesian FSA was an effort to depoliticize the regulatory power in the financial services industry from external interference. In order for the Indonesian FSA to be free of interference, it should attain independent status. This is consistent with the work of Siregar and James (2006) who also argued that a unified financial services authority "must be able to take decisions and carry out its duties without undue outside interference, whether from ministers, parliamentarians, industry leaders, or other government official" (p. 106). According to them, the definition of Indonesian FSA's independence includes the non-interference relationships between it and all related parties in the Indonesian financial sector.

Secondly, Sitompul (2012) further argued that the literature on central bank independence provides a framework for states to continue reforming the financial sector. The central banks in most parts of the world have currently been relishing the independent status, including in Indonesia. However, he also mentioned that there were also discussions that the central banks were being too authoritarian by covering both macro- and micro-banking supervision at the same time. The long debate on the integration or separation of macro- and micro-banking supervision contributed to the discussions on the establishment of the Indonesian FSA. For instance, the proponents of integration advocated that, as the "lenders of last resort" in the banking industry, the central banks needed the authority to oversee both the monetary aspect (macro-banking) as well as the prudential side (micro-banking). On the other hand, the opponents of integration argued that separation of prudential supervision from the central banks would result in the enhancement of the central bank's capacity by focusing only on inflation targeting. The separation view has become popular since at least the last decade and is partly attributable to the failure of central banks across the world to maintain financial stability resulting in financial crisis. Thus, in order to get consistent with the current global financial sector reform, Indonesia also separated the macro- and micro-banking supervision. While the monetary aspect is still under the full domain of Bank Indonesia, the Indonesian FSA has taken authority of the prudential side (micro-banking).

Those three factors mentioned above (the need to supervise financial conglomerates, depoliticizing of the regulator from external interference, and the separation of micro-banking authority from the central bank) are the most important rationales for agents to keep pushing for the establishment of the Indonesian FSA. For instance, Former Chairman of the Indonesian FSA, Dr. Muliaman Hadad, (Hadad et al., 2017) looked back on his critiques of financial services regulators prior to the establishment of the FSA. For instance, he mentioned that Bank Indonesia needed to reform its structure and configuration through separating its monetary authority from its banking supervision. Additionally, he highlighted the use of financial conglomerates to support the establishment of the FSA. Ultimately, the insertion of the Article 34 of the Bank Indonesia Law as quoted earlier was to reflect the push from agents to establish a unified financial services authority. In the next section, this chapter looks at the delays in the establishment of the Indonesian FSA, even though the mandate to establish the institution actually had started in 1999.

Delays in the Establishment of the Indonesian FSA (2004–2010)

Under the administration of President Megawati Soekarnoputri, Indonesia amended Law Number 23 Year 1999 on Bank Indonesia with the enactment of Law Number 3 Year 2004 on Bank Indonesia. As President Megawati Soekarnoputri administration's term ended soon after the enactment of this law, the implementation actually started during the period of President Susilo Bambang Yudhoyono (SBY)'s presidential term (2005–2014). The discussions on the emergence of the Indonesian FSA afterwards were then within the context of President SBY's administration. The most important amendment in this new law that is relevant to the discussions of the institutional emergence (in this chapter) is a deadline change for the establishment of the Indonesian FSA from 31 December 2002 to 31 December 2010 (Amendment to Article 34 of the Law Number 23 Year 1999 on Bank Indonesia). This meant that there was eight years of delay in the establishment process of the FSA from its original proposal. Ordinary public opinion might say that the delay was a result of the lack of government willingness, or perhaps a consequence of the long parliamentary process of approval. Although these changes in government and parliamentary priorities might logically explain the delay, there were other more important occurrences during the duration of the delay.

During these periods of postponement, there were surely changes in priorities of not only the government but also the parliament. To this extent, this chapter looks at the inclusion of the law to establish the Indonesian FSA in the National Legislation Program (Program Legislasi Nasional/Prolegnas). Prolegnas itself listed all the laws that were priorities for the next five-year period to be discussed and/or concluded between the government and the House of Representative. The law to establish the Indonesian FSA had just been formally inserted into one of the items in Prolegnas for the period of 2010–2014 as it missed out on the 2005–2009 period. The delay may be also because of the power shift to the FSA required a comprehensive institutional transition. The Elucidation of the Law Number 23 Year 1999 on Bank Indonesia mentioned that:

> The transfer of the bank supervision function from Bank Indonesia to a supervisory board for the financial services sector shall be phased in after fulfilment of the requirements covering infrastructure, budget, personnel,

> organizational structure, information system, documentation system, and various implementation regulations in the form of legal instruments, and shall be reported to the House of Representatives. (Law Number 23 Year 1999 on Bank Indonesia)

As noted above, while it seems logical for these changes in government and parliamentary priorities to explain the delay in the process, there were other more important occurrences.

As the power and authority of the FSA derived from some parts of the Indonesian MOF and Bank Indonesia's power and authority, FSA agents also mostly came from the MOF and Bank Indonesia. There were different circumstances during the postponement that helped FSA agents gain their independence. From the side of the Indonesian MOF, agents were utilizing the internal reforms carried out to accumulate experience for an integrated financial supervisory agency. They were pushing for independent status while preparing the infrastructure to support the new institution. On the other side, agents from Bank Indonesia were pushing institutional reforms on the central banks. These institutional reforms can be seen firstly, from the continuous debates and discussions as to the separation of macro-banking to micro-banking supervisions. Secondly, they were also a result of a push for reform due to a renowned banking scandal involving the highest-level officials of Bank Indonesia. In addition to these separate circumstances, there were also circumstances involving agents from both institutions. These included an enhanced engagement with the House of Representative, arguably to smoothen the enactment of the FSA Law. These events are elaborated in more detail in the following section.

At the outset, the first circumstance was the internal reform carried out by the Indonesian MOF. The internal reforms here refer to the merger of two Echelon I[2] units into one Echelon I unit under the Minister of Finance. The corresponding units, the Capital Market Supervisory Agency (Bapepam) and the Directorate General of Financial Institutions (Direktorat Jenderal Lembaga Keuangan/DJLK), were merged into the

[2] Echelon is a structural hierarchy within government institutions in Indonesia. In most Ministries, Echelon I units are units under the leaderships level of a Secretary General, or an Inspectorate General, or Director General, or Head of Agency. Echelon I unit is the highest structural hierarchy that the heads directly report to the Minister.

Capital Market and Financial Institutions Supervisory Agency (Bapepam-LK) in 2005. Bapepam was formerly responsible for the regulation and supervision of the capital market industry. Meanwhile, DJLK was mainly regulating and supervising the non-bank financial institutions (insurance, pension fund and financing companies). At that time, the government considered the merger to be an "embryo" for the establishment of the FSA (Bisnis Indonesia, 17 February 2005). The government was of the view that the successful future operations of the FSA relied on the success of the merger. If the merger was successful, then there was a high possibility that the IFSA would perform well in the future. This seems reasonable as, at least, half of the FSA's power and functions were supposed to be from Bapepam-LK, while the other half were supposed to be from Bank Indonesia powers and functions around banking supervision.

During five-year merger period (starting in 2005 until the establishment of the FSA in early 2011), agents from this new Echelon I unit had accumulated the knowledge and ideas for the best possible system of an integrated financial services supervision in Indonesia. In some cases, agents faced institutional limitations on the enforcement of rules and regulations due to institution's limited power. For instance, in order to investigate market manipulation or an unusual market activity case, Bapepam-LK might undertake an examination of the flows of money involved. This would require Bapepam-LK to deal with the banking secrecy provisions that were still the domain of Bank Indonesia. To this extent, in the Indonesian bureaucratic context, it might be an uneasy and long process to ask Bank Indonesia to open the banking secrecy provisions. This could be attributable to the non-interference power of Bank Indonesia as an independent institution. On the other hand, Bapepam-LK still need to go through a higher hierarchy, at least at Minister of Finance or President level, in order to tap into areas covered by banking secrecy. In the process of creating the FSA, agents learned that in order to have an effective financial supervision, a new institution should equip itself with the independent status and a higher degree of power.

For instance, according to an internal document, a former chairman of Bapepam-LK suggested that Bapepam-LK had identified features needed to enhance supervision in the capital market. As a consequence, in the same document, the former chairman further mentioned that the identified features should be present in the FSA. The former chairman particularly noted the following features (pp. 16–19):

> Adanya kewenangan-kewenangan OJK melakukan pengaturan, pengawasan, pemeriksaan, dan tindakan lain terhadap Lembaga Jasa Keuangan, memberi dan mencabut izin, mengenakan sanksi, dan kewenangan tambahan yakni memberikan perintah tertulis kepada LJK, menunjuk dan menetapkan Pengelola Statuter, Penyidikan dan perlindungan Konsumen...Ancaman sanksi pidana berlaku bagi pihak-pihak yang mengintervensi OJK.
>
> [*The existence of authorities of the Indonesian FSA to carry out regulation, supervision, examination and other actions to Financial Services Institutions, approve and revoke licences, give sanctions, and additional authorities that are giving written order to Financial Services Institutions, appointing and designating Statutory Management, Investigation and Consumer protection.... The criminal sanction applies to parties that intervene the Indonesian FSA.*]

On another occasion, agents also experienced difficulties expressing ideas on how to perceive portfolio investment liberalization. For instance, the issue of linking all exchanges trading platforms to achieve a connected trading link among AMS had been an issue since early 2007. From the initiation of the trading link, Bapepam-LK indicated its position not to join the link, particularly due to problems in converging regulations and infrastructures. However, conveying this idea to other AMS could be challenging for Bapepam-LK. Under the Indonesian MOF, Bapepam-LK was unable to act on behalf of the Indonesian MOF in relation to international affairs, including ASEAN initiatives on portfolio investment liberalization. Agents still needed to disseminate the idea to another unit within the Indonesian MOF for the approval of the Minister of Finance, or in some cases to the presidential level, before finally expressing it in an international forum or agreeing to a financial liberalization agreement. In addition, agents' ideas that intersecting with the authority of Bank Indonesia, such as on issues of government bonds settlement, could be even more challenging. To this extent, agents were pushing for the "independent and free" status that would also allow them to attain discretionary power in portfolio investment liberalization.

The second context elaborated here is related to the FSA agents from Bank Indonesia pushing for institutional reforms on the central bank. The push here can be seen from the continuous debates and discussions as to the separation of macro-banking and micro-banking supervision. Sato (2005) also notes that there had been delays in the emergence of the independent authority due to the reluctance of the central banks to hand over their micro-banking authority to the FSA. There were discussions regarding the enormous institutional power of Bank Indonesia, as it seemed to have full power over most monetary and financial dealings. According to Sitompul (2004), the idea of establishing the FSA was actually the result of a compromise to circumvent a deadlock in discussing Law Number 23 Year 2004 on Bank Indonesia by the House of Representative. The idea of separating the banking supervisory function from the central bank actually came from Dr. Helmut Schlesinger, the former Governor of the German Central Bank, who at the time of drafting the law acted as a consultant. Thus, the model used in separating the banking supervisory functions largely imitated the practices in Germany. As a result, there was strong resistance to the process of enacting the law from members of parliament that supported Bank Indonesia retaining full power over banking supervision. As a compromise, it was agreed that the institution which would replace Bank Indonesia in supervising banks was also tasked with overseeing other financial institutions. This compromise was intended to show the public that the separation of the supervision function was not merely an effort to reduce the central bank's authority. It also set a precedent for the future.

The third circumstance, and another factor that related to the agents from Bank Indonesia, is the renowned scandals involving the Board of Governors of Bank Indonesia. For instance, former Bank Indonesia Senior Deputy Governor Miranda Goeltom was involved in corruption committed in 2004. She was then sentenced by the court to three years in prison in 2012. She was considered to have committed the crime of corruption by bribing members of the House of Representative in order to ease her position as a Senior Deputy Governor. Another case was related to former Governor Burhanuddin Abdullah who was sentenced to five years in prison. He was considered to have misused his authority by approving the transfer of Rp. 100 billion to Bank Indonesia from the Indonesian Banking Development Institute (Lembaga Pengembangan Perbankan Indonesia/LPPI). Around more than half of the funds were then used by Bank Indonesia to finance the legal costs of former BI officials. Some significant portion of the funds was also channelled to members of the House of Representative to insert particular amendments in Law Number 23 Year 2004 on Bank Indonesia. Through all of these events (the GFC, the Century Bank bailout as well as other renowned scandals), agents were determined to establish the FSA following the mandate of the Law by the latest 31 December 2010.

Some commentators suggested that there was also a reluctance on the part of agents in Bank Indonesia to establish the FSA. Sitompul (2004) also suggested that, aside from strong resistance from the pro-Bank Indonesia members of the parliament, there was also resistance from internal agents within Bank Indonesia. For instance, one of the former Governors of Bank Indonesia expressed his strong rejection to the establishment of the FSA (Kompas, 29 September 2010). He conveyed this rejection formally during the hearing in the House of Representative. He mentioned that a single financial services authority, like the Indonesian FSA, might be an outdated structure in the current global financial system. He also added that, in some cases such as in the United Kingdom (UK), banking supervision had been transferred back to the Bank of England. The Bank Indonesia Workers Union (Ikatan Pegawai Bank Indonesia/IPEBI) also expressed its resistance to the establishment of the FSA (Kontan, 6 December 2010). The Union's resistance was mostly related to the fact that Bank Indonesia would transfer some of its employees to the FSA, particularly employees within the banking supervision structure of Bank Indonesia. IPEBI claimed that, based on the survey it conducted on around 500 Bank Indonesia employees, almost 80% rejected the idea of moving to the FSA, and just a little more than 10% of them were willing to transfer themselves. The rest, almost 10%, preferred to have early retirement.

The fourth factor was that both the FSA agents from the Indonesian MOF and Bank Indonesia worked together in an increasing engagement with the House of Representative. One of the major examples of this would be that members of parliament conducted comparison studies on other countries' financial services authorities or other equivalent overseas institutions. These comparison studies took place particularly after the draft law inserted into Prolegnas 2010–2014 and aimed at member of the special committee on draft law of the Indonesian FSA. Most of national media in Indonesia have exposed these comparison studies mentioning that there were four countries involved: the UK, Germany, Japan and South Korea. Some of the major agents from both Bank Indonesia and Bapepam-LK were included in the trips along with members of parliament. This was the opportunity for agents and other related players to get together and compromise on the major deadlocks for the enactment of the law. According to Omori (2014), one of the major deadlocks causing delays in the enactment of the law was that "the government and parliament were unable to reach an agreement for the composition of the OJK's board of commissioners and selection mechanism" (p. 1005). In fact, agreements on the deadlocks were eventually reached, and the enactment followed after the conclusion of the comparison studies.

Omori (2014) revealed that two of the major political parties in the parliament have finally agreed to have one representative from Bank Indonesia and one representative from the Indonesian MOF out of the total nine members of the FSA Board of Commissioners. Prior to this, those two major political parties were in objected to having representatives from Bank Indonesia or the Indonesian MOF on the Board of Commissioners, while other small parties supported having government and Bank Indonesia's representatives within the FSA. Both major political parties argued that the insertion would reduce the independence of the institution, because it might lead to government or other institution's interference in Indonesian FSA policymaking. Meanwhile, other small parties acknowledged the need for regulatory harmonization and exchanges of information, in addition to the national interests, as the main reasons behind supporting the representatives. Agents in both Bank Indonesia and the Indonesian MOF (through Bapepam-LK) were undoubtedly pushing for this as it meant continuous involvement in the FSA policymaking. Eventually, the final outcome of this issue was to accommodate the representatives. The Minister of Finance and the Governor of Bank Indonesia would appoint one "ex-officio" official each as representatives of both the government and Bank Indonesia.

Lastly, the 2008 Global Financial Crisis (GFC) also accelerated the establishment of the FSA. As compared to the Asian Financial Crisis, most scholars suggested that the 2008 GFC had affected the Indonesian economy less despite its bigger magnitude (such as Basri & Rahardja, 2010; Tambunan, 2010; Thee, 2012). However, Iyer and Lane (2016) argue that a series of financial scandals by Bank Indonesia high-level officials generated "a consensus that BI [Bank Indonesia] had failed—that its banking supervision was inadequate, and its leaders were untrustworthy—and sentiment mounted for an alternative" (p. 293). Thus, with the GFC in the background, FSA agents were pushing for an independent institution that would take away banking supervision from Bank Indonesia. For instance, the bailout of Century Bank in 2008, as one of the biggest financial scandals, paved the way for the establishment of the FSA (Iyer & Lane, 2016; Omori, 2014). The government's decision to bail out the defaulted Century Bank was a collective decision made by the Coordinating Forum for Financial Sector Stability (FKSSK). The

FKSSK was known as the predecessor of the Financial Sector Stability Committee (FSSC) that is discussed in more detail in a later chapter of this book. The FKSSK, at that time, still consisted of the Indonesian MOF, Bank Indonesia and the Indonesia Deposit Insurance Corporation (IDIC). Later, this bail out decision was considered to have led to financial losses by the Indonesian Corruption Eradication Commission (Komisi Pemberantasan Korupsi/KPK), a special government agency which fights corruption. As a result, high-level officials within the FKSSK were prosecuted. Not only was there a high level of distrust of Bank Indonesia, but also of the government's ability to maintaining a stable financial system.

Thus far, this book has explained that the roots of the rise of the FSA were in Bank Indonesia's independence, which initially was demanded by the IMF as part of its neoliberal structural adjustment programme. A similar degree of independence was given to the FSA. In addition, the government, through the Indonesian MOF, then also transferred its power in the financial services industry to the FSA. This book has explained that there were different circumstances resulting in delays in the establishment of the FSA. These circumstances assisted the merger of independent agents from MOF and Bank Indonesia. The next period analysed covers the period after the enactment of the Indonesian FSA Law. In the next section, this book continues the discussion by explaining the early operations of the Indonesian FSA, or the transition period.

The Transition Period (2011–2013)

After a long process and postponement, the enactment of the Law Number 11 Year 2011 on the Indonesian FSA finally marked the formal establishment of the institution. However, the first two years of its operation was a transitional period for the FSA. In the transitional period, the power of financial sector supervision that was previously under the Indonesian MOF had now been transferred to the FSA. In addition, the power of banking supervision that previously was the domain of Bank Indonesia had now also shifted to the FSA. Thus, the FSA assumed full domestic authority in relation to portfolio investment liberalization. Former Chairman of the Indonesian FSA, Dr. Muliaman Hadad, described his experiences in leading the transitional period as follows:

> Tantangan terbesar dalam melakukan transisi adalah mengatasi adanya kemungkinan munculnya gejolak internal di organisasi yang kontra produktif, dan gejolak eksternal di Industri Jasa Keuangan yang bisa menggangu stabilitas sistem perekonomian nasional. (Hadad et al., 2017, p. 56)
>
> [*The biggest challenge in carrying out transition is dealing with the possibility of internal turbulences in the organisation that are contra-productive, as well as external turbulences in the Financial Sector Industry that may disrupt the national economic system stability.*]

The transition to the FSA was carried out by the "transition team in coordination with the Minister of Finance and Governor of Bank Indonesia" (The Law of the Republic of Indonesia Number 11 Year 2011, Article 60 Verse 1). This transitional provision reflects that, since its establishment, the FSA is actually monitored by the government and the independent Bank Indonesia. This perhaps is attributable to the government's responsibility to ensure a smooth transition. Another factor might be that most of the supporting resources and infrastructure for the transition would come from the MOF and Bank Indonesia. For instance, the Law stated that the transition team should consist of the officers and employees of the MOF and Bank Indonesia (Article 61 Verse 4 and Article 63-64). Thus, in the early period of establishment, the employees of the FSA consisted of only Indonesian MOF (particularly Bapepam-LK) and Bank Indonesia employees. For instance, almost two-thirds of the FSA employees are from the MOF and Bank Indonesia.

Referring to Chart 3.5 from the Indonesian FSA Internal Document, the transitional period itself largely consisted of two main phases. The first phase of the transitional period started from the appointment of the FSA's Board of Commissioners on June 2012 and ended at the end of 2012. During this six-month period of transition, the FSA took over the power of financial sector supervision that was previously under a unit within the MOF (Bapepam-LK). This period of transition covers the regulation and supervision of capital market and non-bank financial institutions (insurance, pension fund, financing institutions and other non-bank financial services institutions) from Bapepam-LK to the FSA. This meant that all the authority and power of Bapepam-LK was also transferred to the FSA. Particularly related to portfolio investment liberalization, the FSA took over all into its possession. These pending matters included those related to the ASEAN Capital Market Forum (ACMF), other initiatives under ASEAN and ASEAN and Partner Countries, as well as international regulatory standards. Hadad et al. (2017) argued that:

> Dalam pembentukan OJK ada sebuah tim beranggotakan 77 orang yang melakukan persiapan pembentukan organisasi. Tim pendahuluan ini sebagian masuk dalam Tim Transisi OJK Tahap I. Tim Transisi inilah yang melakukan proses peralihan pengawasan yang dilakukan Bapepam-LK kepada OJK. (p. 59)
>
> [*In the establishment of the Indonesian FSA, there was a team consisting of seventy-seven people that carried out the preparation for organizational establishment. Most of the members in this advanced team are included in the Indonesian FSA Transition Team Phase 1. The Transition Team carried out duties to transfer supervisory from Bapepam-LK to the Indonesian FSA.*]

Meanwhile, still referring to Chart 3.5, the second phase of the transitional period occurred over the course of 2013. During this second phase, the power of banking supervision that previously had been a domain of Bank Indonesia also shifted to the FSA. In addition, the transition for

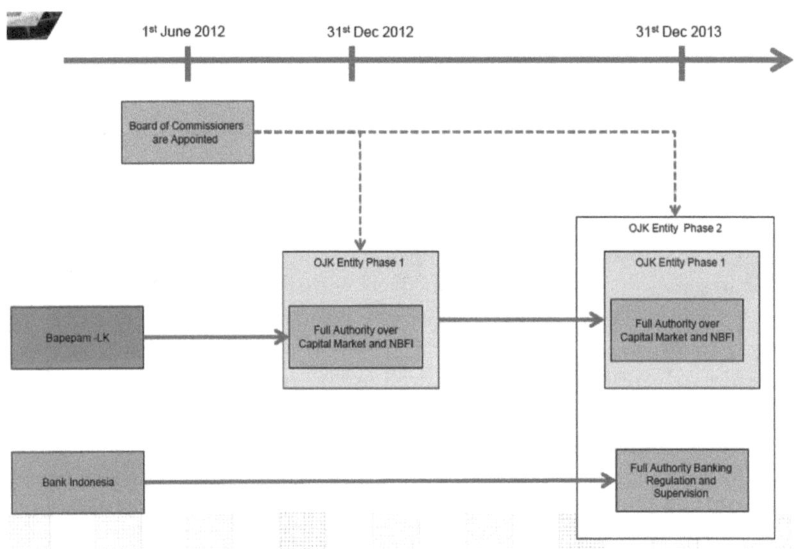

Chart 3.5 The Indonesian FSA transition period (*Source* Indonesian FSA Internal Document)

the power of financial sector supervision as explained in the preceding paragraph also continued. Thus, by the end of 2013, the transition had been completed. The ultimate goals of this transition were to transfer the regulatory and supervisory functions, as well as establish FSA regional offices across Indonesia and representative offices overseas. According to the Progress Report of the Transfer of Banking Regulatory and Supervisory Function from Bank Indonesia to the Indonesian FSA (2013), banking supervision transitional works included (1) banking supervision, (2) banking regulation, licencing and development, (3) data and information system, (4) logistics and documentation and (5) organization and human resources.

Banking supervision transitional works include the formulation of Standard Operating Procedures (SOP) including for FSA regional and representative offices. The working mechanism between banking "compartment"[3] and other "compartments" within the FSA, such as the capital market compartment, was also arranged. The banking supervision transitional works also covered the design of a Memorandum of Understanding (MoU) and a coordination mechanism between the FSA and other institutions, as well as the transfer of supervision of Rural Credit Institutions (Badan Kredit Desa/BKD). Meanwhile, on banking regulation, and licencing and development, the transition activities covered the formulation of the framework on integrated supervision of financial conglomerates. In addition, there was also the mapping of Bank Indonesia's regulations in monetary and payment systems related to banking, as well as the establishment of the Sharia Financial Services Development Committee (SFSDC). Transition work on data and information systems was mostly related to information technology infrastructure, while logistics and documentation dealt with the transition of assets and infrastructures. As for organization and human resources, the transition work was mostly related to the establishment of FSA regional offices and representative offices overseas, as well as the transfer of employees from Bank Indonesia to the FSA.

Another important point to discuss in relation to the transition to the FSA is the budget to finance its operations. The Law itself mentioned that "OJK budget sources are from the State Budget and/or fees from

[3] The use of the term "compartment" here, rather than for instance department, refers to term used formally by the Indonesian FSA during the transition period to address divisions among banking, capital market and non-bank financial institutions.

parties carrying on activities in the financial services sector" (Law of the Republic of Indonesia Number 21 of 2011, Article 34). Further, the Law also explicated that "[t]o support the operational activities of OJK, the Government may perform the initial placement of funds into the OJK" (Article 35). Thus, the State Budget mostly covered the expenses related to the FSA's early operations. Bank Indonesia also shared the burden of some of the FSA's operational costs, particularly those related to banking regulation and supervision transition. After transition periods, or once the Indonesian FSA was ready to collect fees industry, the government gradually ended the "subsidy" to the FSA. In fact, the government ceased subsidizing the FSA in 2016. This meant that starting in 2017, the budget of the FSA completely relies on the fees collected from the financial services industry.

Even after the formal transition period ended, there were still challenges that threatened the existence of the Indonesian FSA. There were external challenges from outside the institution of the Indonesian FSA, as well as internal challenges from within the institution. Externally, the Indonesian FSA experienced an enormous existential challenge in the form of a lawsuit filed in the Indonesian Constitutional Court (Mahkamah Konstitusi/MK). When the FSA was actively pursuing internal consolidation, strengthening the organization and building stakeholders' trust, a lawsuit from the National Economic Sovereignty Defense Team (Tim Pembela Kedaulatan Ekonomi Bangsa/TPKEB) emerged in July 2014. TPEKB itself is a relatively new anti-neoliberal movement group in Indonesia. This group was associated with an anti-neoliberal association, namely the Asosiasi Ekonomi Politik Indonesia (Indonesian Political Economy Association/AEPI). As the Indonesian FSA was basically rooted from the mandate of the IMF, TPEKB saw that the Indonesian FSA was just another neoliberal institution in Indonesia in support of transnational capital. From there, they were building a case to the Indonesian Institutional Court to test the FSA Law against the Indonesian Basic Constitution.

The content of the judicial review from the TPEKB was essentially a request that the FSA be disbanded. TPEKB requested that the Indonesian Institutional Court tests the compatibility of the FSA Law with the Indonesian Basic Constitution. In addition to asking for the FSA to be disbanded, TPEKB also claimed that if it could not be disbanded, then the FSA should only be able to regulate the supervision of the non-bank financial institutions. This meant giving the authority for banking supervision back to Bank Indonesia. After more than a year and through various hearings, the Indonesian Constitutional Court, on 4 August 2015, finally decided that the Indonesian FSA Law was in accordance with the Indonesian Basic Constitution. Therefore, the Indonesian FSA should retain its power and authority as set out in the law. The decision of the Indonesian Constitutional Court serves as a "constitutional" basis for the existence of the FSA. In other words, through this experience of, the existence of the Indonesian FSA now has a stronger legal basis.

Internally, the FSA also experienced an existential challenge in merging ideas and agents that came from different backgrounds. After the transitional period, the FSA consisted of people from the Indonesian MOF, Bank Indonesia, as well as new recruits. Each of them had their own ideas, norms and cultures attached to their preceding institutions. As described in his book, the first Chairman of the Indonesian FSA needed to create a new organizational culture for the FSA. He noticed that there was a "silo" culture during the early transition period. In order to create a better integrated supervisory function, he created a "synergy" culture within the FSA. In the end, the establishment of the FSA was also a response to the growing financial conglomerates in Indonesia. Thus, agents needed to work across industries and financial institutions. He particularly emphasized that agents needed to comprehend the existential purposes of the FSA. One way to manifest this culture was by internalizing the added power and authority of the FSA, as compared to the preceding institution, across all employees.

In the same book (Hadad et al., 2017), Hadad also revealed that the process of internalizing the FSA's organizational culture did not run smoothly. He raised the issue that sharp differences in the perceptions and idealism of employees often inhibited fundamental and meaningful changes. The FSA's organizational culture was, according to him, often misperceived and understood differently. Some employees were accepting and adopted the new culture, some were doubtful and adopted the culture in a perfunctory manner, and some were resistant, choosing to be passive. For instance, he admitted that the process of integrating Bank Indonesia employees into the FSA has not run smoothly. More than a thousand employees were assigned from Bank Indonesia to the FSA. They naturally expected to be permanent employees of the Indonesian FSA. However, in the midst of the transitional period as well as early operations of the FSA, there were still several questions hanging over their heads such as matters related to remuneration, career opportunities and the institutional sustainability of the FSA itself.

Conclusion

This chapter has related the story of the historical emergence of the Indonesian FSA. I have identified that the main agents in the establishment of the Indonesian FSA were coming from the Indonesian MOF and Bank Indonesia. Those two institutions were the main institutional players in the establishment of the FSA. While the Indonesian MOF is part of the government administration, Bank Indonesia is an independent institution as the FSA was established to be. As this chapter has revealed, the emergence of the Indonesian FSA basically relates the 1997–1998 Asian Financial Crisis that hit Indonesia hard. As a consequence, Indonesia had to deal with the IMF and follow the structural reform programmes it mandated. One of those structural adjustment programmes was the enactment of the Bank Indonesia Law. This law endowed the independence on Bank Indonesia, as previously it was under the control of the government. Most importantly, the law also mandated the establishment of the single financial services authority in Indonesia, or the contemporary FSA. This was the first time the concept of the FSA was included in a legal enactment.

There were important circumstances leading to the formal establishment of and transition to the FSA. This chapter provided a story that within those circumstances, agents were involved in the institutional shaping of the FSA. These circumstances were the independent status of Bank Indonesia and the reduced authority of both Bank Indonesia and the government in financial sector supervision. In addition, there were also important milestones during establishment. The Indonesian MOF carried out an internal reform to prepare for moving its authority to the new institution. In Bank Indonesia, there were objections to moving employees to the new institution. Meanwhile, members of parliament conducted comparison studies of other countries' financial services authorities or equivalent institutions. Along the way, another major financial crisis, the GFC, occurred and brought financial sector reform back into the policy priorities of the government. Ultimately, the Indonesian FSA formally emerged in 2011 after an evolution of more than a decade. FSA has evolved to reach its current level of power and key ideas.

However, it is FSA agents who will be using these powers and putting these ideas into effect. Thus, in the next chapter, I explain how agents within the FSA operate and how they may stymie the domestic portfolio investment liberalization process in Indonesia.

References

Akimov, A., & Dollery, B. (2010). Financial sector reforms in Indonesia and South Korea in 1980s and early 1990s. *Journal of Emerging Market Finance, 9*(1), 25–49.

Basri, M. C., & Rahardja, S. (2010). The Indonesian economy amidst the global crisis: good policy and good luck. *ASEAN Economic Bulletin, 27*, 77–97.

Cho, Y.-J., & Khatkhate, D. R. (1989). *Lessons of financial liberalization in Asia: A comparative study* (World Bank Discussion Paper).

Claessens, S. (2003). Benefits and costs on integrated financial services provision in developing countries. *Brookings-Wharton Papers on Financial Services, 2003*, 85–139.

Djiwandono, J. S. (2002). *Role of the IMF in Indonesia's financial crisis*. In H. Soesastro, A. L. Smith, & H. M. Ling (Eds.). *Governance in Indonesia: Challenges facing the Megawati presidency*. Institute of Southeast Asian Studies (ISEAS).

Grenville, S. (2004). The IMF and the Indonesian crisis. *Bulletin of Indonesian Economic Studies, 40*(1), 77–94.

Gultom-Siregar, M. (1993). *Financial liberalization, capital structure and investment: An empirical analysis of Indonesian panel data, 1981–1988*. ProQuest Dissertations Publishing.

Gunawan, A., & Siregar, R. (2009). Survey of recent developments. *Bulletin of Indonesian Economic Studies, 45*(1), 9–38.

Hadad, M., Susetyo, R., & Guritno, G. (2017). *OJK way: implementasi manajemen perubahan di OJK*. Grasindo

Hadiz, V., & Robison, R. (2005). Neo-liberal reforms and Illiberal consolidations: The Indonesian paradox. *Journal of Development Studies, 41*(2), 220–241.

Haggard, S. (2000). *The political economy of the Asian financial crisis*. Institute for International Economics.

Haggard, S., & Maxfield, S. (1996). The political economy of financial internationalization in the developing world. *International Organization, 50*(1), 35–68.

Hall, P. A. (2012). The economics and politics of the euro crisis. *German Politics, 21*(4), 355–371.

Hamilton-Hart, N. (2000). Indonesia: Reforming the institutions of financial governance? In G. W. Noble & J. Ravenhill (Eds.), *The Asian financial crisis and the architecture of global finance*. Cambridge University Press.
Hamilton-Hart, N. (2012). *Hard interests, soft illusions: Southeast Asia and American power*. Cornell University Press.
Hanna, D. P. (1994). *Indonesian experience with financial sector reform*, World Bank.
Iyer, L., & Lane, D. (2016). Indonesia's OJK: Building financial stability. In *Institutions, institutional change and economic performance in emerging markets* (pp. 267–309). World Scientific Publishing Pte.
Kuntjoro-Jakti, D. (1986). The global crisis of the 1980s and Indonesia's response. *Hitotsubashi Journal of Economics, 27*, 101–113.
Mwenda, K., & Fleming, A. (2001). International developments in the organisational structure of financial services supervision: Part 1. *Journal of International Banking Law, 16*(12), 291–298.
Nitisastro, W. (2011). *The Indonesian development experience: A collection of writings and speeches*. Institute of Southeast Asian Studies.
Omori, S. (2014). The politics of financial reform in Indonesia. The Asian financial crisis and its aftermath. *Asian Survey, 54*(5), 987–1008.
Reinhart, C., & Calvo, G. (2000). *When capital inflows come to a sudden stop: Consequences and policy options* (IDEAS Working Paper Series from RePEc).
Resosudarmo, B. P., & Kuncoro, A. (2006). The political economy of Indonesian economic reforms: 1983–2000. *Oxford Development Studies, 34*(3), 341–355.
Rethel, L. (2012). Each time is different! the shifting boundaries of emerging market debt. *Global Society, 26*(1), 123–143.
Rodrik, D., & Velasco, A. (1999). *Short-term capital flows*. National Bureau of Economic Research Working Paper Series (Working Paper 7364).
Sato, Y. (2005). Bank restructuring and financial institution reform in Indonesia. *Developing Economies, XLIII*(1), 91–120.
Sheng, A. (2009). *From Asian to global financial crisis: An Asian regulator's view of unfettered finance in the 1990s and 2000s*. Cambridge University Press.
Simpson, B. (2010). *Economists with guns: Authoritarian development and US-Indonesia relations, 1960–1968*. Stanford University Press.
Siregar, R., & James, W. (2006). Designing an integrated financial supervision agency: Selected lessons and challenges for Indonesia. *ASEAN Economic Bulletin, 23*(1), 98–113.
Sitompul, Z. (2004). Menyambut Kehadiran Otoritas Jasa Keuangan (OJK). *Majalah Pilars, 2*, 12–18.
Sitompul, Z. (2012). Konsepsi dan Transformasi Otoritas Jasa Keuangan [*The conception and transformation of the Indonesian Financial Services Authority*]. *Jurnal Legislasi Indonesia, 9*(3), 343–360.

Stiglitz, J. E. (2001). Failure of the fund: Rethinking the IMF response. *Harvard International Review, 23*(2), 14–18.

Tambunan, T. T. (2010). The Indonesian experience with two big economic crises. *Modern Economy, 1*(03), 156.

Taylor, M., & Fleming, A. (1999). Integrated financial supervision: Lessons of Scandinavian experience. *Finance and Development, 36*(4), 42–45.

Thee, K. (2012). The impact of the global financial crisis on the Indonesian economy and the prospects for the resumption of rapid and sustained growth. In *Indonesia's economy since independence* (pp. 126–136). ISEAS–Yusof Ishak Institute.

Trihayati, T. (1993). Paket Deregulasi Pasar Modal Tahun 1988: Suatu Tinjauan Terhadap Peran dan Penyempurnaanya [Capital market deregulation package 1988: A review of its roles and refinement]. *Jurnal Hukum dan Pembangunan, 4*, 340–348.

Walter, A. (2005). Understanding financial globalization in international political economy. In N. Philips (Ed.), *Globalizing political economy*. Palgrave.

Walter, A. (2008). *Governing finance: East Asia's adoption of international standards*. Cornell.

CHAPTER 4

The Indonesian FSA and Stymied Portfolio Investments Liberalization

The endowment of an "independent and free" status as well the endowment full power over the Indonesian financial sector to the Indonesian FSA has, in contrary to the general expectations of neoliberalism, actually stymied portfolio investment liberalization. Agents in the FSA use their power and authority to stymie liberalization thereby creating domestic implementation gaps. In their operations, agents interact internally with other domestic institutions in Indonesia and externally with foreign regulators in ASEAN. Thus, the early part of this chapter will firstly set out the FSA's power and authority. Later, this chapter looks at how agents interact with the financial environment and finally take positions to stymie portfolio investment liberalization. The financial environment includes domestic pressure, such as from the Indonesian MOF that seems to push back Indonesia's accession to the ASEAN Trading Link, and pressure from market players that use the "unreadiness" argument. Meanwhile externally, there are also pressures from peer financial services regulators in ASEAN, particularly, those that already comply with ASEAN initiatives. To elaborate how agents interact with these influences, this chapter uses the cases of the ASEAN Trading Link, the ASEAN Framework for Cross Border Offering of Collective Investment Scheme (CIS), the ASEAN Disclosure Standards, the ASEAN Banking Integration Framework and other related standards and regulations.

C. Kusuma, *The Rise of the Indonesian Financial Service Authority*, https://doi.org/10.1007/978-981-19-3850-4_4

The later part of this chapter shows that agents within the FSA are harnessing the international standards towards advancing the "national interest" and thus avoiding the implementation of the ASEAN portfolio investment liberalization. This chapter elaborates on the finding that agents employ different approaches to look at the relations between adherence to international regulatory standards and Indonesia's position in ASEAN portfolio investment liberalization. The different approaches here are attributable to how agents treat the circumstances surrounding both international regulatory standards and ASEAN liberalization. As for the international regulatory standards, Indonesia has a long historical engagement. In addition, the standards also have been used as a renowned benchmark globally. Meanwhile, ASEAN liberalization is a relatively new thing for Indonesia as it arose only against the background of the Asian Financial Crisis. Besides, ASEAN portfolio investment liberalizations are non-binding to AMS. It is important to remember that the ultimate purpose of the international standards is mainly to achieve regulatory convergence, while ASEAN portfolio investments liberalization puts heavy emphasis on regional market openness. This chapter shows that in order to build up the domestic market, Indonesian FSA agents are engaging with international standards selectively. The last part of this chapter discusses the existence of the Financial Sector Stability Committee (FSSC). This forum provides another opportunity for the FSA to bring issues related to portfolio investment liberalization back to the table, particularly, those related to the risky overflowing of portfolio investments.

The operationalization of "agents-in-context" approach throughout this chapter is to show the occurrences of bidirectional relationship between agents and the surrounding structural context. The approach starts with the existing Indonesian FSA power and authorities, later to identify the areas of ASEAN financial liberalization where agents particularly stymie the domestic portfolio investment liberalization process. This is particularly showing that given the power and authorities, Indonesia FSA agents use those power and authorities to stymie the domestic portfolio investment liberalization process. This chapter unveils the way the Indonesian FSA agents do that, by analysing the cases where the Indonesian FSA agent empirically proven to be stymieing the process of the domestic portfolio investment liberalization. For each case analysed in this chapter—ASEAN Trading Link, the ASEAN Framework for Cross Border Offering of Collective Investment Scheme (CIS), the ASEAN Disclosure

Standards, the ASEAN Banking Integration Framework and other related standards and regulations—the approach identifies major issues that are halting to move forward. From there, the analysis looks at the positions of Indonesian FSA agents to the issues.

The Indonesian FSA Power and Authorities

The Indonesian FSA Law defines the FSA as "an agency which is independent and free from interference by other parties, having the functions, duties and authorities to regulate, supervise, examine and investigate as referred to in this Law" (Law of the Republic of Indonesia Number 11 Year 2011, Article 1). The scope of works of this agency includes "to establish an integrated regulatory and supervisory system for all activities in the financial services sector" (Law of the Republic of Indonesia Number 11 Year 2011, Article 5). At the centre of this financial services sector is the financial services institutions that the Law also defines as "institutions that carry out activities in the sectors of Banking, Capital Market, Insurance, Pension Fund, Financing Institutions, and Other Financial Services Institutions" (Law of the Republic of Indonesia Number 11 Year 2011, Article 1). Further, the Law equipped this newly-born institution with an "independent and free" status, marking the "de-politicisation" of the financial services regime in Indonesia. As Saputro (2017) argued the Indonesian FSA was an example of the "de-politicised financial authority placed beyond the control of Indonesia's elected government" (p. 202). Thus, "de-politicisation" means that the decisions regarding financial services supervision are not bound to various interests, including political interests (Denk & Gomes, 2017).

A collective and collegial Board of Commissioners leads the operation of the Indonesian FSA. The law itself elucidates that the term "collective" here means that "every decision of the Board of Commissioners is decided jointly by the members of the Board of Commissioners", while "collegial" means "that every decision of the Board of Commissioners is based on a negotiation for consensus, on the basis of equality and unity among the members of the Board of Commissioners" (Law of the Republic of Indonesia Number 11 Year 2011, Elucidation). As graphic below shows, there are nine members to the Board of Commissioners with equal voting rights. There are two ex-officio officials on the Board of Commissioners, one each from the Indonesian MOF (Director General level official) and Bank Indonesia (Member of Board of Governors level). In its Elucidation part, the Indonesian FSA Law stated the following details in relation to the existence of ex-officio officials (Chart 4.1):

> Institutionally, the Financial Services Authority is outside the Government, which means that the Financial Services Authority does not become part of the power of the Government. However, it does not rule out the existence of elements of representative government because essentially the Financial Services Authority is an authority in the financial services sector that has strong relationships and linkages with other authorities, in this case the fiscal and monetary authorities. Therefore, the institution involves representation of the elements of both of these authorities on an Ex-officio basis. Ex-officio existence is meant to ensure coordination, cooperation, and harmonization of policies in the areas of fiscal, monetary, and financial services sector. Ex-officio existence is also necessary to ensure the maintenance of national interests within the framework of global competition and international agreements, the need for coordination, and exchange of information in order to preserve and maintain financial system stability. (Law Number 11 Year 2011 on the Indonesian FSA)

Members of the Board of Commissioners are appointed by the House of Representative considering candidates proposed by the President of the Republic of Indonesia through a Selection Committee. According to a release document from the Indonesian MOF, the Selection Committee itself consists of nine people drawn from various stakeholders' bodies such as the government, Bank Indonesia, as well as the general public (The Indonesian MOF Press Release, 16 January 2017). In the latest

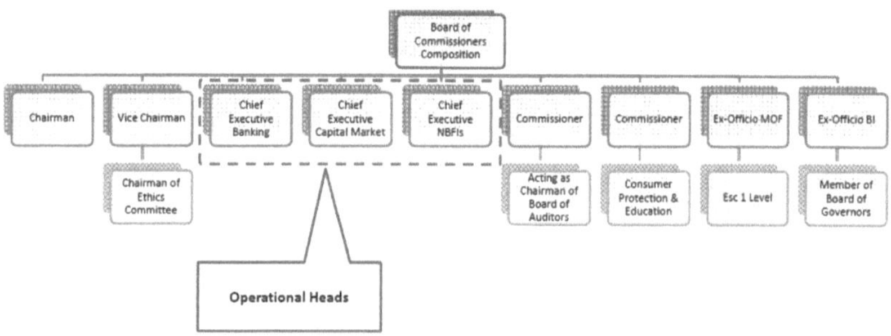

Chart 4.1 The Indonesian FSA organizational structure (*Source* Indonesian FSA Internal Document)

selection for the Board of Commissioners (for the period of 2017–2022), the Selection Committee selected twenty-one candidates to be selected by the President of the Republic of Indonesia. The president then proposed fourteen names to the House of Representative. There were also other selection mechanisms at the House of Representative ranging from administrative selections to a fit and proper test. Only then, the House of Representative selected seven names to be the Members of the Board of Commissioners. Meanwhile, the other two Members of the Board of Commissioners, the ex-officio, were selected and appointed by the respective institutions (the Indonesian MOF for government representative, and Bank Indonesia). From the beginning of the selection process itself until the inauguration of the Board of Commissioners, the process took around six months to complete. Once inaugurated, the Board of Commissioners is equipped with the power and authority to issue forms and regulations in carrying out its duties and functions. These can take the form the Indonesian FSA Regulations, or Board of Commissioners Regulations, or a Board of Commissioners Decree.

With regards to power and authority in international relations, the Law also has specifically endowed privileges on the FSA. For instance, the Elucidation part contains this provision:

> Board of Commissioners is the top leadership of OJK [the Indonesian FSA]. In order to cooperate with the Financial Services Authority in other countries and international organizations and other international institutions in the financial services sector, the members of the Board of Commissioners act as officials representing the state. (Law Number 11 Year 2011 on the Indonesian FSA)

There are two particular articles in the law that endow the FSA with great power and authority (Article 47 and 48). However, the FSA also has a control mechanism here. The law mentioned that "[i]n the event of approval of international agreements in the financial services sector brings legal consequences and impact on the national financial system, OJK must obtain confirmation from the House of Representatives" (Article 47, Section 3). In the Elucidation part to that corresponding Article, the law further refers to "[i]nternational treaties that impact on the national financial system including international agreements that impact on national interests in the field of human resources, control, and ownership in the financial services sector". This particular provision of Article 47 is basically also consistent with the provisions related to ratification of international agreements related to the financial sector as set out in the new Trading Law that was enacted in 2014. The next chapter of this book provides more detailed discussions on the issues related to the new Trading Law and the ratification process.

The power of the FSA principally includes all things related to Indonesian financial services. For instance, in relation to the banking sector, the Indonesian FSA has sole power over the regulation and supervision of domestic banks' institutional arrangements (such as licenses, or business activities), conditions (such as the liquidity, or the minimum capital adequacy ratio, or even the accounting standards), prudential aspects and examination. Although, power over macro-prudential banking regulation (that is, for the interests of the overall soundness of the banking system in Indonesia) is still under the hand of Bank Indonesia. Finance and banking theory mostly argue that there should be alignment and consolidation in micro-prudential and macro-prudential policies (see, for instance: Borio, 2003; Galati & Moessner, 2013; Hanson et al., 2011). Crockett (2000) has advocated that financial services supervisors and regulators should incorporate more macro-prudential considerations in shared efforts to maintain financial stability. He suggested that this incorporation would not necessarily be contrary to the traditional view of focusing solely on micro-prudential concerns. He argued that both micro-prudential and macro-prudential elements can actually supplement each other.

In the case of the Indonesian financial services sector, for those two approaches to align and consolidate, the FSA implemented two strategies. Firstly, at the early stage of its establishment, the FSA signed a Memorandum of Understanding (MOU) with Bank Indonesia. This MOU particularly set out the arrangements related to the transfer of authorities between the two institutions (Nota Kesepahaman antara Bank Indonesia dan Otoritas Jasa Keuangan, 2013). The MOU itself also provides details as to the extent of public and classified data and information that both Bank Indonesia and the FSA need to share for the interests of the transfer of authority. Secondly, at the current stage, the FSA and Bank Indonesia are members of a forum overseeing financial stability in Indonesia, called the Financial Sector Stability Committee (FSSC). This book discusses the FSSC in the last part of this chapter. Meanwhile, in relation to the financial services sector in general (other than the banking sector), the FSA has great power to "conduct supervision, inspection, investigation, consumer protection, and other actions" (Law of the Republic of Indonesia Number

11 Year 2011, Article 9). These powers conclusively cover all actions that supervisors and regulators can perform in managing the financial services industry.

The power mandated to the FSA in financial services integrated supervision has the potential to complicate the process of decision-making related to financial services liberalization. This complication arises from the additional "independent and free" status. Before the establishment of the FSA, the decision-making process related to portfolio investment liberalization fell under the authority of the MOF and of Bank Indonesia in some areas. Meanwhile, the current decision-making process also includes the FSA. In addition, since the Law has mandated the FSA with the sole authority over financial services integrated supervision, it is now the ultimate decision-maker. An official from the MOF explained this complication as below.

> Tapi potensi untuk mempersulit ada. Artinya gini, kalau dulu...Menteri Keuangan dan Gubernur Bank Central, pemainnya hanya dua kan. Dulu kan jasa keuangan di bawah Kementrian Keuangan. Di bawah Menteri Keuangan, artinya lebih gampang...Sementara ini ada ketua OJK...pasti paham tentang Two-Level Games, Robert Putnam, tahun 1988. Two-Level Games itu diartikan sebagai permainan dua kali. Dua steps. Artinya ketika kemudian Menteri Keuangan maupun Gubernur Bank Indonesia mau melakukan negosiasi di tingkat regional karena mereka adalah representasi dari Indonesia, belum tentu kesepakatan itu bisa dieksekusi di dalam negeri. Ini level game yang kedua. Nah game yang kedua pemainnya bertambah. Ada OJK di situ, yang dia adalah penguasa dari jasa keuangan di Indonesia. Belum tentu dia mau mengeksekusi karena dia sekali lagi by the law itu independen. Artinya tidak boleh ada campur tangan.
>
> [*There is a potential to complicate the issue. Previously, there are only two players, the Minister of Finance and the Central Bank Governor. This means easier under the Minister of Finance. Meanwhile, currently, there is also the Chairman of the Indonesian FSA. We surely understand the Robert Putnam's Two-Level Games in 1988. The Two-Level Games means that the game is played two times, or in two steps. It means that when Minister of Finance or even The Central Bank Governor want to carry out negotiations at the regional level, the outcomes of the negotiations may not well be executed within domestic context. This is the second-level game with the additional player, the Indonesian FSA that has the power over Indonesian financial services. There is no guarantee that the Indonesian FSA would be willing to execute the negotiations outcomes, because the Indonesian FSA is an independent body. Independent means that there should be no interference.*]

Each of Indonesia's positions related to ASEAN portfolio investment liberalization must go through and have the approval of the FSA. A high-level official at the FSA confirmed the complication mentioned above. However, he mentioned that the ultimate decision-maker in relation to portfolio investment liberalization is the FSA. Thus, he suggested that, for instance, even though the MOF or Bank Indonesia carried out the negotiations related to portfolio investment liberalization, the two institutions always firstly go through and seek approval from the FSA. He mentioned that:

> …so far, justru pihak-pihak yang pengambilan keputusan yang di atas itu, atau yang kita tidak ikut itu, mostly mesti ngikutin apa yang kita sampaikan. Terkait hal itu juga kan kita yang harus melaksanakan…
>
> [*…so far, the decision makers, or when we are not involved, mostly have to follow what we convey. This is because in the end, we are the one who will implement…*]

Further, an official at the MOF also confirmed the same position: that the FSA will act as an ultimate decision-maker in relation to portfolio investment liberalization. The official explained that:

> …katakanlah di satu momen, Bu Menteri tidak banyak waktu dan dia harus bilang ya atau tidak…Dia putuskan untuk ya. Nah dengan berbagai pertimbangan, OJK bilang "Wah ngga bisa, Bu. Kita ngga bisa ada diek-sekusi". Dengan itu, itu masih boleh karena dia punya mandat itu. Tidak harus tergantung menginduk atau mengikuti apa yang disampaikan Menteri Keuangan…Karena sekali lagi ya, justru yang menarik dari OJK ini adalah terjadi depolitisasi kekuasaan dari Presiden.
>
> [*…say that in one situation, Madam Minister of Finance is running out of time and she has to decide to say yes or no…then she decided to say yes. Later, with various considerations, the Indonesian FSA says "I think we cannot do this, Madam. We cannot execute this." This position is acceptable because the Indonesian FSA has the mandate to do so. The Indonesian FSA does not have the obligation to peg into or follow the positions of the Minister of Finance…Because once more, it is interesting how the Indonesian FSA is depoliticized from the power of the President.*]

This chapter, particularly in the next five sections below, now turns into explaining what and how FSA agents stymie the domestic portfolio investment liberalization process.

ASEAN TRADING LINK

ASEAN elites have agreed to implement the ASEAN Trading Link that electronically connects exchanges in ASEAN countries (ASEAN, 2017; ASEAN Capital Market Forum, 2016). The ASEAN Capital Market Forum (ACMF) has formally documented this agreement in its Action Plan as one of the ASEAN Member States' (AMS) key priorities. ASEAN Finance Ministers have formally endorsed the Action Plan itself. Furthermore, all of the Heads of State/Government of AMS have also officially applauded this Action Plan in their formal Statement (ASEAN Chairman's Statement, 2016).

> The key priorities identified for the ACMF Action Plan 2016-2020 to achieve the ACMF's strategic objectives are set out below... the ACMF will encourage the ASEAN Exchanges Working Group (AEWG) to consider additional measures to enhance the ATL [ASEAN Trading Link]'s value proposition and generate wider participation by ACMF member country exchanges. (ASEAN Capital Market Forum, 2016, p. 2)

Likewise, the ASEAN 2025 Consolidated Strategic Action Plan, an official document setting out steps AMS need to achieve AEC, also discusses the development of the ASEAN Trading Link. "Enhance ASEAN capital market connectivity to support more cross-border activities: Enhance trading linkage for ASEAN stock markets" (ASEAN, 2017, p. 8).

Through the establishment of the ASEAN Trading link, ASEAN expects that there will be one centralized access point in the region to give investors the ease of access to ASEAN capital markets. Currently, only three Stock Exchanges from three AMS (Malaysia, Singapore and Thailand) have joined the ASEAN Trading Link. In reference to data collected from an FSA Internal Discussion Document, at a technical level in ASEAN that is Working Group, the three AMS have put pressure on Indonesia to be the fourth AMS to join the ASEAN Trading Link, citing the strategic importance and the development level of Indonesian markets. However, the FSA has lodged a formal response to other AMS affirming that ASEAN, instead, should "focus on marketing initiatives first (demand side) than those of the technology/technical issues (supply side)" (Indonesian FSA Internal Discussion Document, 2017, p. 36). The supply side of the market generally means initiatives to better support the conduct of the market, including the availability of a reliable trading system like the proposed ASEAN Trading Link. Meanwhile, the demand side deals with initiatives to enlarge the size of the market, such as attracting more investors.

Agreeing to this ASEAN Trading Link means Indonesia needs to adopt a business model that, firstly, allows overseas capital market brokers to trade capital market products directly on Indonesia Stock Exchange (IDX). Secondly, Indonesia needs to adopt the business model requiring Indonesia to deregulate its overseas clearing and payment system to settle capital market products cross-border trading. The following graphic illustrates this business model. Meanwhile, the FSA currently maintains the regime of restricting capital market products trading solely through the domestic capital market broker and using the domestic clearing and payment system for settlement. As to date, the regulatory framework and policies in Indonesia prohibit cross-border trading using overseas capital market brokers or an overseas clearing and payments system. In addition to the equity and debt markets, there are also discussions in ASEAN on moving forward for more "flavoured" products, such as Real Estate Investment Trusts (REITs) or Exchange-Traded Funds (ETFs). However, FSA officials have expressed their reluctance to move forward with the ETFs proposal as they are even being conservative with the plain products (Chart 4.2).

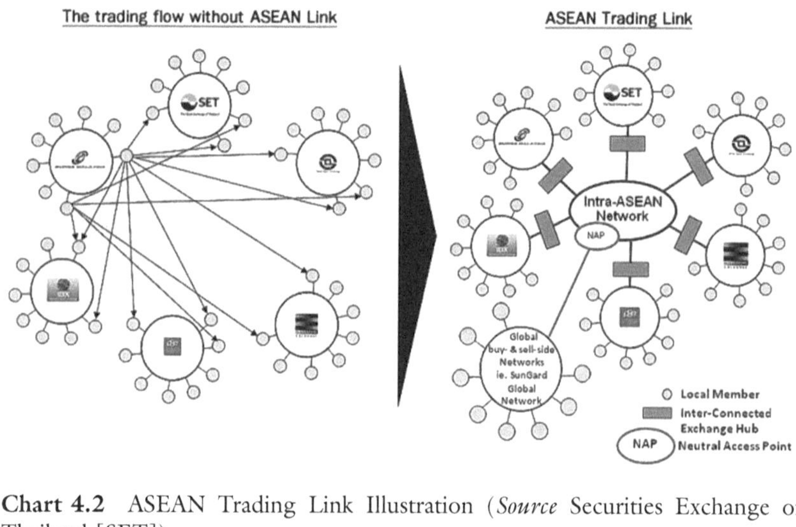

Chart 4.2 ASEAN Trading Link Illustration (*Source* Securities Exchange of Thailand [SET])

In dealing with the ASEAN Trading Link initiative, FSA agents face several challenges internally and externally. Internally, the challenge comes from the "sectoral ego" of other related domestic authorities. The term "sectoral ego" here mostly refers to institutional self-importance: institutions seem to see themselves superior as compared to others. For instance, when asked how exactly the "sectoral ego" affect was to the positions of the FSA generally in financial services liberalization, a high-level official stated that:

> Itukan [memberikan perkembangan terkait liberalisasi] kalau pas meeting aja dari Kementrian Keuangan...Itupun kadang-kadang ego institusinya tinggi banget... Ada beberapa hal yang sebenarnya kalau menurut saya, ini usulannya gini gini gini. Tapi itukan kalau kita enggak bisa begitu karena kita begini begini.
>
> [*Explaining the progress of liberalization was mainly in the meeting with the Indonesian MOF...The institutional egos are very high...There are things that I think should be this way, but then they said we were not supposed to do it that way due to some reasons.*]

The official further implied that the sectoral ego may be unavoidable. However, the official stressed that the FSA has the ultimate authority on implementation and it will exploit that authority in carefully assessing the impact of portfolio investment liberalization.

In addition to the above internal dynamics among related domestic authorities, agents surely have to deal with the pressure from external stakeholders, particularly, other AMS with more financial services openness, such as Singapore. An article from the Financial Times (13 June 2015) mentioned that:

> Ravi Menon, managing director of the Monetary Authority of Singapore, said progress on ASEAN financial integration had been "disappointing" and was lagging behind efforts to integrate trade within the region. He suggested that member countries should build on the Asean Trading Link "by further broadening and deepening post-trade linkages".

A high-level official at the Indonesian FSA also confirmed this situation stating that:

> Karna kayak Singapura, itu kan siapa yang mau ini. Itukan cuman tempat berdagang doang, kan? ...Akhirnya maunya di Singapura semua. Jadi saya sih melihatnya masih ego masing-masing negara.
>
> [*Because like Singapore, who wants the [Trading Link] anyway. That is just a place for the trading transactions, right? In the end, Singapore takes all. In my opinion, this is in the end just the ego of each country.*]

The statement above may also reflect the response of the FSA to external pressures to join a more liberalized regime of portfolio investments in the region.

Despite the fact that ASEAN elites have agreed to implement the ASEAN Trading Link, Indonesian FSA officials basically still seems unconvinced of its benefits. There are at least two main concerns for FSA officials. The first concern is that Indonesia will not gain anything from joining the ASEAN Trading Link. One of the top-level FSA officials even believes that there will be no learning process gained in the ASEAN Trading Link, and that overseas big brokerage companies will presumably get the biggest portion of the market. The official specifically mentioned that:

> Nah kita sudah nanya sama pelakunya, sama Perusahaan efek, kalau direct market access dari investor langsung ke sana, ke Singapore boleh nasabahnya dari broker kita, maka mereka tidak mendapatkan manfaat apapun dan tidak punya skill juga secara pengalaman untuk nanti mengembangkan ke Indonesia sehingga nanti mereka bisa menjadi direct market akses nya. Dan ada kecenderungan mereka akan menjadi...kalaupun melalui, itu melalui broker mendirikan PT atau afiliasi; sister company kek, brother company kek atau apalah di masing-masing negara itu...Jadi ada lesson learn.
>
> [*We have consulted the matter of direct market access to Indonesian securities companies. They believe that if, for instance, Singapore has a direct market access to our investor without the need to go through domestic securities companies, Indonesian securities companies are not going to gain anything or experiences from that kind of scheme. Indonesia will be better off if the scheme is using local incorporated securities companies, affiliations, sister companies or brother companies. In doing so, we can expect a lesson learning from the scheme.*]

The no learning process here is mainly due to the fact that ASEAN Trading Link allows overseas broker to trade directly in Indonesiaand leads to a fierce competition to local brokerage companies in Indonesia.

The official argued that local domestic brokerage companies could maximize the "transfer knowledge" from more advanced overseas brokers when they trade through local brokers. This also means that the FSA wants to ensure that local brokerage companies have the "same direct market access". The official further added that the current success stories of trading linkage, such as Euronext and the Integrated Latin American Market, are completely different to markets in AMS. For instance, Euronext consists of all developed exchanges in addition to the fact that it was established with historical European integration in the background.

One of the highest-ranking officials at the FSA also had previously expressed the same concern publicly through an established media channel in Indonesia. The official said that Indonesia were assessing the benefit of the linkage for Indonesia (*The Jakarta Post*, 2015). The official implied, through that media channel, that there were technical problems linking all the different trading platforms used across AMS. Nevertheless, the official believed that the larger issue would be the fact that the FSA has assessed the disadvantages of the linked trading platform to Indonesia. One issue raised was the inability of the ASEAN Trading Link to provide a dispute resolution mechanism. A dispute resolution mechanism is one of the main components of investor protection. Despite all the concerns above, the three AMS that had previously joined the linkage were very hopeful that Indonesia would be the fourth AMS to get on board. For instance, a high-level official at the Malaysian securities regulator (the Securities Commission) has expressed the importance of Indonesia, as the only members of G20 from ASEAN, joining the linkage (*The Jakarta Post*, 2015).

The second concern of FSA officials is that the ASEAN Trading Link exposes the domestic Indonesian market to more risky portfolio investment flows. As mentioned earlier, the linkage's business model expects big overseas brokerage companies to trade directly into Indonesia accompanied by the deregulation of overseas clearing and payment systems for settlement. Such a business model ultimately allows a freer flow of portfolio investments with less intervention of the government to regulate. For instance, with the current trading system, transaction flows are still restricted under the regulatory of corresponding domestic authorities. Thus, authorities still have the power to intervene in the market. With the proposed linkage, Indonesia can expect that the restrictions as well as the authority to regulate to be removed. A similar tone of uncertainty was also expressed by officials in the Indonesian MOF. For instance, one of senior officials at the MOF suggested that Indonesia is being defensive when it comes to pressure to join ASEAN Trading Link. The official explained that:

> Ya itu tadi, sepanjang dari teknikal AFMM [ASEAN Finance Ministers' Meeting]-nya itu jelas, sebagai contoh Trading Linkage...jadi memang Indonesia defensive. Dan, Indonesia di pertemuan Vientiane, tahun lalu berarti sekarang kan Filipina. Pada saat rapat itu akan di-approved, tahun lalu kan di-approved-nya. Indonesia bilang, "silahkan maju jadi empat tapi tolong di-noted bahwa yang ke empat itu tidak harus indonesia.
>
> [*Thus, as far as the technicalities at the AFMM is clear, for instance in the case of Trading Linkage...Indonesia is indeed being defensive. And, for instance at last year's meeting in Vientiane, or this year in Philippines, we have approved the position since last year. Our position stated that "just proceed to include 4 states, but please note that Indonesia is not obliged to be the fourth state."*]

The official further added that:

> Strategic Action Plan kita itu kalau dicermati, seingat saya, sangat defensif sekali. Jadi bahwa untuk Indonesia itu sangat defensive sekali. Sebagai contoh Trading Link. Silahkan ASEAN mau Trading Link tapi yang keempat cuman Indonesia. Aku yakin itu kan yang udah...itu juga yang menggambarkan bagaimana ke depan apakah kita gain atau...
>
> [*Our Strategic Action Plan, if we are looking thoroughly and to the extent of my memory, is very defensive. Thus, Indonesia' position is very defensive. For instance, in the case of Trading Link. ASEAN can just proceed with the Trading Link, yet ASEAN wants Indonesia to become the fourth state to join. That is just an example of our position. It is to illustrate whether Indonesia to gain or loss.*]

This implies that the MOF official is in full agreement with the position of the Indonesian FSA to decline joining the ASEAN Trading Link. The official expressed that ASEAN can just go ahead with its plan to further add membership to the linkage to four Stock Exchanges, yet it will certainly not be the IDX.

The development of the ASEAN Trading Link system also requires that the ASEAN Exchange Connectivity (hereafter "Connectivity") be in place. The Action Plan, as endorsed by ASEAN Finance Ministers and applauded by all of the Heads of State/Government of AMS, has included the Connectivity as part of ASEAN Trading Link system. The

Connectivity itself aims to integrate the Central Counter Party (CCP) and Clearing System, as well as the Custodian Central Depository (CSD) and Settlement System. In the current cross-border trading mechanism, if a broker from one AMS wants to purchase equities or debt products from another AMS, the domestic corresponding Self-Regulatory Organizations (SROs) where the products originated perform the clearing and settlement system. For instance, if a Malaysian broker purchased an Indonesian listed company's stocks, then the authorized domestic SROs are the Indonesian Clearing and Guarantee Corporation (PT. Kliring Penjaminan Efek Indonesia/KPEI) to do the clearing and Indonesian Central Securities Depository (PT. Kustodian Sentral Efek Indonesia/KSEI) to do the settlement. Meanwhile, the Connectivity will allow the Malaysian broker to use clearing and settlement systems other than KPEI and KSEI.

Currently, other clearing and settlement systems can be used in two ways. Firstly, the Connectivity will allow the use of the clearing and settlement system from where the broker originates. Thus, in the example mentioned above, a Malaysian broker may be able to use the Malaysian clearing and settlement system. Secondly, there is also a proposal to form a single ASEAN clearing and settlement system. Thus, trading performed in ASEAN will inevitably have to use the single ASEAN system. However, the current discussion is tending to allow clearing and settlement SROs other than where the products originated. ASEAN still sees a single ASEAN clearing and settlement system as a longer-term objective once all AMS clearing and settlement systems have converged. The Indonesian FSA has also paid particular attention to the Connectivity as a part of the successful implementation of the ASEAN Trading Link. As is the case with the ASEAN Trading Link, Indonesian FSA officials also seems unconvinced on the need for Connectivity.

If AMS fully join the ASEAN Trading Link as well as the supporting ASEAN Exchange Connectivity, ASEAN surely can expect portfolio investment flow to be freer. Equities and debt transactions will flow easily between AMS. Residents in any AMS can purchase equities and debts originating in other AMS without the need to undergo the scrutiny of each AMS domestic authorization process, for instance, by the existence of the each AMS domestic stock exchanges or brokerage companies, a condition that reflects a risky portfolio investment flow. The Indonesian FSA officials are clearly considering the impact of these risky portfolio investment flows when it comes to deciding to join the ASEAN Trading Link and the ASEAN Exchange Connectivity. In addition, domestic authorities will also have less involvement when it comes to the overall equities and debt trading system. Thus, once risky portfolio investment flow conditions exist, domestic authorities will eventually have less power over these flows. The reduced power of domestic authorities can have limited intervention tools once the market destabilizes. If tools are limited, domestic authorities may then be obliged to turn the stabilizing power over to a higher regional or global authority or organizations. This sounds like Indonesian case with the IMF discussed earlier in this chapter. Secondly, the reduced power of domestic authorities can also make the development of domestic markets difficult. Domestic authorities will eventually have less room to improve domestic markets since overseas players may already occupy the space.

ASEAN Framework for Cross Border Offering of CIS

Like the preceding case with ASEAN Trading Link and ASEAN Exchange Connectivity, ASEAN elites have as well agreed to implement the ASEAN Framework for Cross Border Offering of the Collective Investment Scheme (CIS) (ASEAN, 2017; ASEAN Capital Market Forum, 2016). They are particularly pushing to "[e]nhance market access for funds under the ASEAN CIS Framework" (ASEAN, 2017, p. 9). Currently, three AMS have implemented the Framework, namely Singapore, Malaysia and Thailand. ASEAN expects to add another AMS by 2021 and a fifth by 2025. The three AMS have recognized several technical issues in implementation, such as taxation, or an appropriate dispute resolution mechanism for cross-border trading (Chen et al., 2017). Nevertheless, ASEAN published the ASEAN CIS Handbook in 2014. The publication itself aims "to enable industry practitioners to gain an understanding of the different legislative requirements in each participating jurisdiction and the procedures for the cross-border Offering of ASEAN CIS" (ASEAN CIS Handbook, 2014, p. 3). The formal launch of implementation of the Framework followed.

The Framework introduced a streamlined authorization process for mutual fund managers to make cross-border Offerings to retail investors in the ASEAN region. Among all the initiatives under ASEAN as overviewed in Table 1.1 at the beginning of this book, this Framework has perhaps seen the most progress in terms of implementation. Its procedures rely on mutual recognition between the "Home Jurisdiction" with the "Host Jurisdiction". According to the ASEAN CIS

Handbook issued in 2014, the "Home Jurisdiction" means the jurisdiction where an ASEAN CIS Operator is licensed or registered, while the "Host Jurisdiction" means the jurisdiction of the target country of a cross-border trade. In order to do cross-border trading, an ASEAN CIS Operator needs to classify as a "Qualifying CIS Operator", or a company that fits to the predetermined criteria set out by ASEAN. The products themselves (the CIS) also need to comply with predetermined criteria set out by ASEAN, or the so-called the "Qualifying CIS". Only then, the Framework "allows the units of an ASEAN CIS authorised in its Home Jurisdiction to be offered in other Host Jurisdictions under a streamlined authorisation process, provided that the ASEAN CIS satisfies the set of common standards" (ASEAN CIS Handbook, 2014, p. 3). This is expected to lead to freer flows of through portfolio investments through cross-border trading.

Since its formal launch back in August 2014, currently thirteen ASEAN CIS Operators have received approval from the "Home Jurisdiction" as the "Qualifying CIS" (Table 4.1). These approvals were one of major indications that at least this ASEAN initiative made significant progress. However, based on the latest data provided in 2017, among those thirteen CIS Operators, only five have had approval from the "Host Jurisdiction" regulators. There are several possible explanations for this low rate of approval. Firstly, the "Host Jurisdiction" regulators may not be fully assured of the virtue of the cross-border Offering itself. Thus, it seems that the three AMS that have previously committed to implementing the cross-border Offering are holding on to their current position. These three AMS have deliberated on the cross-border Offering for around five years, yet "Host Jurisdiction" regulators handed out only five of thirteen ASEAN CIS Operators for approval CIS in their own jurisdictions. Secondly, the current ASEAN CIS market is perhaps already in balance. It implies that CIS Operators still prefer to trade using the usual system (no direct cross-border trade and all things related to trading need to go through each AMS domestic scrutiny) instead of the newly introduced ASEAN system.

Overall, the regulatory framework in Indonesia has already been aligned with the standards set in the ASEAN Framework for Cross Border Offering of CIS. For instance, jurisdictions wishing to join the Framework should adhere to the principles issued by a global regulator organization, such as the International Organization of Securities Commission (IOSCO) in its document containing standards for securities regulators (IOSCO, 2010). As to date, Indonesia has adhered to five

Table 4.1 Position of approval from "Home Jurisdiction" and "Host Jurisdiction"

	Malaysia	*Singapura*	*Thailand*	*Total*
Amount of Fund approved as Qualifying CIS	6	6	1	**13**
Home Regulator and Host Regulator Approval to Qualifying CIS	4[a]	1[b]	–	**5**

[a]Approval from Singapore
[b]Approval from Malaysia
Source Indonesian FSA (OJK)

out of seven required principles, with the remaining two in process for broad, if not full, implementation in Indonesia. In addition, Indonesia has mostly fulfilled the technical requirements for joining the Framework. For instance, the Framework regulates the qualification of personnel for the ASEAN CIS Operators. The CEO of the ASEAN CIS Operators need to have at least ten years of experiences in the field of financial and capital market, while the Director and Fund Manager, need to have a minimum of five years of experience in the field of financial and capital markets. According to data from the FSA, Indonesia has complied with those minimum experience requirements. There is also a requirement of ongoing capital adequacy of ASEAN CIS Operators in the Framework to the amount of USD 1 million and 0.1% from the excess of Assets Under Management (AUM). Indonesia also has adhered to this requirement. In another instance, the Framework also regulates the redemption timeframe for the ASEAN CIS. That is the redemption payments take a maximum of seven days. Meanwhile, investors can redeem once each month at a minimum. The Indonesian regulatory framework also has reflected these requirements. In Indonesia, redemption payment takes a maximum of seven days, and an investor can redeem even every day.

Although the regulatory framework in Indonesia may already be in alignment, agents still need to deal with several challenges when it comes to domestic implementation. As the case with the ASEAN Trading Link in the preceding section, an FSA official also identified both the internal and external challenges for the Framework. Internally, the pressures to delay opening the market come from a majority of domestic market players. The official mentioned the following:

> Para pelaku di Indonesia. Ketika kita konsultasi ke para pelaku gitu mereka tanggapannya. Selalu belum siap. Ada sih beberapa yang menyatakan siap, cuma enggak mewakili keseluruhan industri. Hanya yang besar-besar dan asing.
>
> [*The market players in Indonesia. When we had consultations we always have the same response. Always not ready. There are some that declare their readiness, yet they may not represent the overall industry. They are just the biggest and foreign companies.*]

Meanwhile, externally, there were pressures from other AMS that had earlier committed to join and advance the development of the Framework. The official also said that:

> Ya perkembangan terakhir kan yang sudah tanda tangan MOU kan baru tiga - Singapura, Malaysia dan Thailand. Memang yang ditargetin untuk ikut menyusul itu kan Indonesia sama Filipina. Tapi bolak-balik kita diundang diskusi dengan MOU-nya, kan. Soal ini, lagi dipetakan peraturan di kita tuh mana yang belum *comply* dengan standar ASEAN atau pun dari kita pun juga sama.
>
> [*The latest development of [the Framework] is that there are three countries has already signed the MOU – Singapore, Malaysia, and Thailand. They are targeting Indonesia and Philippine to follow them. But, they always invite us, back and forth, to discuss the MOU. In relation to that, we convey that we are still mapping our regulatory framework that may not be following the ASEAN standards or already be converged.*]

Referring to the statement above, when faced with the external pressure from peer AMS, agents tend to delay the move to portfolio investment liberalization initiatives.

Despite of all these instances of adherence to the Framework, the fact is that FSA officials still decline to commit themselves to the framework due to unresolved issues, such as the Assets Under Management (AUM) limitation. The Framework requires an ASEAN CIS Operator to have an AUM of minimum USD 500 million globally and at least five years of experience in managing CIS. Indonesia objected to these requirements, especially the minimum AUM. This is mainly because Indonesia views that such a requirement will only benefit the upper tier of ASEAN CIS Operators. Meanwhile, the majority of operators that are not in the upper tier in terms of AUM will have a hard time struggling to match the requirement. Another main concern related to the implementation of the cross-border Offering of CIS is domestic player readiness. FSA officials seem still unconvinced about the macroeconomic impacts of cross-border CIS trading in Indonesian capital markets. A senior official at the FSA confirmed that Indonesia has no significant issues related to the regulatory framework. The official emphasized that "we [Indonesia] can actually comply with all regulatory requirements as sets out for ASEAN CIS". This means that technically Indonesia can soon follow the path of the three AMS that have previously committed implementation.

The official also implied that Indonesia was in no rush to commit to the Framework considering the unconvincing impacts of cross-border trading on the Indonesian domestic CIS market. As the official further explicated that:

> Kalau dari arahan pimpinan sih kan ya belum jelas memang. Selama ini kita selalu menghindar, kita belum siap. Kemudian kita undang-undangnya belum bisa direvisi. Tapi lama-kelamaan kita juga harus commit pada komitmen kita kan.
>
> [*We have no clear direction from the top officials [of OJK] just yet. So long [in ASEAN CIS] we have been in avoidance that we are not just ready yet. Then, we have not revised our regulatory framework. But, I think in the end we must commit to our commitment.*]

Overall, the above analysis illustrates some evidence to suggest that officials from the FSA are far from ready to allow a more liberalized CIS regime. Even though the official mentioned readiness in terms of domestic regulations, the top-level officials at the FSA still avoided committing Indonesia to the Framework. The reasons for this are explained below.

If AMS fully approve the more liberalized regime of CIS, ASEAN surely can expect that portfolio investment flow will be freer. As discussed earlier in this chapter, the Framework allows mutual fund managers to make cross-border Offerings to retail investors in the ASEAN region without going through domestic scrutiny in each of AMS. Thus, bypassing this domestic scrutiny, portfolio investments can easily flow from one AMS to others. For instance, a Singapore-based "Qualifying CIS Operator" can purchase products of "Qualifying CIS" in Indonesia without the need to register and obtain approval from Indonesian domestic authorities. Similarly, a Singapore-based product of "Qualifying CIS" can be in any other AMS market, almost without restriction, without the need to register and get approval from Indonesian domestic authorities. As per the current CIS regime, each AMS domestic authority exercises the power to accept the registration and approval of both CIS Operators and CIS products in respective markets. Thus, adopting the ASEAN CIS regime means not only a freer flow of investment, but also that the regime is stripping away authority from domestic regulators. In addition, particularly in the case of Indonesia, other considerations to adopt the benefit for Indonesian CIS Operator or domestic players in adopting the ASEAN CIS regime are unclear. The macroeconomic impacts of cross-border CIS trading on Indonesian capital markets are also ambiguous. FSA officials may share the same concerns that there are more risks associated with the ASEAN CIS regime than tangible benefits to Indonesian domestic players and the overall economic condition.

ASEAN Disclosure Standards

ASEAN elites have also agreed to implement the ASEAN Disclosure Standards that aims to facilitate the offering of equity and debt products across multiple states in the region. ASEAN expects that this will provide ease of facility towards issuers, since there will be only one set of prospectuses disclosure standards to prepare for products offering in the region (ASEAN, 2017; ASEAN Capital Market Forum, 2016). As is the case with ASEAN Trading Link, ASEAN Disclosure Standards are one of the key priorities endorsed by the ASEAN Finance Ministers and recognized by the ASEAN Summit.

> Equal and seamless access to regional issuance and investment opportunities is facilitated through the adoption of mutually accepted and cohesive rules and practices for capital market products and services. The ASEAN Disclosure Standards and Common Prospectus Streamlined Review Framework have been introduced to enable multi-jurisdiction offerings of equity and plain debt securities to retail investors using a single prospectus. (ASEAN Capital Market Forum, 2016, p. 3)

A single set of disclosure standards means Indonesia needs to deregulate its own disclosure standards by, firstly, allowing the use of overseas trustees in capital market product cross-border Offerings. Secondly, Indonesia needs to allow overseas capital market professionals to do their business in Indonesia, cross-border, without a physical presence. And, finally,

Indonesia is required to adopt one-approval regime for disclosure. This means that if a capital market product has been offered and approved for trading in one state, it can also be automatically traded in another state without further registration and approval of local authorities. Meanwhile, the current regulatory framework and policy in Indonesia still maintains the compulsory domestic trustee in any capital market product offering, both domestic and cross-border. The same policy of "only domestic actors" also applies to the engagement of capital market professionals. As for one-approval regime for disclosure, officials still maintain the policy of registration and approval with local authorities to any capital market product offered within Indonesian jurisdiction.

Meanwhile, the Common Prospectus Streamlined Review Framework was initiated to streamline the reviewing process of prospectuses if issuers want to list or offer equity and plain debt products. Generally, adoption of this Framework also requires Indonesia to deregulate domestic prospectus-related policies. The deregulation is expected to allow the use of a single prospectus for a cross-border Offering or listing of capital market products. In doing so, ASEAN assumes that portfolio investments will move even more freely within AMS. However, as is the case with ASEAN Disclosure Standards, FSA officials seem reluctant to join the Framework. There are, at least, four aspects related to such reluctance. Firstly, the regulatory aspect will involve complex deregulation, such as on restrictions on foreign capital market professionals, distribution channels and continuous disclosure. However, the FSA has previously affirmed its intention to maintain these restrictions (Indonesian FSA Internal Discussion Document, 2017, pp. 73–74). Secondly, the enforcement aspect will require a set of cross-border dispute settlement mechanisms. This aspect directly relates to the issues of domestic investor protections in cross-border transactions. Thirdly, there should be assessments on the readiness of domestic players. This aspect also includes the assessment of macroeconomic condition under freer portfolio investments flows. Lastly, there are also aspects related to taxation and monetary conditions. These are mostly around how to tax cross-border transactions, as well as how freer portfolio investments flows affect domestic monetary stability.

There are currently three AMS committed to implementing the ASEAN Disclosure Standards and the Common Prospectus Streamlined Review Framework, namely Malaysia, Singapore and Thailand. While the Standards have come into effect from April, 2013, the Framework has been put into trial for implementation since March 2015. The FSA's position of maintaining its restrictive regime also correlates to the fact that there has been no substantial implementation of either the Standards or the Framework since commencement. There are two possible explanations for this lack of implementation. Firstly, each AMS is holding back from fully operating under the Standards and the Framework. Despite ASEAN's campaign to move to closer financial integration, AMS officials are cautious about portfolio investments moving more freely within AMS. There are risks associated with the freer flow of portfolio investments, for instance, the "hot money" flows or the risks of having less authority over the domestic market. Thus, AMS officials treat implementation with high caution, resulting in slow progress.

The second explanation is that companies wishing to issue their product can just live with the conventional product issuance rather than take risky steps using a newly introduced cross-border issuance. A senior official at the Indonesian FSA agreed that there are actually several good regulatory ideas within the Standards and the Framework. However, the official opts for only those ideas rather than fully adopting the Standards and the Framework. The official mentioned that:

> Kalau ada international standard yang mereka buat, misalnya, kita dalam proses adopsi. Tapi adopsinya itu dalam rangka untuk penggunaan domestik sebetulnya. Kayak misalnya ASEAN Standard, ASEAN Disclosure Standards, itu kita adopsi loh. Cuman penggunaannya jadi lebih ke untuk yang domestik offering dulu.
>
> [*If they (ASEAN) make an international standard, for instance, then we are in the process of adopting the standard. However, the purpose of the adoption is only to strengthen our domestic regulatory framework. For instance, in the case of ASEAN standard, the ASEAN Disclosure Standard, we actually adopted the standard. However, currently the operationalization of the adoption is only for domestic offerings.*]

Further, the official also explained that the only problem in opening up the current restrictive regime is the lack of willingness from the top decision-makers in the FSA. At present, the official added that there is no clear direction to open up current restrictive disclosure requirement to foreigners or further liberalize the portfolio investment regime.

Market players in ASEAN, in one occasion, have also voiced reluctance to take risky steps using a newly introduced cross-border issuance mechanism. In a meeting in early 2016, market players in ASEAN, through the ACMF Industry Consultative Panel (AICP), provided inputs to the officials (Indonesian FSA Internal Discussion Document, 2017). AICP suggested that domestic oversubscriptions might be the main reason for the lack of substantial implementation of both the Standards and the Framework up to date. Domestic oversubscription may mean that there are parts of the domestic CIS market still untapped. Thus, the first priority for Indonesia and the industry communities should be to tap into these parts before committing to the Standards and the Framework. Further, AICP also added that there is no need to standardize the current approval regime for the purpose of raising more funds in ASEAN. Thus, AICP implied that a single set of disclosure standards is unnecessary. However, AICP came up with alternatives that ASEAN instead should focus more on "flavored" products, such as for Real Estate Investment Trusts (REITs) or the development of Private Placement.

If AMS fully adopt the Standards and the Framework, ASEAN surely can expect portfolio investment flows to be freer. Allowing a single set of disclosure standards means that not only players can operate freely within the ASEAN region but also that products can find markets without much needed scrutiny. For instance, a Singapore-based listed company can issue equities or debt and market them to the Indonesian market with less control from Indonesian authorities. Thus, capital expects to flow seamlessly within the ASEAN region. This is a condition that sounds familiar, "hot money" flows. In addition, a single set of disclosure standards also means that Indonesia must deregulate overseas capital market professionals. Again, this is stripping away regulatory power from domestic authorities. In the case of economic instability, with less regulatory power, it would be hard to imagine that domestic authorities can freely exercise policies to stabilize the market. The worst-case scenario, Indonesia may need to turn to international financial organizations to get out of the prolonged instability. In addition to the matters covered in this section (external peer pressure from other AMS and rejection from domestic market players), internally there are also concerns in relation to the Indonesian MOF. When asked about the relationships between the FSA and the IMOF, an official from the FSA briefly mentioned that:

> Oh, ada yang mau ngegas, ada yang mau ngerem gitu, kurang lebih... kita sih enggak ada yang pingin nge-judge.
>
> [*Oh, there are those that want to move forward, there are also those that want to put the brakes on...we do not want to judge each other on this.*]

ASEAN Banking Integration Framework

The AEC Blueprint 2025, as approved by the highest-level governance structures in ASEAN, has mandated closer financial integration among AMS. Particularly in regard to banking sector integration (ASEAN, 2015, p. 8), ASEAN expects the integration to:

> [p]rovide greater market access and operational flexibility for Qualified ASEAN Banks (QABs) through the ASEAN Banking Integration Framework (ABIF), based on each country's readiness and on a reciprocal basis, thereby reducing gaps in market access and operational flexibility across ASEAN[.]

Further, as part of ASEAN's Strategic Action Plan for 2016–2015, ASEAN expects that by 2020 onwards at least the ABIF will have already implemented these arrangement and significant number of banks have qualified as QABs. Meanwhile, pre-2020, the ABIF will focus the work to formulate the guidelines for implementation. On its initial development in 2014, the ABIF was optimistic about creating a multilateral agreement framework using a single set of standards that will apply to all AMS. Thus, by the existence of this multilateral agreement framework, all the QABs will have better access and able to operate in a greater market across all AMS. QABs themselves shall meet the minimum capital requirement as well as comply with a set of pre-agreed regulatory requirements, including, for instance, other prudential measures. However, after technical discussions, AMS officials reported to higher-level governance structures in ASEAN that it might not be possible to move forward with the multilateral agreement framework. This was mainly attributable to the fact of wide differences in domestic banking regulatory frameworks among AMS.

In order to provide alternative arrangements to the multilateral agreement framework plan, ASEAN then agreed to pursue a more modest way of liberalizing its banking regime. Thus, instead of directly pursuing the multilateral agreement framework, ASEAN has come to push AMS to conclude bilateral arrangements between one state and another state. The expectation is that bilateral arrangements will eventually lead to a multilateral agreement. Through these bilateral agreements, QABs anticipate enjoying special access and operational ease. This does not necessarily mean that banks other than QABs may not be able to perform a cross-border banking operation, yet states will treat QABs with privileges. For instance, under the ABIF, Indonesian authorities signed a bilateral agreement with Malaysia on August 2016. An official release from the Indonesian FSA stated that "[t]he scope of the agreement covers the regulations on market access and banking activities related to the process that banks have to comply with when applying for QAB permits[.]". Thus, both Indonesia and Malaysia reserved special reciprocal privileges for banks that qualified as QABs. Meanwhile, other banks will have to follow the normal procedure to perform cross-border banking operations. Indonesia and the Philippines are currently also heading into the same bilateral agreement under the ABIF with the signing of the Letter of Intent (LoI) to kick-off the discussion. Other AMS are notably pursuing the same arrangement, such as the Philippines and Thailand or Philippine and Malaysian bilateral agreements.

Apart from the ASEAN's optimistic view of the ABIF, it is also undeniable that there is a concern for regional stability in future associated with facilitation of the freer flow of investments. Thus, Indonesian FSA officials seem to want to halt the development of the ABIF in terms of the plan of fully integrating the banking system. Nevertheless, they are partially open to the idea of the QABs. Currently, officials prefer to opt for bilateral agreements. The idea of bilateral agreements came from technical level officials to the highest-level governance structures. This suggests that that officials are open to the idea of providing greater market access and more flexibility to banks, yet there are also other concerns to notice. Firstly, AMS, including Indonesia, are not ready to integrate their banking system regionally. Each AMS has not only different regulatory frameworks but also a different level of banking sector development. Secondly, the story of "hot money" flows in European banking has become a reason for caution on the part of officials. In future, the ABIF may suggest a scenario of regional collapses throughout financial sector. This implies that officials will have to seek a more comprehensive monitoring and surveillance system to safeguard their own domestic financial sectors.

With those two concerns in the background, Indonesian FSA officials appear to use bilateral agreements as a long term-strategy to escape from the trap of the multilateral agreement framework. A senior official at the FSA confirmed that, in fact, there is almost no further substantial banking sector liberalization made through the bilateral agreements. The official particularly mentioned that:

> Tapi sebenarnya, pada kenyataannya, apa yang ada di dalam bilateral agreement itu, dituangkan dalam SOC... bisa baca di paket ke-enam. Itulah isinya bilateral agreement... Mungkin seremonial aja. Kick off meeting lah sebenarnya. Sebelum dua-dua nya step down itu.
>
> [*As a matter of fact, the contents of the bilateral agreement is as the same as those committed in the Schedule of Commitment (SOC) Sixth Package of the ASEAN Framework Agreement on Services (AFAS). We can just read that document and conclude that the contents are the same. The bilateral agreement is perhaps only a ceremonial. It actually only is a kick off meeting. It will then serve as a legacy for both Indonesian and Malaysian Financial Services Authority's leaders.*]

For instance, the substance of Indonesia's bilateral agreement with Malaysia is merely a reflection of the current state of banking sector liberalization in ASEAN. This means that neither Indonesia nor Malaysia are offering a freer flow of investments through the banking sector by signing the agreement. The official further explained that the bilateral agreement was largely attributable to the needs of reporting to a higher-level structure in ASEAN. In doing so, at least Indonesia is making progressive contribution to the development of the ABIF. The official even mentioned that the agreement is no more than a "ceremonial" or "kick-off meeting" for many rounds of negotiations and discussions to come. A similar explanation also may apply from the Malaysian the point of view.

This strategy of pursuing more bilateral agreements for a freer flow of investments itself is perhaps already deep-rooted given the example of the World Trade Organization (WTO). For instance, the failure of the WTO to conclude a multilateral agreement among its members made way for the development of Regional Trade Agreements (RTAs). As a result, regionals started to arrange their very own Free Trade Agreements (FTAs). As a result, the WTO hopes to turn the "spider's web" effect of regional trading into a multilateral agreement in a long-term. ASEAN is no exception to pursuing regional arrangements. The RTAs are expecting the "spider's web" effect of bilateral trade arrangements. Applying this to here, the ABIF expects that bilateral trade agreements, such as the Indonesia and Malaysia agreement mentioned earlier, will grow to form a multilateral agreement framework. Indonesian officials are surely aware of this strategy. Thus, rather than opposing the multilateral agreement framework as mandated by the highest-level of governance in ASEAN, they opted to utilize bilateral agreements, even though the agreements are considered to be merely "ceremonial".

If AMS fully implement the multilateral agreement framework under the ABIF, ASEAN surely can expect portfolio investment flow to be freer. The banking sector is the backbone of the payment and settlement system for portfolio investment products. The banking sector is thus part of the infrastructure required for a successful liberalization of portfolio investment. The banking sector also accounts for external lending and borrowing transactions. The banking sector, in fact, still dominates the development financing needs in AMS. In Indonesia, for instance, the banking sector accounts for the majority of the total asset composition, or nearly 80%, of the Indonesian financial sector (Chart 4.3). From the capital market area, security companies account for around 10% of the asset composition. Investment funds, multi-finance companies, pension funds and other non-bank financial institutions (NBFI) share the rest. Overall, considering its importance and dominance, banking sector integration is an integration priority for ASEAN. It is also important to note here, as discussed at the beginning of this chapter that early episodes of financial liberalization in Indonesia started with banking sector deregulation. Further, the Asian Financial Crisis also hit Indonesia hard because the dominance of the banks in the wider financial sector. Thus, once the crisis affected the banking sector, the overall economic condition was destabilized.

Up to this point, the external factor being overviewed here is mostly related to the pushback from other regulators in AMS as well as the strategy employed by the FSA's agents in dealing with the pushback. In addition to that external factor, agents also have to deal with an internal factor due to the fact that matters covered by the ABIF was used to be the domain of Bank Indonesia and central banks in AMS. An Indonesian FSA official mentioned that in one instance, Bank Indonesia decided for the Indonesian FSA related to the establishment of a working committee for banking under ASEAN. This may attributable to the fact that the Indonesian FSA was still in a transitional period. Particularly, the official mentioned the following:

> ABIF itu mau dibikin working committee sendiri... saya termasuk orang yang mempertanyakan urgency itu. Untuk apa dibikin lagi working committee ABIF? ...yang jelas kayaknya bukan inisiatif OJK ya. Kayaknya itu inisiatif pertemuan Bank Sentral itu... Dia membentuk suatu prosedur atau mekanisme sendiri yang, nah ini ada kritik juga nih mengenai organisasi di ASEAN itu ya.

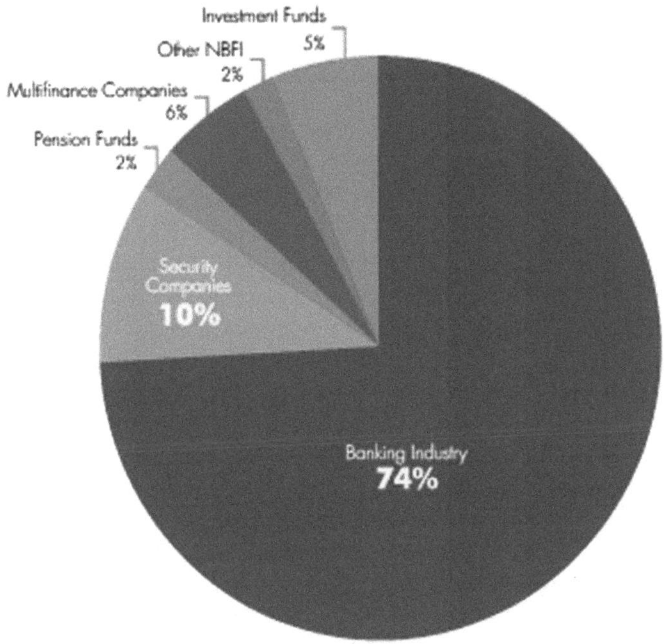

Chart 4.3 Asset Composition of the Indonesian Financial Services Sector * (*Source* Indonesian Financial Services Sector Master Plan 2015–2019; *Data as of 2014)

> [*That ABIF wants to make its own working committee...I am one of those questioning the urgency of that. Why would we need a new working committee on ABIF? ...Clearly that was not the Indonesian FSA's initiative. It might be initiative from the Central Banks meeting...They made their own procedure or mechanism; this is a critique to ASEAN organizational arrangement.*]

The official further suggested that agents at the Indonesian FSA, have suggested to Bank Indonesia that they may also need to be actively involved in meetings among ASEAN central banks, particularly, if the issues of banking sector liberalization are to be discussed.

Other Related Flows

For other related flows, such as external borrowings and lending in the banking sector, ASEAN elites have agreed to a further liberalization of the remaining restrictions (ASEAN, 2016, 2017). This means that ASEAN elites committed to open all of Indonesia's banking sector transactions, including in trade credits, loans, currency, deposits and other assets and liabilities. In general, Indonesia has allowed external lending and borrowing in trade credits. However, domestic implementation gaps are mostly in transactions other than trade credit. For instance, Indonesia still maintains a limitation on bank's foreign loans of up to 30% of reserve. There is also a restriction to put Indonesian Rupiah deposits from Indonesian Rupiah foreign exchange purchasing. Another instance would be restrictions on loans to non-residents for consumer credit and domestic use purposes. All of these restrictions are expected to be liberalized under the commitment made by ASEAN elites, thus leaving an implementation gap in Indonesia. In the above-mentioned implementation gaps, Indonesian FSA officials clearly exhibit a more conservative approach to portfolio investment liberalization than that deliberately committed to by ASEAN.

In general, these instances of the liberalization of other monetary flows are widely included in the capital account liberalization efforts under ASEAN. Within the governance structure of ASEAN, capital account liberalization has its own technical level discussion (Working Committee on Capital Account Liberalization/WC-CAL). This Committee reports to higher-level structures from the ASEAN Finance Ministers' Meeting (AFMM) up to the ASEAN Summit. The final aim of CAL in ASEAN is to support freer capital flows including current account, foreign direct investment (FDI), portfolio investments and other investments. In another part of ASEAN, there are also efforts to liberalize financial services in particular. Through its own technical level discussion (Working Committee on Financial Services Liberalization/WC-FSL), efforts to liberalize financial services mainly aim to enable the free flow of financial services. The term financial services here includes those that support portfolio investment liberalization through, for instance, liberalization of capital market brokers and investment managers. Similar to WC-CAL, this Committee also reports to the higher-level structure from the ASEAN Finance Ministers' Meeting (AFMM) up to the ASEAN Summit.

It is expected that those main initiatives to liberalize portfolio investments in ASEAN, such as those mentioned early in this chapter (ASEAN

Trading Link, ASEAN Framework for Cross Border Offering of CIS, ASEAN Disclosure Standards, and ABIF), will further hasten the achievement of wider CAL and FSL objectives. For instance, under the ABIF, ASEAN can expect that capital account liberalization will be achieved. Alternatively, ASEAN Disclosure Standards strongly correlate with financial services liberalization through the deregulation of capital market brokers and investment managers. In another particular instance, agreements under the ABIF may also cover further deregulation of external borrowings and lending in the banking sector. Thus, although the scope of CAL and FSL seems wider than just portfolio investments, officials paid particular attention to both of them. CAL and FSL can anticipate no further progress until development in the main initiatives is visible. In the next sections, this book looks at the way agents harness the international standards towards the "national interest", and avoid implementing the ASEAN integration initiatives.

International Financial Standards And Regional Financial Integration

The following sections feature case studies using the following international regulatory standards: (1) The Basel Committee on Banking Supervision Standards; (2) IOSCO Objectives and Principles of Securities Regulation; and (3) IAIS Insurance Core Principles. These international standards were chosen based on the following considerations. Firstly, they are the most discussed sectors related to the portfolio investment liberalization. There are a number of initiatives in these sectors, and the standards are historically evolving over time. The Basel Standards represents the banking sector. Meanwhile, IOSCO applies to the capital market sector, one of the most highly discussed sectors in ASEAN portfolio investment liberalization. In addition, IAIS applies to the insurance sector, also one of the favoured sectors for closer integration and liberalization in ASEAN.

Another consideration is that the three international standards are perhaps among the most recognized international standards related to portfolio investment liberalization with worldwide assessments and applications. The Basel Standards can be traced back to the mid-1970s. Meanwhile, IOSCO was established in the early 1980s. Though the IAIS may be a relatively new standard setter through its establishment in the early 1990s, it is the most prominent organization for insurance regulators in the world. While the ultimate goal of these standards is regulatory convergence leading to closer financial integration, Indonesian FSA officials applying the standards as one of the tools for developing their own domestic market. Thus, even though legally and in practice Indonesia already adheres to the standards, it is also not attracted to financial integration. An Indonesian FSA official claimed that:

> Dengan melihat kepatuhan kita terhadap standard setting boddies, itu ya memang kita menunjukan itikad yang baik dan komitmen yang luar biasa untuk bisa terciptanya integrasi…Beberapa assessment yang dilakukan belakangan ini, dua tahun terakhir ini, menunjukan bahwa kita alhamdulillah hasilnya bagus…Kita benar-benar mencoba untuk comply terhadap international standard setting bodies.
>
> [*By looking at our compliance to the standard setting bodies, it shows our good willingness and tremendous commitment for creating an integration…Several latest assessments, in the last two years, show that we are doing good…We are really trying to comply with the international standard setting bodies.*]

This implies that there should be a positive correlation between adherence to international regulatory standards and Indonesia's position on ASEAN financial integration. However, this section suggests that the correlation is actually in different directions. At the very least, this book is unable to confirm the positive correlation through findings in the field.

To this extent, there are several rationales behind the existence of these different directions between adherence to international financial standards and the pursuit of regional financial integration. These rationales serve as factors affecting the way FSA agents behave to stymie regional financial integration. From the point of view of the international standards, there have been a long historical engagement not only with the standards themselves but also with the international financial organizations issuing the standards. For instance, Indonesia's engagement with the IOSCO as the international financial organization issuing the IOSCO Objective and Principles of Securities Regulation dated back to early in 1980s. Although, Indonesia might be an exception in the case of IAIS Insurance Core Principles attributable to the relatively late development of the insurance industry. On the other hand, Indonesian engagement with ASEAN regional financial integration has relatively recent. Indonesia's regional engagement with ASEAN financial integration only started post the Asian Financial Crisis in 1997–1998.

Another rationale is that the international financial standards evolved over time and have been used been used as international benchmarks for a long period. As a result, regional financial integration has to relate to the international financial standards. For instance, admission to the Framework for Cross-Border Offering of CIS is based on compliance with IOSCO Objectives and Principles of Securities Regulation. Meanwhile, despite AMS commitments and peer pressure, ASEAN initiatives are non-legally binding. In other words, Indonesia has no legal obligation to domestically implement ASEAN initiatives as this book has discussed in the preceding sections. Thus, agents can easily opt out from joining the ASEAN Trading Link or delay the accession to the Framework for Cross Border Offering of CIS. This is unlikely be the case for the international financial standards because not only has there been a long engagement with the standards but also regional initiatives reference them. Although, for instance, Indonesia's engagement with ASEAN particularly can be traced back to as early as 1967, the overall concept of the ASEAN financial integration was just introduced by ASEAN members in the early 2000s as a response to the Asian Financial Crisis.

In addition to the two rationales elaborated above, there is also a rationale related to the ultimate purposes of international financial standards as compared to regional financial integration. The ultimate purpose of the international financial standards is mainly to achieve a regulatory convergence among states. It is true that a regulatory convergence may serve as a prerequisite for closer financial integration. However, there is still a long way to go even to have regulatory convergence across one region. Regulatory convergence can also mean that a state is adopting international best practices into its domestic regulatory framework. Meanwhile ASEAN, particularly with the AEC for instance, is clearly aiming for a more open and liberal international portfolio investment flow (ASEAN, 2015, 2016). The idea of regulatory convergence is rather compelling than opening and liberalising the domestic market. Therefore, it is more compelling for Indonesia to comply with the international regulatory standards, rather than to pursue non-binding ASEAN regional initiatives. In the next three sections, this book demonstrates the application of these rationales.

Basel Committee on Banking Supervision Standards

Starting in the banking area, the standards discussed here are perhaps the most recognized and practicable international standards for banking regulation, The Basel Committee on Banking Supervision (BCBS) Standards. According to Goodhart (2011), the establishment of the Committee on Banking Regulations and Supervisory Practice (CBRSP) or today's BCBS was attributable to the greater financial interconnectedness among countries post-World War II. However, the regulations were unable to match the speed with which financial interconnectedness occurred. As a result, the early objective of the CBRSP was to bridge this unbalanced pace between the regulations and financial interconnectedness through cooperation among countries (Goodhart, 2011; Toniolo, 2005). In the next development of this cooperation, BCBS has issued, up to date, several sets of international standards for banking regulation. Adapting from Penikas (2015), the development itself, at least, consisted of three major periods, namely the Concordat (1974–1986), the Basel Standards (1987–2011) and the Post-Basel period (2012–onwards). To date, the latest Basel III standards continue to evolve to match with current developments in the banking industry, increases in cross-border banking operations, as well as regulatory and supervisory needs.

Like other banking regulators in the world, Indonesia is certainly subject to the Basel Standards. In overall, according to the latest available reports (FSB, 2014; IMF, 2012b), Indonesia generally has taken steps to ensure full compliance with Basel III. For instance, assessment under the Financial Sector Assessment Program/FSAP (IMF, 2012b) put Indonesia at the highest-level of compliance (or the "Compliant") on six out of thirty Basel Core Principles assessed. The IMF put most of the assessment results just one grade below the highest-level of compliance (or the "Largely Compliant"). There were eighteen out of thirty Basel Core Principles in this grading category. While there were four principles still in the category of "Materially Non-Compliant", only two principles are in the category of "Non-Compliant". One of these principles was related to country and transfer risks, and the IMF stated that the "risk is largely unaddressed in the banking system" (IMF, 2012b, p. 24). The other principle with a "Non-Compliant" grading was the interest rate in the banking book. The IMF commented that:

> Regulations on risk management in banks do not explicitly cover interest rate risk in the banking book (IRRBB); banks do not actively manage this risk and the supervisors do not adequately focus on this risk. (IMF, 2012b, p. 24)

The Indonesian FSA together with Bank Indonesia is working to address the two principles that are still in "Non-Compliant" grading. For instance, the Financial Stability Board/FSB (2014) has recorded that Indonesia has taken steps to address the principles of IRRBB. The report particularly mentioned that Indonesia has come up with a method to measure the IRRBB and then later to incorporate the measurement into the overall risk assessment. In addition, the report also highlighted at least two other factors that were critical to Indonesia. One was the transition to the Indonesian FSA. In an earlier chapter, this book covered how and why the new institution emerged. Domestic financial system stability was the second factor. In a later section, this book explains the existence of the Komite Stabilitas Sistem Keuangan or Financial Sector Stability Committee (FSSC). It provides a legal forum for interaction among the corresponding domestic institutions related to portfolio investment liberalization. Through highlighting these two critical factors, along with steps to ensure further compliance to the international standards, the report generally has given a good impression on Indonesia's adherence to international financial regulatory standards.

From the discussion above, Indonesia seems to have a great willingness and commitment to adhere to international financial regulatory standards. However, full compliance with Basel III did not necessarily mean that FSA officials favour regional financial integration. A high-level FSA official, regarding adherence to international financial regulatory standards, stated that:

> Kalau itu [arahan Dewan Komisioner OJK terkait integrasi keuangan] iya, tetapi ada garis bawahnya. Jangan menjadi pasar kita jadi bulan-bulanan lah. Intinya gitu...Tolong diperhatikan dan jangan membuat komitmen yang lebih dibandingkan dengan yang lain-lain...Prinsip yang harus kita anut adalah mutual [benefit].
>
> [*There are directions from the Indonesian FSA Board of Commissioners, yet they underline few things. Our domestic market is the most important...Please pay closer attention and do not make a commitment that is above other states' commitment...We admit the mutual benefit principle.*]

The impression was that the Indonesian FSA is generally willing and committed to ensuring that Indonesia takes steps to adhere to the international financial regulatory standards. However, considering national interests first, the FSA still seems reluctant to commit to international financial regulatory standards if the standards particularly resulted further liberalizing financial services. This reluctance also is accurate in regard to portfolio investment liberalization, such as the ASEAN Disclosure Standards. Thus, in this case study, FSA officials are expressing the same positions to ASEAN in reference to the positions to the international regulatory standards. As a result, FSA officials still block further commitment to ASEAN banking sector integration or liberalization.

IOSCO Objectives and Principles of Securities Regulation

The relationship between the IOSCO and Indonesia can be traced back to 1984, or just a year after the establishment of IOSCO itself (OECD, 2016). Indonesia became one of the earliest members of IOSCO through Indonesian involvement in the forum. The history of the IOSCO itself started with the establishment of a forum for securities regulators in western nations, led by the United States. However, in its development, the IOSCO has evolved to include more countries in other hemispheres and thus became worldwide since then (Sommer, 1996). As mentioned in its By-Laws, the main objectives of the IOSCO are:

> To cooperate in developing, implementing and promoting adherence to internationally recognized and consistent standards of regulation, oversight and enforcement…; to enhance investor protection and promote investor confidence in the integrity of securities markets…; and to exchange information at both global and regional levels on their respective experiences… (p. 2)

From the objectives above, it may seem that the IOSCO has less involvement in portfolio investment liberalization. One can argue that the IOSCO is simply an international standard setter related to portfolio investments. However, regulatory convergence remains the most important tool in achieving global liberalization or integration. This is plausible since once the world achieves regulatory convergence, then it is easier to open markets. In addition, in order to achieve its objectives, the IOSCO is working with other international financial institutions (IFIs) advocating liberalization or integration.

As arguably the most prominent forum in the world for securities regulators, the IOSCO collaborates closely with and mostly integrates its agenda with the Group of Twenty (G20) and the FSB. These collaborations among the IOSCO, G20 and FSB are particularly related to issues of interconnectedness in setting up global regulatory standards. For instance, issue of portfolio investment volatility fall under the authority of the securities regulators. However, under the scrutiny of the G20 and the FSB, financial market volatility, in general, is an important factor for global financial stability. Most of the global financial standards as set by the IOSCO are consistent with discussions at the G20 and the FSB. Thus, although the IOSCO has non-binding regulatory instruments, its member jurisdictions, including Indonesia, seem to regard IOSCO instruments as one of the most important international regulatory standards (Costi, 2015). This is especially evident in the capital market and in financial institutions where other global or regional fora are using the IOSCO instruments as a benchmark, or even one of the pre-conditions to get into a global or regional initiative. For instance, ASEAN uses the IOSCO instruments as one of the pre-conditions to join the ASEAN Framework for Cross Border Offering of CIS.

There are currently two main instruments being utilized by the IOSCO. These instruments are: (1) IOSCO Objectives and Principles of Securities Regulation (or later referred to as the Principles) and (2) IOSCO MMOU. The IOSCO introduced the principles to its members in 1998. In total, there are eleven headings that break down to thirty-eight principles. An assessment of Indonesia, however, still used the earlier version of thirty principles (IMF, 2012a). Based on this assessment, Indonesia received the highest grading, or the "Fully Implemented" grading, for one-third of the total number of principles assessed, or ten principles. Meanwhile, the IOSCO put the other thirteen principles in the grading immediately below the highest grading or the "Broadly Implemented" grading. IOSCO then assessed the rest of the principles as either "Partly Implemented" or "N/A". Indonesia received no "Not Implemented" grading in the assessment. One of the principles that received the "Partly Implemented" grading is the one that related to the ASEAN Framework for Cross Border Offering of CIS (Principle 20). The principle itself stated that regulation should ensure that "there is a proper and disclosed basis for assets valuation and the pricing and the redemption of units in a collective investment scheme" (IMF, 2012a, p. 19).

As for the MMOU, IOSCO has listed Indonesia in Appendix A, along with the other 121 jurisdictions, as of 14 January 2014. Appendix A itself generally means that members have fulfilled and practiced all the requirements set forth in the MMOU. There is also Appendix B for those members who are still unable to fulfil and practice all the requirements set forth in the MMOU. Yet, to be listed in Appendix B, these members need to lodge formal intentions to be listed in the Appendix A. Currently, there are only nine members still in Appendix B. The Philippines is currently the only member from the ASEAN-5 that is still under Appendix B. In order for a member to be listed on Appendix A, the member needs to lodge a formal application to the IOSCO. The IOSCO Verification Team (VT) will then decide to assess and verify all the legal requirements as well as practical observations to ensure that the corresponding member has fulfilled and practiced all the requirements set forth in the MMOU. The process for Indonesia's application to be listed in Appendix A itself lasted around eight years or from 2005 to 2014 (Indonesian FSA Internal Presentation Document, 2015).

According to that same document, there were three main issues that Indonesia needed to address. Firstly, the issues were on the independent status of the securities regulator in relation to providing information to foreign authorities without interference and/or dependence on any parties. Secondly, there were also issues relating to obtaining confidential banking data in the context of securities inspection and investigation processes. Lastly, there were issues as to the ability to provide information to foreign authorities regarding securities inspections and investigations being carried out by such authorities. While the securities regulator was still under government control, the issues of independence and the power to obtain and provide information posed problems due to government restrictions. However, with the enactment of the Indonesian FSA Law and the establishment of the FSA itself, Indonesia can finally settle all these issues through the power and authority given to the FSA. After several discussions and verification processes, the IOSCO finally granted Indonesia's application under the newly-established FSA.

The FSA also continued to work on other initiatives that used IOSCO instruments. For instance, in the case of the ASEAN Framework for Cross Border Offering of CIS, there is pre-condition that AMS should be listed in Appendix A of the IOSCO MMOU. In addition, AMS needs to get a grading of at least "Broadly Implemented" on the principles related to the CIS, such as for Principle 20 mentioned in the earlier paragraph. There are also other requirements, such as the exclusion of AMS from the list of "non-cooperative country" as issued by the Financial Action Task Force (FATF). An official document has mentioned that Indonesia has fulfilled all the requirements to join the ASEAN Framework for Cross Border Offering of CIS (Indonesian FSA Internal Discussion Document, 2017). Yet again FSA officials also implied that Indonesia is in no rush to commit to the Framework considering the unconvincing impacts of cross-border trading on the untapped domestic CIS market. As the official further explicated that:

> Kalau dari arahan pimpinan sih kan ya belum jelas memang. Selama ini kita selalu menghindar, kita belum siap. Kemudian kita undang-undangnya belum bisa direvisi. Tapi lama-kelamaan kita juga harus commit pada komitmen kita kan.
>
> [*We have no clear direction from the top officials [of the Indonesian FSA] just yet. So long [in ASEAN CIS] we have been in avoidance that we are not just ready yet. Then, we have not revised our regulatory framework. But, I think in the end we must commit to our commitment*.]

To this extent, FSA officials seem to consider that the improvement made by committing to the international regulatory standards should be enough to fulfil Indonesia's obligation to international pressure. Thus, the Indonesian FSA would deliberately delay domestic implementation of the regional initiatives, or even perhaps opt to reject implementation in the case of CIS.

IAIS Insurance Core Principles

Before moving forward to a discussion of the IAIS Insurance Core Principles, this section needs to restate the importance of the insurance industry within the context of portfolio investment liberalization in Indonesia. In another part of ASEAN, there are also efforts to liberalize financial services through technical level discussion, such as the WC-FSL. A government source stated the following:

> FSL itu berbicara tentang liberarisasi terintegrasi dan lain-lain...Yang paling depan untuk untuk liberarisasi integrasi.
>
> [*FSL is discussing the integrated liberalization and other things...At the forefront is for integration liberalization.*]

These efforts to liberalize financial services mainly aim to enable the free flow of financial services. The terms financial services here certainly cover those that support portfolio investment liberalization through, for instance, liberalization of pension funds and insurers. In addition, the pursuit of a freer flow of portfolio investment itself was mainly a result of IMF LOIs for Indonesia to develop its non-bank financial institutions, including the capital market, financing and insurance companies. The aim was to overcome the over-reliance on the banking system. Since then, portfolio investment liberalization is moving forward at a faster rate, providing perfect timing for ASEAN to tie down AMS to liberalize their markets and push for closer financial integration. Another thing is that insurance companies are investing in portfolio investments, and these investments are occurring cross-border among countries. Though in some countries, including Indonesia, there are heavy restrictions on cross-border transactions for insurance companies. Thus, discussions on the liberalization or integration of the insurance industry became one of the important parts within the context of portfolio investment liberalization in Indonesia.

Now that this section has restated the importance of the insurance industry within the context of portfolio investment liberalization in Indonesia, the following discussions elaborate Indonesia's engagement with the IAIS. Unlike in the two previous global standard setters (the BCBS and the IOSCO), Indonesia's membership in the IAIS is relatively new, only around six years old. Indonesia became a member of the IAIS just back in 2012, or almost 20 years after the establishment of IAIS in 1994. According to its By-Laws (2018), the IAIS has the mission to:

> a. promote effective and globally consistent supervision of the insurance industry in order to develop and maintain fair, safe and stable insurance markets for the benefit and protection of policyholders; and to
> b. contribute to global financial stability. (p. 2)

Although membership in the IAIS for insurance supervisors is voluntary the IAIS is also one of the members of the FSB. Thus, the issuance of the IAIS's international regulatory standards is subject to the FSB's endorsement. In addition, the IMF-WB also regularly observe countries' compliance with the IAIS international regulatory standards through the Financial Sector Assessment Program (FSAP) program. The standards commonly applied here are the IAIS Insurance Core Principles.

The IMF-WB has carried out its first observance of Indonesia's compliance with the IAIS Insurance Core Principles in 2018. A recent report of the assessment (IMF, 2018) concluded that there is a need to improve significant areas in Indonesia's insurance supervision. Particularly, the report noted the need to make an amendment to the current Law of the Republic of Indonesia Number 40 Year 2014 on Insurance. This current law was, however, already amended in the previous Law of the Republic of Indonesia Number 2 Year 1992 on Insurance Business. The report mentioned that the main approach to insurance supervision in Indonesia is not compatible with the international regulatory standards. While the international regulatory standard's approach places "protection of policyholders" as the ultimate objective of insurance supervision, Indonesia's regulation "has other objectives and particularly the objective of market development seems to have caused conflict with the objective of policyholder protection" (IMF, 2018, pp. 4–5). However, the IAIS also acknowledges that Indonesia has so far carried out necessary steps to ensure changes in the ultimate objective of Indonesia's insurance supervision. Indonesia has drafted and lodged a Bill to address the issue. In the same report (IMF, 2018), the IAIS wrote the following:

> A new bill is being drafted to develop industry wide policyholder protection funds in accordance with Article 53 of the Insurance Law. The MOF is currently developing a draft Bill to improve policyholders' protection by establishing policyholder protection funds. It will also widen the ambit of resolution powers that can be applied to insurers and establish new institutional responsibility for insurer resolution. The Bill is due to be enacted by October 2017. (p. 15)

It is also important to note here that the enactment of a new Bill may take some years to finalize. Thus, even though the report said that the amendment would take effect in 2017, the fact is that the Bill may still be under internal discussion in the government. This section now provides more details of the principles assessed under the observance process. This will show that not only has the IAIS acknowledged significant improvements made by Indonesia but also that it has graded Indonesia in the top tiers.

Table 4.2 summarizes the observance status of Indonesia to the IAIS Insurance Core Principles. Indonesia currently has achieved the highest observance status, the "Observed" for six out of the twenty-six principles, or at a bit more than 20%. Meanwhile, for most of the other principles, the IAIS graded Indonesia in the status of "Largely Observed" (thirteen principles fell under this grading), or "Partly Observed" (seven principles fell under this grading). Though Indonesia has mostly achieved grading in the top-two levels, it still needs to deal with the very basic approach to insurance supervision. Thus overall, the IAIS has acknowledged the development of the Indonesian insurance industry as well as the recent regulatory reform. However, as mentioned earlier, the IAIS noted the remaining assignments to be addressed. Specifically, the IAIS stated in its report (IMF, 2018) that:

> Insurance regulation and supervision have been remarkably improved since the establishment of OJK and the enactment of the new Insurance Law...However, the assessment has identified a significant number of shortfalls in observance with the Insurance Core Principles. Some deficiencies are due to the lack of effective group regulation and supervision of insurance groups... The Indonesian insurance sector is still vulnerable to a number of material risks... The mission recommends that OJK improve the effectiveness of supervision. (pp. 4–5)

As is the case with the IOSCO, the IAIS also uses an earlier instrument in ensuring that countries are consistent with the international regulatory standards. Before the application of the Insurance Core Principles, the IAIS utilized the IAIS MMOU. This MMOU basically similar objectives

Table 4.2 Indonesia observance status to the IAIS insurance core principles

Observed (O)	6
Largely observed (LO)	13
Partly observed (PO)	7
Not observed (NO)	0
Total	26

Source IMF (2018)

to the IOSCO MMOU. These objectives are mainly related to "practical arrangements concerning cross-border cooperation and information exchange" (IAIS, 2014, p. 4). However, unlike the IOSCO MMOU that Indonesia is already one of the signatories, Indonesia's has current plan to become the signatory of the IAIS MMOU is unclear. Although, the FSB report (FSB, 2014) has suggested that Indonesia consider the option to formally apply to become a party to the IAIS MMOU. In addition, the Indonesian FSA already had several bilateral MOUs with insurance supervisors in other countries, such as with Dubai, Japan, Korea and others. In the same tone, the recent IAIS report (IMF, 2018) also stated:

> It is recommended that: OJK expand the scope of MOU, for example by joining in the IAIS MMOU, and offering its analysis (such as key results of inspection results) to the home supervisors to enhance the cooperation with home supervisors. (p. 23)

In sum, it is fair to conclude that Indonesia's compliance with the international regulatory standards in insurance supervision seems lower than the compliance in the banking and capital market area. Yet, this case may attributable to the relatively recent engagement of Indonesia in the IAIS. In addition, regulatory convergence is getting more intense and is moving forward in the Indonesian insurance industry. The IAIS has also graded Indonesia under the grading of mostly "Observed" or "Largely Observed". To this extent, this section has demonstrated that the Indonesian FSA would still have a lot of work to do, such as the Law amendment and the application to become a signatory to the IAIS MMOU, although Indonesia has made notable progress in relation to the adherence to international regulatory standards in insurance sector regulation and supervision. This progress is as reflected in the most recent assessment of the IAIS. The remaining work may well be completed in future though some assignments can be challenging, such as the enactment of a new Bill that may take some years to finalize. This suggests that FSA officials are actually using progress towards adherence to global standards as a benchmark for its position in the ASEAN financial liberalization initiatives. As a result, discussion of liberalization under the ASEAN's WC-FSL seems unable to move further. A long-time researcher in the area of financial services liberalization mentioned that:

> Kayaknya gitu [enggak maju-maju sih itu. Liberalisasinya maksudnya jalan di tempat saja sih gitu]. Dan andaikan pun mereka menulis, gitu ya, terbuka tapi ternyata hambatan di dalamnya regulasinya berat.
>
> [*It seems that the liberalization [in ASEAN] is not moving forward. It means that liberalization [under WC-FSL] stay as it is now. And, even if [ASEAN] claimed that members have agreed to liberalize, apparently there are substantial domestic regulation restrictions*.]

Up to this point, this book has argued that the Indonesian position on ASEAN portfolio investment liberalization legally and practically is now in the hands of the FSA. In the next section, this book continues the discussions by further analysing the roles of the contemporary Indonesian MOF and Bank Indonesia, particularly on their current involvement in ASEAN portfolio investment liberalization efforts.

The Roles of the Indonesian MOF and Bank Indonesia in Portfolio Investment Liberalization Post the Establishment of the Indonesian FSA

After ceding its authority to the FSA, the MOF's role in portfolio investment liberalization is as a financial services policy coordinator. As the financial services coordinator, the MOF is responsible for coordinating the flow of information particularly between ASEAN and Indonesia institutions including portfolio investment liberalization. Note that the FSA is not part of the formal structure of ASEAN. Thus, only the MOF, and recently Bank Indonesia, can represent Indonesia formally at the ASEAN level. This includes representation at high-level meetings, such as at the Ministerial level and the ASEAN Summit. Meanwhile, the authority to regulate and supervise is already in the hands of the FSA. With this in mind, this section explains the current roles of the MOF within the frame of ASEAN portfolio investment liberalization, particularly as the financial services policy coordinator in Indonesia.

Within the general scope of ASEAN financial services liberalization, the coordinator or focal point for Indonesia is the MOF under the purview of the AFMM. The name AFMM itself entails that the central corresponding authority is the Ministry of Finance (MOF). To this end, the MOF, led by the Minister of Finance acts as the coordinator to the AFMM. However, the FSA and Bank Indonesia are also actively involved in the process. In practice, high-level officials of the FSA and Bank Indonesia attend the

AFMM along with the Minister of Finance and MOF officials as the Indonesian Delegation. According to an official at the MOF, the roles of the Indonesian MOF can actually take the form of, firstly, there are certain matters that can only be resolved internally by the Indonesian MOF, and secondly, that needs to go through coordination with other parties outside the MOF. The internal Indonesian MOF settlement only means that the MOF is the ultimate decision-maker with regards to issues discussed in ASEAN. Meanwhile, coordination with other parties outside the MOF may suggest that the MOF is not the ultimate decision-maker, rather only conveys data and information between ASEAN and the ultimate decision-maker.an example of this is the relationships between the MOF and the FSA with regards to the ASEAN Trading Link as explained in the preceding section.

Referring to the most recent AEC Blueprint 2025 (ASEAN, 2015) as well as the Joint Statement of the 4th ASEAN Finance Ministers' and Central Bank Governors' Meeting/AFMGM (2018), there are a significant number of matters that are for internal Indonesian MOF settlement only. Among the most notable, and perhaps the top priority for the current ASEAN Chair, is related to "resilience and innovation". For instance, there are initiatives to strengthen financial, disaster and cyber resilience. Financial resilience focuses on establishing an ASEAN regional safety net in order to ensure financial stability in the region. Disaster resilience relates to the high number of natural disasters in the region. ASEAN needs to establish a regional disaster management system to minimize the impacts of natural disasters to a member and the region as a whole. For instance, ASEAN is currently developing the ASEAN Disaster Risk Financing and Insurance body (ADRFI). Cyber resilience aims to strengthen regional resilience to increased internet traffic in the region. This particularly relates to the rapid growth of financial technology (FinTech). These resilience initiatives are currently under the direct purview of the Indonesian MOF. This means that the MOF is the focal point for these matters. Though there may be an intersection with other related institutions in Indonesia, the MOF is the ultimate decision-maker. Thus, the MOF can settle these issues internally.

Another example is the innovation initiatives. The most important part of these initiatives is the development of FinTech and financial inclusion. Both initiatives aim to provide direction to ASEAN on how they can be developed as a region. For example, the direction to include a larger number of Small and Medium Enterprises (SMEs) to take advantage of FinTech. There are a number of practical issues to be resolved. For example, FinTech and financial inclusion are closely related to the domestic payment system. Thus, in order to establish an ASEAN FinTech and financial inclusion, one of the main prerequisites is to connect the domestic payment systems of its members. This is the part where, in future, the Indonesian MOF may not be the ultimate decision-maker. Indonesia's domestic payment system is currently under the macro-supervision of Bank Indonesia and the micro-supervision of the FSA. However, it seems unlikely to advance to the practical parts in the next few years as the ASEAN discussion of FinTech and financial inclusion is still at an early stage. The innovation initiatives, at least their general parts, are currently also under the direct purview of the Indonesian MOF. This also means that the Indonesian MOF is the focal point for these initiatives. Though there may be an intersection with other related institutions in Indonesia, the MOF is the ultimate decision-maker. Therefore, the Indonesian MOF can settle general issues internally. Nevertheless, there may be a need for further exploration in future once the discussions of the practical aspects move forward. To this extent, as portfolio investment liberalization is currently not under its authority, the Indonesian MOF can only settle issues that are outside this area.

Meanwhile, coordination with other parties is mostly related to the financial integration and liberalization agenda, including portfolio investment liberalization and agendas that are under the purview of the Governor of Bank Indonesia. In fact, this perhaps is the only agenda for which the MOF is the focal point, nor the ultimate decision-maker. Thus, the MOF's job is mostly arranging coordination meetings to stay updated with the latest issues and discussion related to financial integration and liberalization. An official at the Indonesian MOF confirmed the procedure for arranging the coordination meetings as mentioned in quotes below.

> Rapat koordinasi itu kan tidak hanya satu kali, dua kali atau tiga kali. Nah gunanya rapat koordinasi itu sebenarnya lebih dari satu tujuan. Jadi pertama itu rapat koordinasi untuk saling berbagi perkembangan. Yang kedua untuk merumuskan masukan dan posisi Indonesia, agenda yang harus dibahas. Nah setelah rapat koordinasi itu jadilah dirumuskan menjadi suatu posisi Indonesia. Berarti Kementerian Keuangan biasanya mengundang direktori terkait untuk datang ke kita, untuk berbagi sharing informasi perkembangan yang mereka punya, sekaligus merumuskan secara bersama

posisi Indonesia. Nah kenapa perkembangan itu penting kita dengar dari mereka? Karena tidak semua forum itu kita hadir di tempatnya mereka, maupun di tempat kita. Jadi, ada gap di masing-masing unit itu yang harus diisi melalui rapat koordinasi.

[*Coordination meetings was rarely only a one-time meeting. The meetings could take two or three times. The aim of the meetings was multi-purpose. Thus, the first meeting intended to share current development. The second meeting aimed to formulate Indonesia's positions and inputs of the corresponding agendas. Only after the coordination meetings that Indonesia could formulate positions. This means that the Indonesian MOF invited all the related directories to share their current development as well as formulate Indonesia's positions in consensus. Why was sharing the current development important? This was because we might not be able to attend all the [Technical Committees and Forums]. Thus, there were [informational] gaps in each institution that the coordination meetings would fill.*]

This implies that coordination with other parties outside the Indonesian MOF can be an exhaustive and time-consuming process. There were times when the coordination meetings were not working as expected. In such cases, the MOF commonly relied solely on the information as provided by the ASEAN Secretariat. As a result, the Indonesian MOF would be unable to take a considered position in the AFMM.

As for the case of Bank Indonesia, pre-2015 ASEAN's formal structure still excluded Bank Indonesia, as well as other ASEAN central banks, from the discussion of the AFMM. As such the initiatives related to portfolio investment liberalization were almost exclusively the domain of the Indonesian MOF. This was even though some of the initiatives also fell under the authority of Bank Indonesia, for example, external borrowings and lending in the banking sector, capital account liberalization and the ABIF. At that time, officials of Bank Indonesia could only participate in fora subordinate to the AFMM, namely the ASEAN Finance and Central Bank Deputies' Meeting (AFDM). It means that if Bank Indonesia wishes to have any input related to portfolio investment liberalization it must be via the MOF. Although in practice, representatives of Bank Indonesia might attend the AFMM as a part of the Indonesian delegation, they held no rights to speak or represent Indonesia's position.

Through a first joint meeting in 2015, gradually ASEAN started to recognize the central banks in its formal structure, namely through the ASEAN Finance Ministers' and Central Bank Governors' Meeting (AFMGM). This first joint meeting took place on 21 March 2015 under the Malaysian chairmanship of ASEAN (Joint Statement of the 1st AFMGM, 2015). Through its Joint Statement, this meeting formally acknowledged the involvement of the central banks. This involvement covered any initiatives that are under the purview of AFMM, including portfolio investment liberalization. At present, ASEAN has even formally recognized the incorporation of the central banks to its formal structure through the latest edition of the ASEAN Charter (The ASEAN Charter, 2018). The Charter has updated its Annex 1 on ASEAN Sectoral Ministerial Bodies to include both the ASEAN Central Bank Governors' Meeting (ACGM) and AFMGM under the AEC Council. Thus, initiatives related to portfolio investment liberalization are no longer exclusively the domain of the Indonesian MOF. At least ASEAN has formally included other agents in the frame with the incorporation of the central banks. Thus far, there are still limited discussions on incorporating other important agents such as the FSA. Incorporation of other agents may as well be feasible in future, especially with the case study of the Indonesian FSA and its financial services integrated supervision as discussed in the earlier part of this chapter.

The incorporation of Bank Indonesia into the framework of the AEC Council along with the Indonesian MOF is, for instance, happened in the case of ABIF. In the preceding chapter, this book explained that the ABIF was optimistic about creating a multilateral agreement framework using a single set of standards that will apply to all AMS. In recent developments, however, ASEAN has come to push AMS to conclude bilateral arrangements. The expectation is that bilateral arrangements will eventually lead to a multilateral agreement. In order to discuss details of the multilateral agreement framework as well as to administer the bilateral arrangements between AMS, ASEAN formed the Task Force on ABIF. This Task Force reports to the ACGM and AFMGM. A source stated that:

> Task Force ABIF ini isinya orang Bank Central...Ini karena ABIF ini dibahasnya di forum Bank Central. Menteri Keuangan enggak tahu-menahu.
>
> [*Task Force on ABIF consists of central bankers...This is particularly because the discussions on ABIF is in central banks forum. The Minister of Finance has less knowledge on the contents of the discussions.*]

The statement above implies that the ABIF, particularly in at technical level has become the sole domain of Bank Indonesia. This means that ASEAN has acknowledged the role of the central banks in the discussion of portfolio investment liberalization. And, with the existence of the Task Force on the ABIF as well as the ACGM and AFMGM, the Indonesian MOF now has reduced, if not eliminated, its involvement in the discussion of banking liberalization under the ABIF. The Indonesian MOF acts as the policy coordinator filling particular information needs related to banking liberalization. Thus, ASEAN also needs to recognize the central banks, along with the MOFs, in its institutional framework.

However, banking liberalization is the issue on which of Bank Indonesia is incorporated into the formal institutional framework of the AEC Council. Other issues related to portfolio investment liberalization would still be under the Indonesian MOF as the domestic financial policy coordinator in Indonesia. This being the case, the involvement of other corresponding domestic authorities is limited to the level of Technical Committees and Fora under the higher governance structure, such as the AFMM. An official conveyed the following:

> Sebagai contoh yang paling tren saat ini, paling baru, paling recent, financial inclusion. Financial inclusion itu di working level yang duduk tiga; Kementerian Keuangan, Bank Indonesia dan OJK. Jadi sudah ada plot tiga kursi di working level.
>
> [*As an example, on the recent trend, the newest, the most recent, is the financial inclusion. In the working level discussion on financial inclusion, Indonesia has three seats; the Indonesian MOF, Bank Indonesia, and the Indonesian FSA. Thus, Indonesia already has three seat slots.*]

The above statement highlights a new agenda under the purview of the AFMM and AFMGM that is the financial inclusion agenda. Indeed, Indonesia may have more seats in technical discussions, allowing more involvement from other institutions, such as Bank Indonesia and the Indonesian FSA. However, as mentioned above, financial inclusion is currently still classified as an internal Indonesian MOF matter only. Thus, at the higher level of governance in ASEAN, the Indonesian MOF is not only the policy coordinator or focal point but also the ultimate decision-maker.

In conjunction with the explanation of the central banks and corresponding domestic institutions in general, there are also discussions on the relationship among the corresponding domestic institutions to ASEAN and Partner Countries. The case is almost identical when it comes to the ASEAN and Partner Countries. Identical in that the Indonesian MOF is the financial services policy coordinator, particularly within the context of portfolio investment liberalization. In addition, the other corresponding domestic institutions, namely the Indonesian FSA and Bank Indonesia, have very limited involvement despite being the ultimate decision-makers domestically. Officials at the Indonesian FSA are basically well aware of this situation, yet they just follow the governance process. In the end however, they are the ultimate decision-makers. A high-level official of the Indonesian FSA said:

> Akhirnya seperti itu yang terjadi. Jadi ASEAN, karena kami tidak mempunyai, dalam tanda kutip, jalur ke atas enggak punya track, enggak punya jalan, akhirnya untuk yang RCEP, untuk yang ASEAN Plus, segala macam diambil BKF dan Bank Indonesia.
>
> [*Consequently, this is what happens. So, in ASEAN, because we do not have "tracks to the higher level", thus for RCEP [Regional Comprehensive Economic Partnership] and ASEAN Plus [Three], everything is under Fiscal Policy Agency [the Indonesian MOF] and Bank Indonesia.*]

It is notable to also mention the well-known ASEAN Plus Three initiative called the Chiang Mai Initiative Multilateralisation (CMIM). The next few paragraphs on CMIM serve to better explain the contemporary roles of the Indonesian FSA and Bank Indonesia in financial integration in general, particularly after the rise of the FSA. The CMIM itself is one of the major outputs from ASEAN and its cooperation with Partner Countries, in this case, the Plus Three (China, Japan, South Korea) countries. The CMIM, in brief, is a regional financial safety net system for ASEAN Plus Three countries providing a platform for multilateral currency swaps among member countries. With the Asian Financial Crisis in the background and taking the momentum of the aftermath of the GFC, CMIM was launched in early 2010. CMIM itself is expected to be another regional financial resort to deal with member countries' balance of payment and short-term liquidity problems, or the regional IMF alike. In order to achieve that main objective, ASEAN Plus Three countries are pooling a fund from the contributions of member countries. In proportion to their financial contributions to the pooling fund, countries are given voting rights in the governance and operation of the fund. Currently, the fund pool has doubled from its original and now amounts to US$ 240 billion. The Plus Three countries are still the biggest financial contributors with 80% of the total amount, while the whole AMS only contribute.

The ASEAN+3 Macroeconomic Research Office (AMRO) supports the CMIM by conducting a yearly economic consultation with members of the CMIM, as explained by an official of AMRO. In doing so, AMRO is able to assess regional economic and financial conditions and determine the overall risks in the East Asia region and individual members. Focusing on developing a mechanism for overcoming the short-term financial liquidity problems and providing a regional safety net in East Asia, the CMIM itself gives voting power to both the central banks and the MOFs. An Indonesian MOF official mentioned the following in relation to the relationship between Bank Indonesia and the Indonesian MOF at the CMIM:

> CMIM itu, itu dikasih vote loh dua-duanya. Dikasi voting power loh untuk di Menteri Keuangan maupun BI. In case mereka dispute; yang satu sepakat bantu negara lain, sedangkan yang satu ngga, yang ngetok Menteri Keuangan. Tapi jangan salah, CMIM itu hanya bisa berjalan kalau antar central banks itu buka accounts. Lah kalau ini ngga mau, ok account-nya ditutup sama dia, dia enggak bisa dong ngasih negara meskipun Menteri Keuangan-nya udah ok.
>
> [*In the CMIM, we have two votes. The voting powers are for both the Minister of Finance and Bank Indonesia. In a case of dispute, for instance one vote agrees to help one member [in needs of financial liquidity], while the other vote not to help, then the Minister of Finance still has the ultimate power to decide. Nonetheless, in practice, CMIM can only work if members' central banks open an account. If a central bank decides not to follow Minister of Finance's decision, then the central bank just needs to refuse to open an account.*]

The above statement implies that in any cases under the CMIM, the Indonesian MOF would still be the focal point as well as the ultimate decision-maker. This is, perhaps, mostly attributable to the fact that the Indonesian MOF is the representative of the Government of Indonesia in ASEAN as well as with its Partner Countries. Meanwhile, most AMS and Plus Three countries commonly see central banks as free and independent institutions from the government, including in the case of Indonesia. However, ASEAN Plus Three also acknowledges the vital role of the central banks for the practical implementation of the CMIM in opening bank accounts to exercise the currency swap mechanisms among the members of the CMIM. The CMIM itself relies on the currency swap mechanisms in overcoming the short-term financial liquidity and regional safety net in East Asia. Thus, for the purpose of the CMIM, ASEAN Plus Three endowed the central banks with voting rights along with the MOFs in shaping the decision of the CMIM. In the next section, this book explains the FSSC and looks at how portfolio investments liberalization-related authorities interact among particularly post the establishment of the Indonesian FSA.

The Financial Sector Stability Committee (FSSC)

The last part of this chapter discusses the existence of the FSSC. The FSSC is important because it is one of the fora that the three central institutions (the Indonesian FSA, Indonesian MOF, and Bank Indonesia) are legally members, along with another government institution, the Indonesian Deposit Insurance Corporation (IDIC). Thus, the FSCC provides a legal forum for interactions among domestic institutions in Indonesia. The legal provision of the FSCC itself is under the Law of the Republic of Indonesia Number 9 of 2016 on Prevention and Resolution of Financial System Crisis. Article 4 of the Law particularly mandated that:

> (1) in pursuance of this Law, the Financial System Stability Committee is established. (2) The Financial System Stability Committee as referred to in section (1) performs the prevention and resolution of Financial System Crisis for the economic interests and resilience of the country.

This formal forum of coordination among authorities related to the Indonesian financial sector facilitates the operation of the FSA. Thus, in relation to our aim in this chapter to explain how agents operate within the FSA, the FSSC provides a self-actualization stage for the existence of the FSA. This forum basically creates a policy space for both agents of the FSA and Bank Indonesia to operate in and exercise their power and authority, including in portfolio investment liberalization. Firstly, the existence of this forum and the inclusion of the FSA a form of affirmation on the FSA's existential presence. Secondly, as a new institution, agents need a place, or a stage, or a facility, for their voices to be heard nationally and internationally. To this end, this section elaborates the work and coordination mechanisms of the FSSC.

This section looks further to the coordination arrangements among the institutions related to portfolio investment liberalization. According to a document provided by the Secretariat of the FSSC, it started with the establishment of the IDIC in 2004 through the enactment of the Law of the Republic of Indonesia Number 24 of 2004 on IDIC. To further strengthen the coordination mechanism, the Indonesian MOF, Bank Indonesia and IDIC then set up a coordination framework through the issuance of Joint Decrees in 2007 (Ridwan, 2017). Later, with the establishment of the FSA, the initiation of the FSSC incorporated the FSA with the other three preceding institutions These four institutions were coordinating and interacting with each other through a forum called the Coordinating Forum for Financial System Stability (Forum Koordinasi Stabilitas Sistem Keuangan/FKSSK) (FSB, 2014). The FKSSK itself seemed to be just a transitional forum to wait for the enactment of the Law Number 9 of 2016 that would give a legal basis for the institutions to coordinate and interact through the establishment of FSSC (Ridwan, 2017).

Chart 4.4 describes the current coordination mechanism with regard to financial system stability in Indonesia. The Indonesian Minister of Finance is the coordinator for the FSSC. Meanwhile, the Governor of the Central Bank, the Chairman of the Indonesian FSA and the Chairman of the IDIC are members of the FSSC. Though the three other institutions are all members to the FSCC, the Chairman of the IDIC is the only member with no voting right in the FSCC. The non-voting status of the IDIC is mainly attributable to the fact that the IDIC is not a regulatory body with authority to enact regulation in the regulatory structure, like the Indonesian FSA and the Central Bank. Article 4 of the Law Number 24 of 2004 simply mentioned that "[t]he functions of the IDIC are: (a) insure customers' deposits; and (b) actively participate in maintaining the stability of banking system in accordance with its authorities." In addition, a high-level official at the FSCC Secretariat confirmed that:

> Because, based on our assessment, IDIC function is heavier on executing policy, not making policy, meaning that the policy action that can be made by the IDIC is quite limited compared to other 3 members... The other consideration is, in our decision-making process, even though we deliberate to reach consensus, but if we fail to make consensus, the decision will be made by majority vote. Therefore, we need to have odd number to get the majority vote.

Chart 4.4 Indonesia financial system safety net framework: coordination mechanism (*Source* Adapted from Law Number 9 of 2016 & Indonesian MOF Internal Document)

Particularly related to portfolio investment liberalization, the FSCC is indirectly tapping into the issues. This means that the coordination and interaction among the corresponding domestic authorities may not actively assess the positions related to portfolio investment liberalization. However, the scope of the FSCC actually covers issues related to portfolio investment liberalization. In addition, one of the roles of the FSCC itself is actually also to promote greater international cooperation, both bilaterally and multilaterally. Thus if, for instance, the FSCC decides that an initiative related to portfolio investment liberalization may disrupt domestic financial stability, then the FSCC will look at the initiative in depth and more detail. A high-level official at the FSCC Secretariat stated that:

> ...dalam konteks dia memelihara stabilitas sistem keuangan, kan itu kan memang menjadi bahasan-bahasan juga yang di luar enggak hanya meng-assess kondisi stabilitas sistem keuangan. Kadang-kadang beberapa isu topik yang diangkat juga memang dibahas... Kalau ada situasi yang bisa meng-create instability, nah ini baru dibahas, KSSK bisa melakukan pencegahan.
>
> [*"...in the context that it maintains financial system stability, the coverage of the issues discussed are not limited only to assessing the financial system stability condition. There are also some issues raised and discussed...If there are any situations that may create instability, FSCC can also take preventive actions."*]

This situation above provides the opportunity for the Indonesian FSA to bring issues related to portfolio investment liberalization back to the table, particularly those related to the risky overflowing of portfolio investments.

As illustrated in Chart 4.5, the coverage of the FSCC includes four main areas, namely macroeconomics, financial institutions, financial markets and financial infrastructure. Under financial markets, there are sub-areas on the capital market, money market and government bond market. The issues of portfolio investment liberalization itself may fall under the coverage of the capital market. That said, if the FSCC sees that an issue related to portfolio investment liberalization may impact domestic financial system stability, then it can escalate and look at the issue more closely. This is partly a preventive action that the FSCC can carry out in exercising its duties. A high-level official at the FSCC Secretariat illustrated the preventive action as the "swimming pool analogy". He stated that the "swimming pool analogy" includes financial deepening, financial inclusion and financial stability. He argued that financial deepening refers to widening the pool area or making the pool deeper so that people can explore more areas in the pool. He further explained that financial inclusion refers to the number of people that can get into the swimming pool. Lastly, he said that financial stability ensures that there is no leak in the pool, or that the water is mild for swimming.

The corresponding domestic authorities coordinate and interact each other affecting their behaviour in the overall case of portfolio investment liberalization. Although the Minister of Finance acts as Coordinator in the FSCC coordination mechanism, the other corresponding institutions, namely Bank Indonesia and the FSA, have their own authority and powers. These authorities and powers are also free from the interference of the government. Thus, this condition creates a policy space for both agents of the Indonesian FSA and Bank Indonesia to operate and exercise their power and authority, including over portfolio investment liberalization. For instance, when financial stability demands improved banking practice, the regulatory power to decide and implement will still be in the hands of the FSA. To this end, the committee may not be able to override each institutions' power and authority. In addition, the establishment of the FSA itself already created policy space for agents in banking industry liberalization, as previously banking industry liberalization was the sole domain of Bank Indonesia. Micro-regulation and supervision, including that related to liberalization, are currently under the authority of the FSA. However, the macro-regulation and supervision of the banking industry

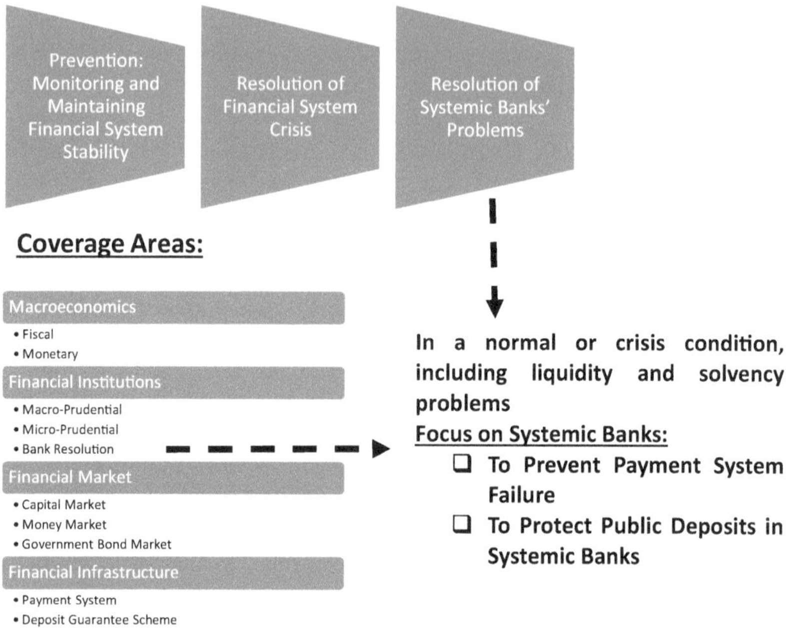

Chart 4.5 FSCC Coverage (*Source* Indonesian MOF Internal Document)

are still under Bank Indonesia. This separation of the micro and macro, in turns, affects how agents operating in each the Indonesian FSA and Bank Indonesia see portfolio investment liberalization.

Nevertheless, the case of Indonesia clearly shows that interaction requires the coordination among financial regulatory authorities. Coordination and interaction among financial regulatory authorities is not uncommon throughout the world. Edge and Liang (2017) have recorded that currently there are a total of forty-one countries throughout the world adopting the model of coordination and interaction among financial regulatory authorities or the "Financial Stability Committees" (FSCs) model. Referring to Table 4.3, the adoption of the FSCs model increased significantly following the financial crisis. Table 4.3 shows that 2008 and 2013 saw the most significant increases. During the global financial crisis in 2007–2008, eleven new countries adopted the FSCs model. Meanwhile, another eleven countries also adopted the model in 2013, perhaps as the result of the Eurozone financial crisis the previous years. Of these

Table 4.3 Financial Stability Committees (FSCs) in the world

FSC or Single Agency		*Year FSC formed*		*Chair-or-chair FSC*[a]		*No. of agencies that vote on FSCs*	
(A)		*(B)*		*(C)*		*(D)*	
FSC	41	≤2008	11	Central Bank	18	2	6
Formal	32	2009	1	CB is a PR	10	3	8
DeFacto	9	2010	4	Ministry of Finance[b]	25	4	17
Single agency	15	2011	3	Prudential regulator	1	5	7
Central Bank	14	2012	3	Other	2	≥6	3
CB is a PR	14	2013	11				
Prudential regulator	1	2014	4				
Informal	2	2015	4				
Total	58	Total	41			Total	41

[a]Sums to more than 41 because for three committees the central bank and ministry of finance are co-chairs and for one committee the central bank and prudential regulator are co-chairs
[b]Includes the First Deputy Prime Minister who chairs the FSC of the Russian Federation
Source Edge and Liang (2017)

forty-one countries, their MOF was the leader or coordinator with more than half of the total number.

Conclusion

This chapter began with an explanation of the Indonesian FSA's power and authority. The Indonesian FSA basically covers anything that relates to financial services supervision and regulation. The scope of these financial services includes all sectors, banking and non-banking. This chapter has explained the matters in which FSA agents operate and, thus, stymie the domestic portfolio investment liberalization process in Indonesia. Agents are exercising their power and authority as the "independent and free" ultimate decision-maker in portfolio investment liberalization. As such, agents opted to reject, or halt, or delay the implementation of the ASEAN portfolio investments liberalization initiatives, in turn, creating domestic implementation gaps. In order to demonstrate this chapter looked examples of recent ASEAN initiatives in the area of portfolio investments liberalization. This chapter uses the ASEAN Trading Link, the ASEAN Framework for Cross Border Offering of CIS, the ASEAN Disclosure Standards and the ABIF as well other related bodies. The first six sections of the chapter illustrate that Indonesian FSA officials clearly exhibit a more conservative approach to portfolio investment liberalization than that committed to in ASEAN. In addition, agents also operate within the Indonesian FSA by harnessing the international standards for "national interests" and avoiding the regional portfolio investments liberalization.

In the case of Basel Standards, Indonesian FSA agents still seem reluctant to commit to any standards if they particularly resulted in opening up further financial services liberalization. As for IOSCO Objectives and Principles of Securities Regulation, agents consider that the improvement made by committing to the international regulatory standards should be enough to fulfil Indonesia's obligation to international pressure. Consequently, agents take deliberate actions to delay, or even reject, the domestic implementation of regional initiatives. Meanwhile, related to IAIS Insurance Core Principles, agents are using adherence to the principles as a benchmark for its position on the ASEAN financial liberalization initiatives. Therefore, the discussion of liberalization under ASEAN's WC-FSL seems unable to move further. In addition, this chapter also discussed the roles of the contemporary Indonesian MOF and Bank Indonesia, particularly their current involvement in the ASEAN portfolio investments liberalization efforts. This chapter revealed that agents' operation within the Indonesian FSA also make the Indonesian MOF, as the international financial policy coordinator for Indonesia, reliant on advice from the FSA. In the last part of the chapter, this book discussed the existence of the FSSC. This formal forum of coordination among authorities related to the financial sector in Indonesia facilitates the operation of the FSA. This forum basically creates a policy space both agents of the FSA and Bank Indonesia to operate and exercise their power and authority, including in the case of portfolio investment liberalization. Chapter 5 captures the enactment of the new Indonesian Trading Law as an emerging challenge to further domestic portfolio investments liberalization in Indonesia. The chapter suggests that agents are using one of the main features of the new law, the involvement of the House of Representative, to halt or delay domestic implementation of ASEAN portfolio investment liberalization.

References

ASEAN. (2014). *ASEAN Collective Investment Scheme (CIS) handbook.*

ASEAN. (2015). *ASEAN economic community blueprint 2025.*

ASEAN. (2017). *ASEAN economic community 2025 consolidated strategic action plan.*

ASEAN. (2018). *The ASEAN Charter* (23rd Reprint).

ASEAN Capital Market Forum. (2016). *ACMF action plan 2016–2020.*

Borio, C. (2003). Towards a macroprudential framework for financial supervision and regulation? *Cesifo Economic Studies, 49*(2), 181–216.

Chen, V., Godwin, A., & Ramsay, I. (2017). An ASEAN framework for cross-border cooperation in financial consumer dispute resolution. *Asian Journal of Comparative Law, 12*(1), 167–196.

Costi, E. M. (2015). Institutional evolution and characteristics of the International Organization of Securities Commissions (IOSCO). *Comparative Law Journal of the Pacific/Journal de Droit Comparé du Pacifique, 21*, 199–232. https://www.victoria.ac.nz/law/research/publications/about-nzacl/publications/cljpjdcp-journals/volume-21,-2015/Egli-Costi.pdf

Crockett, A. (2000). *Marrying the micro- and macro-prudential dimensions of financial stability.* Bank for International Settlements Speeches. https://www.bis.org/review/rr000921b.pdf

Denk, O., & Gomes, G. (2017). *Financial re-regulation since the global crisis?: An index-based assessment* (OECD Economics Department Working Papers, No. 1396). OECD Publishing.

Edge, R. M., & Liang, N. (2017). *New financial stability governance structures and Central Banks* (Hutchins Center Working Paper, No. 32). Brooking Institutions. https://www.brookings.edu/wp-content/uploads/2017/08/es_20170808_liang_newfinancialstabilitygovernancestructures.pdf

Financial Stability Board (FSB). (2014, February). *Peer Review of Indonesia: Review report.*

Galati, G., & Moessner, R. (2013). Macroprudential policy—A literature review. *Journal of Economic Surveys, 27*(5), 846–878.

Goodhart, C. (2011). *The basel committee on banking supervision: A history of the early years 1974–1997.* Cambridge.

Hanson, S. G., Kashyap, A. K., & Stein, J. C. (2011). A macroprudential approach to financial regulation. *Journal of Economic Perspectives, 25*(1), 3–28.

Indonesian Financial Services Authority Internal Discussion Document. (2017). Otoritas Jasa Keuangan.

Indonesian Financial Services Authority Internal Presentation Document. (2015). Otoritas Jasa Keuangan.

International Association of Insurance Supervisors (IAIS). (2014). *IAIS multilateral memorandum of understanding on cooperation and information exchange (IAIS MMOU)*, February 2007. Revised July 2014.

International Monetary Fund (IMF). (2012a). *Indonesia: Financial sector assessment program—Implementation of the IOSCO objectives and principles of securities regulation—Detailed assessment of observance* (IMF Country Report No. 12/189).

International Monetary Fund (IMF). (2012b). *Indonesia: Financial sector assessment program—Basel core principles assessment—Detailed assessment of compliance* (IMF Country Report No. 12/335).

International Monetary Fund (IMF). (2018). *Indonesia financial sector assessment program—Detailed assessment of observance—Insurance core principles* (IMF Country Report No. 18/74).

IOSCO. (2010). *Objectives and principles of securities regulation*. https://www.iosco.org/library/pubdocs/pdf/IOSCOPD323.pdf

Organisation for Economic Co-operation and Development (OECD). (2016). *International regulatory co-operation: The role of international organisations in fostering better rules of globalisation*. OECD Publishing.

Penikas, H. (2015). History of banking regulation as developed by the basel committee on banking supervision in 1974–2014 (Brief overview). *Estabilidad Financier, 28*, 11–47.

Ridwan, D. (2017). *An empirical analysis of market discipline imposed by stakeholders in the Indonesian banking sector*. PhD Thesis, Victoria University.

Saputro, E. (2017). *Indonesia and ASEAN plus three financial cooperation domestic politics, power relations, and regulatory regionalism*. Palgrave Macmillan.

Sommer, A. A., Jr. (1996). IOSCO: Its mission and achievement. (International Organization of Securities Commissions) (Symposium: Internationalization of Securities). *Northwestern Journal of International Law & Business, 17*(1), 15–29.

The Jakarta Post. (2015, March 14). *RI still reluctant to join ASEAN trading link*. http://www.thejakartapost.com/news/2015/03/14/ri-still-reluctant-join-asean-trading-link.html

Toniolo, G. (2005). *Central bank cooperation at the Bank for International Settlements 1930–1973*. Cambridge.

CHAPTER 5

Emerging Challenges to Domestic Implementation of Portfolio Investments Liberalization

This chapter explains that the enactment of the new Trading Law has emerged as a stumbling block to further domestic implementations of ASEAN portfolio investment liberalization. As revealed throughout the discussions in this chapter, Indonesian FSA agents are using one of the main features of the new law, the involvement of the House of Representative, to halt or delay the domestic implementation of ASEAN portfolio investment liberalization. This new Trading Law also provides another context for agents to act, mainly through the possibility of wider institutional involvement throughout the adoption of portfolio investment liberalization into domestic regulatory framework. Thus, the enactment of this new Trading Law in Indonesia may pose a further stumbling block for ASEAN to achieve a more liberalized regional regime of portfolio investments. In order to elaborate how FSA agents halt or delay domestic implementation of ASEAN portfolio investment liberalization using the new Trading Law, this chapter differentiates two periods of the domestic legal ratification process in Indonesia, the pre-2015, and the post-2015. In Indonesia, all the bilateral, regional and global agreements related to financial liberalization require domestic legal ratification. Once domestic legal ratification is concluded, only then can the agreements be translated into the domestic regulatory setting.

Pre-2015, this process of ratification, including of portfolio investment liberalization, only needed the approval of financial elites. This elite

C. Kusuma, *The Rise of the Indonesian Financial Service Authority*,
https://doi.org/10.1007/978-981-19-3850-4_5

approval would take the form of a Presidential Decree. However, post-2015, particularly with a recent amendment (Law of the Republic of Indonesia Number 7 of 2014 on Trading), ratification is required to go through higher scrutiny by escalating the process for the approval to the parliament. Thus, there are significant additional steps to be carried out by seeking parliamentary approval. The output of the parliament's approval can be either in the form that the parliament agrees for the government to move forward without a parliamentary process, or that parliament decides that the ratification needs to go through a parliamentary process. While the former can then take the form of a Presidential Decree, the latter requires the government to draft a Bill to be enacted by the parliament. The latter can certainly be challenging however: the enactment of a new Bill may take some years to finalize. To this end, there is one important background note to make regarding the Indonesian legal system. It works in the civil system of law, and not common law as in some Western justifications. This means that case precedent and judicial interpretation has far less impact than in common law. This also means that the detailed codification of laws and regulations is a process that countries under civil systems must do so more systematically.

This chapter further discusses the implications of the recent legal amendment. For instance, the recent amendment means tighter political controls over the liberalization process, suggesting a more intense interaction between agents and political power. Nevertheless, higher scrutiny also implies a slower translation to the domestic regulatory setting. For instance, if Indonesia finally can agree on the ABIF, then the ABIF agreement needs to be ratified by the approval of the parliament for domestic regulatory translation. This then takes the form of law enactment. In order to give a clearer overview of the process of the ratification itself, the last section in this chapter discusses the case of the ratification of the Protocol to Implement the Packages of Commitment on Financial Services under ASEAN Framework on Services (AFAS). In doing so, this book will present an example of the implications of the shift in the policymaking process in Indonesia. Through this case of the AFAS, this chapter is also able to distinguish the differences in the process between pre-2015 and post-2015. The case demonstrates that until the Fifth Financial Services under AFAS Protocol and SOC, Indonesia still ratified agreements into domestic regulation through the issue of Presidential Decrees. Meanwhile, the product of the ratification to the Sixth Financial Services under AFAS Protocol and SOC was in the form of Law instead of Presidential Decree. This is because the Sixth Financial Services under AFAS Protocol and SOC and all the AFAS Protocols and SOCs following it were already the subject of the recent legal amendment (Law of the Republic of Indonesia Number 7 of 2014 on Trading). However, before moving to explain the above in more detail, it is also important to explain the process that led to the new Trading Law being adopted. Thus, the section immediately below sets out the overall background of the law's adoption.

The operationalization of "agents-in-context" approach throughout this chapter deals mainly with the wider structural contexts. To this point, the book has operationalized "agents-in-context" approach emphasizing on the "mutually shaping" relationships between Indonesian FSA agents and the institution, Indonesian FSA. In this chapter, the approach is operationalized through identifying other wider structural contexts that are used by the Indonesian FSA agents to stymie the domestic portfolio liberalization process. Again, through the identification, the empirical evidences shown in this chapter exhibit how FSA agents halt or delay domestic implementation of ASEAN portfolio investment liberalization using the identified other wider structural contexts. In doing so, this chapter completes all the operational steps of "agents-in-context" approach.

The Enactment of the New Trading Law

For almost 70 years from independence, Indonesia did not have its own national trading law except that of the Dutch colonial legacy. This is perhaps one of the foremost rationales for Indonesia pushing to have its own national law related to trading. After a long process, the House of Representative, on 11 February 2014, finally enacted the Law of The Republic of Indonesia Number 7 Year 2014 on Trading. In its Elucidation part, the Trading Law explicitly stated that:

> Sejak kemerdekaan Indonesia pada tanggal 17 Agustus 1945, belum ada undang undang yang mengatur tentang Perdagangan secara menyeluruh. Produk hukum yang setara undang-undang di bidang Perdagangan adalah hukum kolonial Belanda *Bedrijfsreglementerings Ordonnantie* 1934 yang lebih banyak mengatur perizinan usaha...Oleh karena itu, perlu dibentuk undang-undang yang menyinkronkan seluruh peraturan perundang-undangan di bidang Perdagangan untuk mencapai tujuan masyarakat adil

dan makmur serta dalam menyikapi perkembangan situasi Perdagangan era globalisasi pada masa kini dan masa depan.

[*Since the independence of Indonesia on 17 August 1945, there is no law that regulate issues related to Trading comprehensively. Product of law that as the same degree as a Law is the law product of the Dutch colonial Bedrijfsreglementerings Ordonnantie 1934 regulating more into business licensing…Therefore, it is necessary to establish a law that synchronize all the regulations in the Trading sector to achieve the welfare of the society as well as to response to the current and future Trading globalization era.*]

Another important rationale for the enactment of the new Trading Law was the growing sense of protectionism in relation to domestic policies related to trading in general. Patunru and Rahardja (2015) wrote in a report that:

Indonesia's attitude to trade and investment in recent years has been characterised as "sitting on the fence." On the one hand, the country is an active member in the G20, APEC, and ASEAN. Such participation has in the past encouraged domestic policy reforms that ensured Indonesia benefited from greater economic integration with other countries…On the other hand, there is a growing trend towards protectionism. Most of the policies reflective of this trend are non-tariff measures, as tariffs are already very low. The introduction of a more restrictive cap on certain sectors, the ban on raw mineral exports, and the provision of greater authority for ministers to issue intervention and monitoring policies are just a few examples. (p. 2)

Presumably, there were agents pushing for more restrictive domestic trading policies. However, as this book only concerns portfolio investment liberalization or the financial sector in general, it is clearly beyond its scope to start exploring the rationale behind this growing sense of trading protectionism in general. It must be acknowledged however, that the growing sense of protectionism was among the reasons for the enactment of the new Trading Law. This book is simply concerned with the issue of the House of Representative's involvement. A former Minister of Trade mentioned in an internal document that:

Struktur perjanjian perdagangan internasional intinya meningkatkan akses pasar dan melindungi dan mengamankan kepentingan nasional. Untuk itulah kerjasama perdagangan harus melalui perjanjian perdagangan internasional dengan negara lain, lembaga atau organisasi internasional. Dalam hal ini, Pemerintah dalam melakukan perundingan perjanjian perdagangan internasional berkonsultasi dengan DPR. Pemerintah juga dapat meninjau kembali dan membatalkan perjanjian perdagangan internasional dilakukan dengan persetujuan DPR jika persetujuannya dilakukan dengan UU. Tanpa persetujuan DPR jika pengesahannya dilakukan dengan Peraturan Presiden. Pemerintah juga dapat memberikan preferensi perdagangan secara unilateral kepada negara kurang berkembang dengan tetap mengutamakan kepentingan nasional.

[*The core structure of an international trading agreement is to widen market access as well as protect and secure national interests. Thus, trading cooperation shall take the form of international trading agreement with other countries, institutions, or international organizations. In this case, Government in negotiating an international trading agreement shall consult to the House of Representative. Government may review and withdraw from the international trading agreement with the House of representative's approval, if the agreement was enacted in the form of a Law. Or, without the approval of the House of representative if the agreement was initially adopted through the enactment of a Presidential Decree. Government may also provide preferential unilateral trading to least developed countries while continue prioritizing national interests.*]

ASEAN Portfolio investment liberalization efforts are included within the scope of this new Trading Law because, firstly, the World Trade Organization (WTO) classifies portfolio investments under the general heading of Trade in Services (TIS). ASEAN also follows the WTO system in arranging its portfolio investment liberalization. Secondly, as the product of the international agreement related to portfolio investments is consequently under TIS, then the corresponding international agreement is the subject of the new Trading Law and the House of Representative's involvement in the ratification process. Particularly on the provisions that regulate the ratification process of an international agreement, more control towards liberalization efforts is now in place by allowing House of Representative involvement in the process. In addition, there are other features of the new Trading Law that are basically adding more control towards liberalization efforts. Pangestu et al. (2015), who was also a former Minister of Trade under the former President Susilo Bambang Yudhoyono, argued that the new Trading Law:

...gives the Ministry of Trade more control, strengthens previous government import and export regulations on quotas and bans, allows the temporary changing of tariffs to improve national competitiveness, and

> stipulates that trade negotiations must be approved by parliament. The government also attempted to reintroduce local-content requirements. Of course, it is too early to speculate on how many of these policies will be implemented, especially given the boundaries already set by Indonesia's international commitments. (p. 255)

In its status as the first national law related to trading in general, there were undoubtedly issues and discussions around enactment. However, in the following sections, to the extent to which it is relevant, this book's concerns are limited only to the provisions that regulate the House of Representative involvement in the ratification of particular international agreements, including those of portfolio investments liberalization.

Domestic Legal Ratification Process in Indonesia

This section discusses two different periods of the domestic legal ratification process. One focuses on the ratification process pre-2015. Following this, the focus will be on the ratification process after the enactment of the new Trading Law or the period of post-2015. While the outputs of the earlier period were in the form of Presidential Decrees, the later period's outputs depend on the parliament's approval. For instance, if the parliament allows the government to go ahead without enacting a law, then the government can directly enact a Presidential Decree. However, if the parliament resolves that an agreement related to financial liberalization requires enacting a new law, then the government must follow such a process. There are seven steps to follow if the parliament resolves to enact a law. As exhaustive as the process and the scrutiny can be, this shift in the policymaking process means that tighter political control of liberalization, suggesting a more intense interaction between agents and political power throughout the process. In addition, the ratification process through the House of Representative here has shaped FSA agents' approach to portfolio investments liberalization.

Pre-2015, this process of ratification, including for portfolio investment liberalization, only needed the approval of financial elites. This elite's approval would then take the form of a Presidential Decree. The story here should start with an explanation of the domestic provision in Indonesia related to international agreements. According to Law Number 24 Year 2000 on International Treaties, Indonesia defines the adoption of an international agreement into the domestic regulatory framework through four categories as follows: (1) Ratification; (2) Accession; (3) Acceptance and (4) Approval (Undang-Undang Nomor 24 Tahun 2000 tentang Perjanjian Internasional, Article 1). In its Explanation, the Law explained the four categories as below:

> (a) ratifikasi (ratification) apabila negara yang akan mengesahkan suatu perjanjian internasional turut menandatangani naskah perjanjian (b). aksesi (accesion) apabila negara yang mengesahkan suatu perjanjian internasional tidak turut menandatangani naskah perjanjian. (c). penerimaan (acceptance) dan penyetujuan (approval) adalah pernyataan menerima atau menyetujui dari negara-negara pihak pada suatu perjanjian internasional atas perubahan perjanjian-perjanjian internasional berlaku setelah penandatanganan. (Undang-Undang Nomor 24 Tahun 2000 tentang Perjanjian Internasional, Explanation)
>
> [*(a) ratification applies if a country adopting an international agreement is also a party signing the agreement manuscript (b) accession applies if a country adopting an international agreement is not a party signing the agreement manuscript (c) acceptance and approval are statements to accept or approve from parties to an international agreement upon changes made to the agreement after the signing.*]

According to this, ratification includes the bilateral, regional and global agreements related to portfolio investment liberalization. All members agreeing to further liberalize portfolio investments in ASEAN commonly signed the agreement manuscript. In the case of Indonesia, it is the content of this agreement manuscript that later needs adoption to the domestic regulatory framework.

There are particular areas where the Law mandated that adoption into the domestic regulatory framework shall require a legal enactment. Still, according to the Law on International Treaties (Undang-Undang Nomor 24 Tahun 2000 tentang Perjanjian Internasional, Article 10):

> Pengesahan perjanjian internasional dilakukan dengan undang-undang apabila berkenaan dengan : a. masalah politik, perdamaian, pertahanan, dan keamanan negara; b. perubahan wilayah atau penetapan batas wilayah negara Republik Indonesia; c. kedaulatan atau hak berdaulat negara; d. hak asasi manusia dan lingkungan hidup; e. pembentukan kaidah hukum baru; f. pinjaman dan/atau hibah luar negeri.
>
> [*The adoption of international agreements is carried out by Law if related to: a. issues on politics, peace, defence, and state security; b. changes to territory or boundaries determination of the Republic of Indonesia; c. sovereignty*

or state sovereign right; d. human rights and natural environment; e. the making of new legal norms; f. foreign loans and/or grants.]

According to this Article, the bilateral, regional and global agreements related to portfolio investment liberalization are not in the classification of those international agreements that require legal enactment. As the Law only mandates that adoption of an international agreement can only take the form of either Law or Presidential Decree (Undang-Undang Nomor 24 Tahun 2000 tentang Perjanjian Internasional, Article 9), then adoption of portfolio investment liberalization agreements shall take the form of a Presidential Decree.

What are the implications of using a Presidential Decree instead of a Law? There are at least two. Firstly, a Presidential Decree is less time-consuming. The reason for this is because going through Parliament means there are additional steps that the government needs to carry out. In addition, there are also associated costs. There are at least seven additional steps to go through. By using a Presidential Decree, the government can arrange adoption of the regulatory framework with only approval from the President of the Republic of Indonesia. Overall, some sources revealed that a shift of the policymaking process to the parliament consumes more time and money as compared to using a Presidential Decree. For instance, some sources stated:

> Jadi kita bikin perjanjian, perjanjian udah ditandatangan segala macam, tinggal ratifikasinya melalui Perpres...Perpres, iya. Lebih cepat. Proses konsolidasinya lewat RPP [Rancangan Peraturan Pemerintah] gitu-gitu.
>
> [*So, we made agreements, and the agreements has been signed, only need ratifications through Presidential Decrees...Yes, Presidential Decree. It is faster. The consolidation process only goes through like the Government Regulation Draft.*]

> Iya, betul. [Proses ratifikasi ke DPR] [l]ama dan mahal.
>
> [*Yes, that is true. Ratification process through the Parliament is time-consuming and costly.*]

Secondly, a Presidential Decree involves fewer parties, with the relevant Minister becoming the main decision-maker. The process may start directly by the relevant domestic ministries submitting an international agreement to be adopted in the form of a Presidential Decree. Upon submission, a related body in the government then verifies the urgency of the submission and determines its relevance to the administration's priorities. Once these verifications and determinations have been completed, the President of the Republic of Indonesia directly signs the Presidential Decree. For instance, in the case of an agreement related to portfolio investment liberalization, the Indonesian MOF was perhaps the only main actor in the whole process of a Presidential Decree. Once the liberalization agreement seemed to be urgent and fit government priorities, there were no further discussions necessary. Even if there were discussions on its urgency and government priorities, they were perhaps about merely administrative issues. Since the body in the government that performed the verification and determination was also an integral of the government, discussions were rapidly resolved. Above all, the President, Ministers and chairmen of related government bodies are coordinating frequently, even outside the discussions of the Presidential Decree.

The mark of the post-2015 period was the enactment of the Law of the Republic of Indonesia Number 7 of 2014 on Trading. The Law mandated that the domestic ratification process go through higher scrutiny by escalating the process for the approval of the parliament. The Trading Law specifically stipulates that (*Undang-Undang Republik Indonesia Nomor 7 Tahun 2014 tentang Perdagangan*, Article 84):

> (1) Setiap perjanjian Perdagangan internasional sebagaimana dimaksud dalam Pasal 82 ayat (2) disampaikan kepada Dewan Perwakilan Rakyat paling lama 90 (sembilan puluh) hari kerja setelah penandatanganan perjanjian.
> (2) Perjanjian Perdagangan internasional yang disampaikan Pemerintah sebagaimana dimaksud pada ayat (1) dibahas oleh Dewan Perwakilan Rakyat untuk memutuskan perlu atau tidaknya persetujuan Dewan Perwakilan Rakyat.
>
> [*(1) Each of the international Trading agreement as referred to Article 82 Verse (2) is submitted to the House of Representative at the latest 90 (ninety) working days after the signing of the agreement.*
>
> *(2) The international Trading agreement submitted by the Government as referred to Verse (1) is assessed by the House of Representative to decide the necessity for the approval of the House of Representative.*]

Particularly in the area of portfolio investment liberalization, the enactment of this Law means that any international agreements that involve more relaxed portfolio investment regulation need to go through the scrutiny of the House of Representative. According to an internal document of the Indonesian MOF, the ratification process involves seven steps before Indonesia finally decides to adopt an international agreement affecting portfolio investment liberalization.

As illustrated in Chart 5.1, the first step starts with the formal request from the Government of Indonesia to ASEAN, through the ASEAN Secretariat, to issue a certified true copy of the corresponding international agreement. The issuance of this certified true copy is basically a tool to confirm the authenticity and content of the agreement. The next few steps after acquiring the certified true copy are directly related to the House of Representative's involvement. In the second step, the government needs to formally submit all the required documents for the ratification to the House of Representative. Only then, in the third step, will the House of Representative assess and decide whether there is a need for its approval. In the fourth step, the House of Representative returns the documents for further processing by the government. If the House of Representative decides that no approval is needed, then the President of the Republic of Indonesia can go ahead and ratify the agreement through a Presidential Decree. Meanwhile, if the House of Representative decides that approval is necessary, then the government need to carry out further steps.

Once the House of Representative returns the documents, in the fifth step, the government prepares the necessary documents to formally propose a Bill to the House of Representative. These documents include most importantly, among others, the academic script, the translation of the agreement into Bahasa Indonesia and the Bill itself. After the submission of all those documents, the next step is the alignment process. This step is just one step away from the discussion of the Bill in the House of Representative. The objective of the alignment process itself is mainly to incorporate all inputs from related parties, particularly line ministries or institutions within the government. Thus, there are even more institutions, and more scrutiny, involved in the process. The later section of this chapter particularly discusses the implications of this scrutiny. Once this step is finalized, the ultimate step is the discussion of the Bill in the House of Representative. As perhaps the case with most Bills in Indonesia, it can take a few years depending on the urgency from the House of Representatives' point of view. To this end, it is also common to expect the political process surrounding the Bill will involve discussion between the government and the House of Representative.

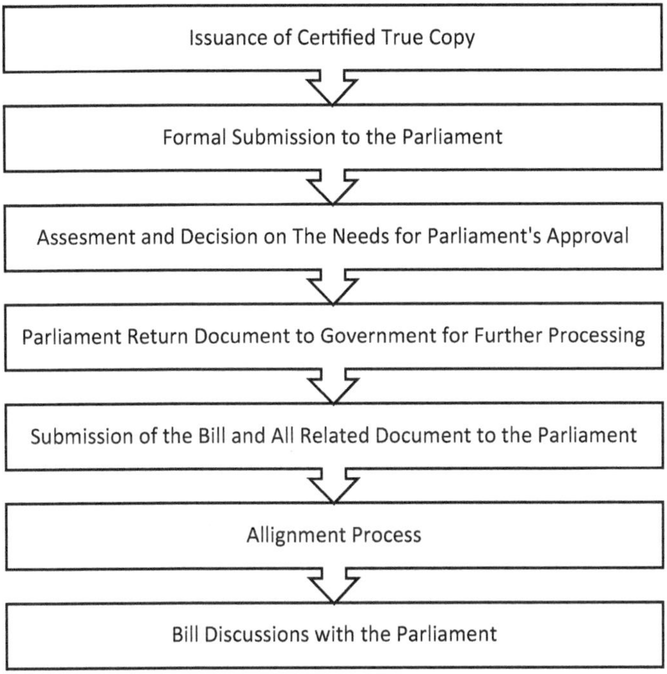

Chart 5.1 Illustration of the domestic ratification process in Indonesia (post-2015) (*Source* Adapted from Indonesian MOF Internal Document)

The enactment of the law brings several challenges to the domestic implementation of portfolio investment liberalization. Firstly, there is a wider involvement from related parties throughout the process. For instance, the alignment process needs to incorporate all inputs from related parties, particularly line ministries or institutions within the government. This means that, in the case of the portfolio investment liberalization agreement, the Indonesian MOF is not the main actor alone. The process Parliamentary debate on the Bill discussions also invites the wider participation of the public. Surely there will be a public consultation. Parliament also commonly invites experts and academics, and other related institutions to speak on the Bill during the discussions. At the very least, the whole process of adoption into the domestic regulatory framework is now not exclusively the domain of the executive administration. The new law has stripped away this exclusivity by involving the Parliament early on the process. From early on, the government has to formally submit all the required documents for the ratification to the House of Representative. Then, the House of Representative will assess and decide whether there is a need for its approval. By stripping away this exclusivity out of the executive, agents can have discretionary opportunities to provide their independent decisions and responses.

Secondly, if the process goes through the higher scrutiny of parliament, then other related institutions can also have the opportunity to get involved in the process. Pre-2015, even with the early establishment of the Indonesian FSA, the exclusive rights for the adoption of a portfolio investment liberalization agreement to Indonesian regulatory framework was still in the hands of the Indonesian MOF. This was because adoption can only take the form of a Presidential Decree with fewer outsiders' involvement. With the new Trading Law, other related institutions can now also formally take part. This means that a formal independent institution like the FSA can be actively involved in the process. After all, the FSA is the current ultimate regulatory and supervision power in portfolio investments. It can exercise its power and authority over the portfolio investments industry. The previous adoption process limited the exercise of this power and authority. So, for instance, the FSA can now express its different opinions either during the alignment process or even before the government submits the Bill to the Parliament. In addition, it is not only formal independent institutions like the FSA that can be actively involved but also other institutions, such as the market player associations or even the non-governmental organizations (NGOs).

Thirdly, if the process goes through the higher scrutiny of parliament, it may become a valid reason for AMS to delay the ratification process of a liberalization agreement. The government can make a formal excuse to the rest of the AMS and in the ASEAN meetings blaming the ratification delay on parliament. A well-known and respected academic based in Singapore mentioned when asked about the different positions between commitments in high-level governance with those in the technical level meetings that:

> ...another possible alternative explanation might be the Dani Rodrik one which is his argument that it's not whether you globalize, it's how. The sequencing becomes very important. When do you liberalize the timing? Indonesia might be actually hiring Dani Rodrik as the consultant and, therefore, when you look at the experience of countries that type of

> time, liberalizing sectors carefully. You want to protect up to a certain point...You don't want to just obey the rules and say that you liberalize now, even though in ASEAN documents you may have said yes, right? So, just to invite you to think about that as a potential alternative explanation. What Indonesia is doing is not puzzling. It is the smart thing to do.

The statement above suggests that, at technical level discussions, the government might use any reason to stall the portfolio investment liberalization from moving forward. In the next section, this chapter looks at implementation and examines real case studies of the involvement of the House of Representative in scrutinizing the ASEAN financial liberalization agreements.

The Case of Ratification of the AFAS Protocol and SOC

The first ratification of the AFAS to Indonesia's domestic regulation was on 30 December 1995 through Presidential Decree Number 88 Year 1995 on Ratification of AFAS. The ratification itself referred to the translation of the original AFAS agreement in English signed on 15 December 1995 (Keputusan Presiden Republik Indonesia Nomor 88 Tahun 1995, Article 1). Meanwhile, the ratification for the First AFAS Protocol and SOC to Indonesia's domestic regulation happened around three years later on 31 March 1998 through Presidential Decree Number 53 Year 1998 on Ratification of the Protocol to Implement the Initial Package of Commitments under the AFAS. From there until the Fifth Financial Services under AFAS Protocol and SOC, Indonesia ratified the agreements into domestic regulation through Presidential Decrees. The length of time for ratification varied from only months to the longest around three years. As predicted, the longest period was starting from the Sixth Protocol and SOC because that was the time Indonesia started to have the legal enactment process for the adoption of portfolio investment liberalization agreements into the domestic regulatory framework. The AMS signed the Seventh AFAS Protocol and SOC 23 June 2016, and the ratification process is still on-going in Indonesia without a clear prediction of the conclusion date.

Table 5.1 shows the duration of each ratification from the date of the signing of the original documents in English until incorporation in Indonesia's domestic regulations. Until the Fifth Financial Services under

AFAS Protocol and SOC, ratification was by Presidential Decree. As seen in Table 5.1, the Third AFAS Protocol and SOC took longer to ratify than the others (three years). Other than this unusually long period, the process of ratification through Presidential Decree should take less time compared to the legal enactment process. The most likely explanation for the three years it took to ratify the Third AFAS Protocol and SOC was because during 2004–2006, the Indonesian MOF was going through major organizational reform. This organizational reform was related to the regulation and supervision of the capital market and non-bank financial institutions. Though both regulation and supervision are under the MOF, both are also under different units (Director General Level). Formerly, the regulation and supervision of the capital market were under a unit called the Capital Market Supervisory Agency (Bapepam), while the regulation and supervision of the non-bank financial institutions were under the Directorate General of Financial Institutions (DGFI). During 2004–2006, the MOF merged the two units. As a result, the merger might have caused delays in the ratification process of the Third AFAS Protocol and SOC.

Table 5.1 Ratification of AFAS protocol and SOC—Indonesia

No	*Agreement*	*Signing*	*Ratification outcome*
1	AFAS	Bangkok 15 December 1995	Presidential Decree No. 88 Year 1995
2	First AFAS Protocol and SOC	Kuala Lumpur 15 December 1997	Presidential Decree No. 53 Year 1998
3	Second AFAS Protocol and SOC	Yangon 6 April 2002	Presidential Decree No. 81 Year 2002
4	Third AFAS Protocol and SOC	Vientiane 6 April 2005	Presidential Decree No. 51 Year 2008
5	Fourth AFAS Protocol and SOC	Danang 8 April 2008	Presidential Decree No. 6 Year 2009
6	Fifth AFAS Protocol and SOC	Hanoi 4 May 2011	Presidential Decree No. 47 Year 2013
7	Sixth AFAS Protocol and SOC	Kuala Lumpur 20 March 2015	Law No. 4 Year 2018
8	Seventh AFAS Protocol and SOC	Hanoi 23 June 2016	Law No. 13 Year 2020

Source Adapted from Indonesian MOF Internal Document

Still referring to Table 5.1, unlike the previous five protocols and SOCs, the ratification of the Sixth Financial Services under AFAS Protocol and SOC was in the form a Law instead of a Presidential Decree. The fact that it was a Law means that the House of Representative was involved in the ratification process. There is no House of Representatives' involvement in the case of Presidential Decree. Indonesia enacted the Law on 25 May 2018, or around three years after the signing of the original English documents on 20 March 2015 in Kuala Lumpur (Undang-Undang Republik Indonesia Nomor 4 Tahun 2018, Article 1). The ratification through legal enactment is consistent with the Law of the Republic of Indonesia Number 7 of 2014 on Trading, as discussed earlier. As mentioned in the earlier part of this chapter, in the third step of the ratification process, the House of Representative will assess and decide whether there is a need for its approval. There are a series of long and exhaustive working meetings between the government and the House of Representative during the assessment. Only after these meetings, can the House of Representative decide whether there is a need for its approval if or the President can just go ahead and issue a Decree.

In the case of the ratification of the Sixth Financial Services under AFAS Protocol and SOC, an internal document revealed that there were different positions between the government and the House of Representative. Both the internal document and a source reveal that while the government insisted on ratifying only by Presidential Decree, the House of Representative maintained the position of ratifying by legal enactment. The House of Representative argued that the agreement widely affected the nation's life as well as burdened the state budget. This is perhaps particularly due to important points in the agreement related to the ABIF. An official stated that:

> Jadi, masalah kenapa sih pakai undang-undang? Sebenarnya karena di tengah jalan itu muncul ABIF itu. ABIF antara Indonesia-Malaysia...Nah, itu jadi agak seru memang pembahasannya karena ada ABIF. Waktu itu kan Pak Marto yang masih ini ya, negosiasinya. Itu menurutku sih good deal banget lah untuk Indonesia...Berarti ini kami firm bahwa ini tidak berdampak luas terhadap aspek kehidupan dan beban negara.
>
> [*So, why did it (the ratification) have to be in the form of the Law? Because in the middle of its process appeared the ABIF, between Indonesia and Malaysia...Thus, the discussion was fierce because of the ABIF. The former Governor Agus Martowardojo led the negotiations (of ABIF) itself at that time. I personally think that it (ABIF Indonesia and Malaysia) was a*

> *good deal...This means we held a firm position that it (ABIF Indonesia and Malaysia) does not widely impact the nation's life as well as not burden the state budget.*]

If AMS fully implements the ABIF, ASEAN surely can expect freer flows of portfolio investment. The House of the Representatives then decided that the ratification of the Sixth Financial Services under AFAS Protocol and SOC needed to go through higher scrutiny via legal enactment. As the House of Representative decided so, the government then carried out further steps to prepare for the Bill.

Subsequently, the MOF conducted the alignment process in support of the Bill. The alignment process involved other government ministries and institutions. These relevant government ministries and institutions included the FSA, Bank Indonesia, the Indonesian Ministry of Law and Human Rights, the Indonesian Ministry of Foreign Affairs, as well as the Indonesian Ministry of State Secretariat. The whole alignment process itself took almost a full year to finish. While the meeting between the government and the House of Representative took place during January 2016, the Indonesian MOF concluded the whole alignment process in late November 2016. The ultimate step is the discussion of the Bill in the House of Representative. Most discussions in Indonesia can take a few years, depending on the urgency of the House of Representative's point of view. The discussion in the case of the ratification of the Sixth Financial Services under AFAS Protocol and SOC started with the formal process of lodging the Bill with the House of Representative. The President of the Republic of Indonesia finally lodged the Bill on April 2017.

It took almost another year after the lodgement of the Bill, in February 2018, for the House of Representative to have the first meeting with the government to discuss the Bill. During a series of meetings with the House of Representative, the government delivered presentations to explain the general substance and commitments of AFAS, particular commitments under the Sixth Financial Services under AFAS Protocol and SOC, as well as future policy implications resulting from the ratification of those particular commitments. The MOF, the FSA and Bank Indonesia represented the government in these meetings. According to the MOF Internal Document, the series of meetings finally concluded with the following three agreements. Firstly, most of the members of the House of Representative believe that ratification of the Sixth Financial Services under AFAS Protocol and SOC has the potential to benefit

Indonesia. However, the House of Representative highlighted areas of concern, including the development of the domestic banking industry to compete with ASEAN banks. Secondly, the House of Representative scheduled a meeting with financial industry players to directly hear their input and opinion of the plan to ratify the Sixth Financial Services under AFAS Protocol and SOC. Lastly, in particular for the ABIF, the House of Representative requested the government to refine the explanatory parts of the Bill in order to better explain additional commitments under the Sixth package.

After all these processes, the House of Representative formally ratified the Sixth Financial Services under AFAS Protocol and SOC through the enactment of the Law of the Republic of Indonesia Number 4 Year 2018 on the Ratification of Protocol to Implement the Sixth Package of Commitments on Financial Services under the ASEAN Framework Agreement on Services. In particular, this Law highlighted arrangements related to the ABIF. ASEAN has well-documented the high-level mandates to push for a closer banking sector integration. Meanwhile, rather than opposing the idea of the multilateral agreement framework as mandated at the highest level in ASEAN, Indonesian FSA officials just opted to use the bilateral agreements as a long-term strategy to escape from the trap of closer integration with ASEAN banking sector as the ultimate objective of ABIF. Thus, under this Law, Indonesia also specifically acknowledged the current bilateral agreement with Malaysia regarding market access and operational coverage of QABs in both countries. The Law mentioned the provision regarding the bilateral agreement as follows (Undang-Undang Republik Indonesia Nomor 4 Tahun 2018, Explanation):

> a. Indonesia dan Malaysia sepakat untuk mengizinkan tiga QAB beroperasi di masing-masing negara. Malaysia yang saat ini telah memiliki dua QAB yang beroperasi di Indonesia baru diizinkan untuk menambah QAB ketiga di Indonesia setelah tiga QAB Indonesia beroperasi penuh di Malaysia; b. QAB Indonesia akan diperlakukan sama dengan bank domestik Malaysia dalam operasionalnya. Hal yang sama juga dilakukan Indonesia untuk QAB Malaysia, begitu pula sebaliknya untuk QAB Malaysia di Indonesia; dan c. QAB Indonesia mendapatkan kelonggaran untuk memenuhi persyaratan modal minimum perbankan di Malaysia secara bertahap.
>
> [*a. Indonesia and Malaysia agreed to allow three QABs to operate in each state. Malaysia, that currently has already two QABs operating in Indonesia, is only allowed to add the third QAB in Indonesia after full operational of three Indonesian QABs in Malaysia; b. Indonesian QABs shall have the same*

treatments as Malaysian domestic banks in their operational and vice versa; and c. Indonesian QABs shall relinquish the gradual concession for minimum banking capital requirements in Malaysia.]

The Law also highlighted the importance of not only the prudential principle in relation to financial services liberalization generally but also of putting domestic interests above liberalization. In particular, the Law stated that (Undang-Undang Republik Indonesia Nomor 4 Tahun 2018, Explanation):

> Dalam perluasan akses pasar jasa keuangan di berbagai forum internasional (multilateral, regional, dan bilateral), Indonesia selalu berpegang pada prinsip-prinsip: (i) penambahan komitmen baru senantiasa memperhatikan komitmen Indonesia pada World Trade Organization (WTO) sebagai patokan, (ii) ikut sertanya Indonesia dalam perluasan akses pasar tidak terlepas dari pandangan ASEAN bahwa Indonesia adalah negara yang memiliki peran yang signifikan dalam mewujudkan Masyarakat Ekonomi ASEAN (peran leadership), (iii) perluasan akses pasar ditujukan pada pengembangan dan/atau penyehatan industri keuangan nasional, penerapan best practice operasional jasa keuangan, dan penciptaan lingkungan yang mendorong daya saing dan inovasi penyedia jasa keuangan domestik, (iv) membuka peluang bagi penyedia jasa keuangan dalam negeri yang memiliki kapasitas memadai untuk melakukan ekspansi ke negara ASEAN lainnya…dan (v) peningkatan jumlah dan kualitas produk jasa keuangan yang terjangkau bagi konsumen dalam negeri baik dalam kedudukannya sebagai produsen maupun konsumen akhir.
>
> [*In the expansion of access to the financial services market in various international forums (multilateral, regional and bilateral), Indonesia has always adhered to the principles that: (i) the addition of new commitments have to look at the Indonesia's commitment in the World Trade Organization (WTO) as a benchmark, (ii) Indonesia's participation in expanding market access is inseparable from ASEAN's view that Indonesia is a country that has a significant role in realizing the ASEAN Economic Community (leadership role), (iii) expanding market access shall aim at the development and/or the soundness of the national financial industry, implementation of best practices in financial service operations, and the creation of environments that encourages competitiveness and innovation in the domestic financial services providers, (iv) opening opportunities for the domestic financial service providers who have sufficient capacity to expand their business to the other ASEAN countries … and (v) increasing the quantity and quality of affordable financial services for domestic consumers, both as producers and final consumers.*]

As the ratification process for the Sixth package has finally been concluded, there is already another ratification process underway. On 23 June 2016, ASEAN signed the Seventh Financial Services under AFAS Protocol and SOC. Again, this required domestic legal ratification. As of now, among the members that have signed the Seventh package, Indonesia is the only state among ASEAN members that has not ratified the package into its domestic legal system. The ratification process for the Seventh package is currently just at the third step where the House of Representative assesses and decides whether there is a need for its approval. While the Sixth package was concerned mainly with the banking industry through the ABIF scheme, the area of concern in the Seventh package is the insurance industry. As with the Sixth package, for this Seventh package, the government again argued that the additional commitments in the insurance industry will not impact on the nation's life and will not result in an additional burden on the state budget. The House of Representative thinks otherwise. Thus, the ratification of the Seventh Financial Services under AFAS Protocol and SOC as well entailed a series of long and exhaustive working meetings between the government and the House of Representative. The process itself has already taken around four years before finally concluded in the 2020.

The majority of sources also confirmed that adoptions of portfolio investment liberalization agreements into the Indonesia regulatory framework through engagement with the parliament and legal enactment are long and exhaustive processes:

> Tiga kali panjang lah sekali...Eh, empat kali sebenarnya. Terus habis itu, empat kali rapat panjang, raker, akhirnya itu selesai Mei 2018 lah.
>
> [*Three times, so long...four times actually. Then, after long four times meeting, then also working meeting, finally done on around May 2018.*]

> Itu banyak yang ratifikasinya tertunda karena ada sebuah prosedur baru di sini di mana harus melibatkan DPR...Jadi akhirnya legal engagement-nya itu lama gitu.
>
> [*There are many delays in ratifications because there is a new procedure here that we have to engage with the House of Representative...Thus, it takes longer for the legal engagement.*]

> Ada beberapa kasus memang seperti itu, dan itu konsekuensi dari demokrasi. Zaman Pak Harto, mungkin itu [bisa] cepet, meskipun enggak ada proses sampai ke sana ya. Nah sekarang dengan adanya sharing of

power antara legislatif dan eksekutif, takes time. Jadi, butuh waktu dan sebagainya. Kalau kita ngomongin internal, ya pasti kemudian masing-masing unit butuh waktu yang agak lama. Belum lagi kalau harus undang-undang loh ya , ratifikasi dalam bentuk undang-undang itu butuh waktu lagi ke DPR.

[*There are few cases like that [the process takes longer], and it is a consequence of democracy. In the [Old Order] President Soeharto perhaps it can be swift, thought at that time we were not using the process [up until House of Representative's approval]. Currently, with the power sharing between legislative and executive, [the process] takes time. If we are talking about internal, surely each unit need longer period of time. This is not to mention if the process needs to go through law enactment as ratification in the form of laws requires more time to the House of Representative.*]

However, despite the criticisms of the long and exhaustive process by this power-sharing between the government and the parliament, agents have been endowed with discretionary opportunities in articulating their ideas to represent the national interest. Firstly, there is a wider involvement from related parties during the process. For instance, in the adoption case of Sixth Financial Services under AFAS Protocol and SOC, the House of Representative scheduled a meeting with financial industry players to directly hear their input and opinions. This wider involvement means that the process has more institutional representation. In addition, wider involvement can also mean that there are expectations of greater institutional support. Wider involvement can also increase the participation of non-government actors. Note that, for instance, industry players have only an informal legitimacy in ASEAN portfolio investment liberalization agreements. Thus, through the wider involvement, Indonesia is actually re-engineering the legitimation process by involving other parties largely ignored by ASEAN. An official from the Indonesian MOF even admitted:

Kalau ASEAN kan seolah-olah hanya negara...Memang belum ada [private berkontribusi di inisiatif regional]. [Ada yang kayak ASEAN Bussiness Council atau apalah tapi more into informal], bukan decision-making]. Saya belum melihat ya terus terang di ASEAN , mungkin saya juga salah. Tetapi sejauh yang saya lihat itu belum ada, keterlibatan itu di ASEAN.

[*If in ASEAN, it seems only the State matters...There are no private sector contributions in its regional initiatives. There is a thing like the ASEAN Business Council, or whatever, yet it is more informal, not in the decision-making. I, honestly, have not seen one in ASEAN, I might be wrong. Yet, so far, I have not seen one, the involvement [of the private sector] in ASEAN.*]

Secondly, other relevant institutions can also have the opportunity to be involved in the process. For instance, the Indonesian MOF conducted the alignment process in support of the Bill. The alignment process involved other relevant government ministries and institutions. These related government ministries and institutions included the FSA, Bank Indonesia, the Indonesian Ministry of Law and Human Rights, the Indonesian Ministry of Foreign Affairs, as well as the Indonesian Ministry of State Secretariat. Several sources also confirm the involvement of relevant government ministries and institutions, such as below:

> Jadi waktu itu, kita kan mengajukan nih, permohonan ratifikasi dong, DPR, sesuai dengan Pasal 84 dan juga itu surat-suratnya. Terus sehabis itu, DPR akhirnya memanggil waktu itu Pak Bambang Brodjonegoro. Menterinya masih Pak Bambang dulu. Terus Pak Thomas Lembong, Menteri Perdagangan, Pak Agus Marto, Gubernur BI, sama Pak Nelson, OJK.
>
> [*So, at that time we proposed the ratification to the House of Representative, according to Article 84 [of the Law of the Republic of Indonesia Number 7 of 2014 on Trading] and also all the related papers. Subsequently, the House of Representative, at that time, summoned Mr. Bambang Brodjonegoro. He was the Minister of Finance at that time. And then Mr. Thomas Lembong, the Minister of Trade; Mr. Agus Marto, the Governor of Bank Indonesia, and Mr. Nelson of the Indonesian FSA.*]

As this section has demonstrated in the case of the Sixth Financial Services under AFAS Protocol and SOC, the whole alignment process itself took almost a full year to finish. On another instance from the same case, during a series of meetings with the House of Representative, the government delivered presentations to explain the general substance and commitments of the AFAS, in particular commitments under the Sixth Financial Services under AFAS Protocol and SOC, as well as future policy implications resulting from the ratification of those particular commitments. There are, at least, the Indonesian MOF, the Indonesian FSA and Bank Indonesia representing the government in these meetings.

Thirdly, agents can also have a valid reason for delaying the ratification process of a liberalization agreement. In the case of Sixth Financial

Services under AFAS Protocol and SOC, ASEAN has to patiently wait for Indonesia to finally ratify the agreement after three years. ASEAN knew that the parliamentary process is one that ASEAN and AMS cannot control and push other AMS. The same with the current ratification of the Seventh Financial Services under AFAS Protocol and SOC where Indonesia took around 4 years to finally ratify the Protocol. Debates about the long and exhaustive process of this power-sharing between the government and the parliament are clearly outside the focus of this section and the entire book. Nevertheless, this section closes with the statement below from an official at the Indonesian Ministry of Foreign Affairs:

> Perubahan politik itu menurutku yang paling matter...Tapi kan kita sebenarnya mengarah ke demokrasi. Dari situ terjadi power diversion, jadi kekuasaan yang kemudian terpecah. Nah ini kemudian juga berefek banyak ke bagaimana menentukan posisi kita ke luar negeri.
>
> [*I think political changes matter the most...But, we are heading into democracy. From there on, there is power diversion, so power is shared. This, in turn, mostly affects our positions of foreign affairs.*]

Conclusion

This chapter depicted the enactment of the new Indonesian Trading Law as an emerging challenge to further domestic portfolio investment liberalization in Indonesia. This latest development on the enactment of the law is largely consistent with Indonesian FSA agents' efforts to stymie portfolio investments liberalization. To that extent, the chapter explained not only the current domestic ratification process of an international financial liberalization agreement, but also to account for the possibility of FSA officials utilizing the process to further stymie portfolio investments liberalization. As demonstrated above, FSA agents are using one of the main features of the new law, the involvement of the House of Representative, to halt or delay domestic implementation of ASEAN portfolio investment liberalization. Thus, the enactment of this new Trading Law in Indonesia may pose a further stumbling block for ASEAN to achieve a more liberalized regional regime of portfolio investments. The chapter started with the explanation of the domestic process in Indonesia that led to this new Trading Law being enacted back in 2014.

As a result, this chapter differentiates two periods of the domestic legal ratification process, the pre-2015, and the post-2015. The main focus here is the difference in the adoption process of a portfolio investments liberalization agreement into the Indonesian regulatory framework between those two periods. Pre-2015, this process of ratification, including for portfolio investment liberalization, only needed the approval of financial elites. This elite's approval would take the form of a Presidential Decree. However post-2015, particularly with the recent legal enactments, ratification is required to go through higher scrutiny by escalating the process for approval to the House of Representative. Thus, there are significant additional steps to be carried out by going for parliament's approval. Indonesian FSA agents are using this as an opportunity to provide resistance to ASEAN portfolio investment liberalization initiatives. In the end, ASEAN knew that the domestic parliamentary process is a process that ASEAN and AMS cannot control. In order to give a clearer overview of the process of the ratification itself, the last section in this chapter discussed the ratification case study of the Protocol to Implement the Packages of Commitment on Financial Services under AFAS.

References

Pangestu, M., Rahardja, S., & Ing, L. (2015). Fifty years of trade policy in Indonesia: New world trade, old treatments. *Bulletin of Indonesian Economic Studies, 51*(2), 239–261.

Patunru, A. A., & Rahardja, S. (2015). *Trade protectionism in Indonesia: Bad times and bad policy*. Lowy Institute for International Policy.

CHAPTER 6

Conclusion

The Agents-in-Contexts

The puzzle identified at the outset of the book posited that Indonesian political elites have kept agreeing to ASEAN initiatives for a more open and liberal international portfolio investment regime as favoured by ASEAN's leaders, while the domestic authorities in Indonesia have worked at the bureaucratic level to maintain the existing regime. As a consequence, I raised the question: Why are there domestic implementation gaps in Indonesia? In Chapter 1, I provided in detail most of these observable implementation gaps within the scope of ASEAN portfolio investment liberalization. I answered the question by arguing that the emergence of the Indonesian FSA, as a single authority overseeing all financial services in Indonesia, has resulted in domestic implementation gaps. Indonesian FSA agents have actually stymied portfolio investment liberalization, rather than advance it. This is particularly attributable to the endowment of "independent and free" status to the institution, as well as its role as the ultimate decision-maker in financial services liberalization in general, including portfolio investment liberalization. Thus, the central discussion of this book was on the historical emergence of the contemporary Indonesian FSA.

In order to explain that emergence, I needed to employ an appropriate theoretical framework. In Chapter 2, I surveyed most of the major existing literature that has considered and observed the existence of

C. Kusuma, *The Rise of the Indonesian Financial Service Authority*,
https://doi.org/10.1007/978-981-19-3850-4_6

domestic implementation gaps in the context of regional governance. The emergence of the Indonesian FSA is the story of institutional changes as a result of the interplay between relevant agents and institutions, as well as other wider structural contexts. To that extent, I chose to employ an approach that is able to explain the institutional changes leading to the rise of the Indonesian FSA. As concluded in the chapter, historical institutionalism served as one of major theoretical anchors to comprehend the creation of the Indonesian FSA as the rationale for the existing domestic implementation gaps. Consequently, I utilized an approach that expands the account of historical institutionalism. This included features that can incorporate both the bidirectional relationship and the surrounding structural context. This is the approach that Bell and Feng (2013) termed the "agents-in-context" approach. There were two theoretical steps I employed in this book. Firstly, drawing on historical institutional theory, I identified the nature of the relevant agents as well as the norms and value of their institutions involved in the rise of the FSA. Secondly, I traced out the bidirectional relationships between agents and their institutions, as well as the broader structural contexts surrounding these relationships.

In Chapter 3, I then moved to empirical analysis to explain the contemporary historical emergence of the Indonesian FSA. I identified the main agents in establishment of the FSA were from the MOF and Bank Indonesia. Those two institutions constituted the main institutional context surrounding the establishment of the FSA. While the MOF is part of the government administration, Bank Indonesia is also an independent institution as is the FSA. The emergence of the FSA was basically rooted in the 1997–1998 Asian Financial Crisis that hit Indonesia hard. As a consequence, Indonesia had to deal with the IMF and follow the structural reform programs it mandated. One of those structural adjustment programs was the enactment of the Bank Indonesia Law. This law endowed independent status to Bank Indonesia, as previously it was under the control of the government. Most importantly, the law also mandated the establishment of the single financial services authority in Indonesia or the FSA.

There were a number of important background factors that intervened along the way to the formal establishment and transition to the FSA. Within those background conditions, agents were involved in the institutional shaping of the FSA. These conditions included the independent status of Bank Indonesia and the reduced authority of both Bank

Indonesia and the government in financial sector supervision. In addition, there were also important events prolonging the establishment of the FSA. The MOF carried out internal reform to prepare for transferring its authority to the new institutions. In Bank Indonesia, there was resistance to moving employees to the new institutions. Meanwhile, members of parliament conducted comparative studies with other countries' financial services authorities or other overseas equivalent institutions. Along the way another major financial crisis, the GFC, occurred and brought financial sector reform back into government priorities. Ultimately, the Indonesian FSA formally emerged in 2011 after more than a decade-long process. In the next chapter, this book continued to explain how agents within the Indonesian FSA had operated and had stymied the domestic portfolio investment liberalization process.

In Chapter 4, I continued its empirical analysis to explain how agents within the Indonesian FSA are using its "independent and free" status to stymie the domestic portfolio investment liberalization process. Agents are exercising their power and authority as the "independent and free" ultimate decision-maker in portfolio investments liberalization. As such, agents opted to reject, or halt, or delay the implementation of the ASEAN portfolio investments liberalization initiatives, in turn, creating domestic implementation gaps. In order to demonstrate these conditions, this chapter took the case studies on the recent ASEAN initiatives in the area of portfolio investments liberalization. This chapter utilized the ASEAN Trading Link, the ASEAN Framework for Cross Border Offering of CIS, the ASEAN Disclosure Standards and the ABIF as well other related arrangements. Overall, FSA officials clearly exhibited a more conservative approach to portfolio investment liberalization than that deliberately promoted by ASEAN. In addition, agents also operate within the FSA by harnessing the international standards for the "national interest" and avoiding regional portfolio investment liberalization.

I confirmed that FSA agents also continuously shape the form of the FSA by adopting positions and strategies that are in line with their power and authority. In addition, FSA agents also interact with other institutions. For instance, this chapter discussed the roles of the contemporary Indonesian MOF and Bank Indonesia on their current involvements in the ASEAN portfolio investments liberalization efforts. This chapter revealed that the Indonesian MOF, as the international financial policy coordinator for Indonesia, relies advice from the FSA. In the last section of the chapter, I also discussed the existence of the FSSC. This formal forum of coordination among authorities related to financial sector in Indonesia facilitates the operation of the FSA. This forum basically creates a policy space for agents of the FSA and Bank Indonesia to operate and exercise their power and authority, including in the case of portfolio investment liberalization.

Chapter 5, the last among the empirical chapters in this book, analysed the enactment of the new Indonesian Trading Law as an emerging challenge to further domestic portfolio investments liberalization. This latest development on the enactment of the law is somehow consistent with the FSA agents' efforts to stymie portfolio investments liberalization. The legal enactment now requires that portfolio investment liberalization agreements go through a domestic ratification process in the House of Representative instead of enactment by Presidential Decree. Legal enactment creates another domestic stumbling block for ASEAN's portfolio investments liberalization agenda. FSA agents may now have a valid reason to halt or delay domestic implementation of ASEAN portfolio investment liberalization by due to the long process of the domestic ratification. Thus, this chapter explained, not only the current domestic ratification process of an international financial liberalization agreement, but also the possibility of the Indonesian FSA officials utilizing the process to further stymie portfolio investments liberalization. This chapter examines a particular case of ASEAN financial services liberalization to better illustrate the challenges related to domestic ratification process.

The Domestic Implementation Gap

As this book throughout uses Indonesian portfolio investments liberalization as a case study, perhaps a question remains: are the arguments and findings I unfolded here in this book applicable generally to AMS, other than Indonesia? The answer is perhaps, at the very least Indonesia is not uncommon for having gone through domestic contestations in the domestic regulatory framework. Domestic contestations of international commitments can surely happen in other countries and other types of intergovernmental organization. However, through the employment of modified historical institutionalism in the case study of Indonesian portfolio investment liberalization, I demonstrate that, in many cases, emphasis on both agents and institutions is equally important. Agents and institutions have a bidirectional relationship, and there are obviously structural contexts surrounding agents and institutions. ASEAN can surely expect that domestic contestations will happen in future and in other AMS. These contestations are, to some extent, played out in ASEAN at multiple levels—recognizing that governance outcomes in ASEAN are necessarily multi-factorial, and not able to be simplified or generalized to one or two countries.

Another general application to AMS other than Indonesia, and perhaps as well as to ASEAN as a regional intergovernmental organization, is the fact that there are still mixed perceptions regarding further portfolio investment liberalization in ASEAN. The debates on the impact of portfolio investment liberalization itself are well outside the scope of this book. However, the existence of mixed perceptions implies that ASEAN is not entirely coherent heading toward a more liberalized regime of portfolio investment in the region. For instance, even though high-level officials in ASEAN have agreed to further pursue portfolio investment liberalization, the AMS bureaucratic level officials may have different ideas on how they perceive the Asian Financial Crisis. Rather than keep pushing for a closer financial integration by liberalizing the portfolio investment regime, at the bureaucratic level officials seem to focus on improving weak domestic financial systems while anticipating another regionally contagious effect in the occurrence of a crisis. In the end, these mixed perceptions may become the biggest challenges to ASEAN and AMS moving forward with its integration plan, particularly in the area of portfolio investment liberalization.

There is another puzzling question that perhaps needs further research in relation to the work I have carried out: How does ASEAN so far, and in future, deal with domestic implementation gaps? Like it or not, ASEAN has to admit that domestic contestations are one of the major challenges to moving forward with regional integration generally and, in particular, financial integration. In the end, the shape of ASEAN regional governance remains dynamic, subject to how far the effects of domestic contestations are felt (such as those explored by Jones & Hameiri, 2019; Nesadurai, 2014). At least, in the case of Indonesia, not only there has been domestic contestation but also there are factors which may lead to further contestation in future going forward. For instance, with the emergence of the FSA, ASEAN can expect more domestic contestation in Indonesia. Even further, ASEAN itself as a regional intergovernmental organization also may interact with other countries in East Asia or the wider region, and it would be interesting to explore if the regional context can also affect the position of domestic agents and the context in which they operate.

For instance, ASEAN also interacts with other countries in East Asia region through ASEAN Plus Three. The ASEAN Plus Three initiatives may seem appealing to agents in Indonesia as the initiatives focus more on regional financial stability mechanisms or domestic market strengthening instead of market integration or liberalization. Based on the literature and assumptions about future economic initiatives proposed by Japan, China or South Korea, this book can provide some insight into the complexities and dynamics which could be expected in Indonesia, as well as to other domestic contexts where law, parliaments and other domestic political agents/mechanisms have an important role in the pace and ultimate developments of such initiatives. Therefore, while one can look at agreements made at the elite level—I suggest looking to further empirical analysis of these processes to see how they play out.

Even further, the findings in this book may also serve as a preliminary inquiry into how officials navigate the domestic implementation gaps at the ASEAN level. For instance, I have explained how agents within the Indonesian FSA operate within their institution to stymie the ASEAN liberalization of portfolio investments process. In relation to this, I have also shown that Indonesian officials at ASEAN's formal governance structure have reflected their positions by opting-out or delaying the implementation of the ASEAN initiatives. Such condition may then also pose a query on how the Indonesia's domestic implementation delays were actually negotiated at the ASEAN level. Although I might have provided an overview of how Indonesian officials were using the opting-out or delaying strategy for the negotiation, further research on how ASEAN was responding to the Indonesian delays may seem requisite at the other end. In doing so, further research may also consider an examination of the agent-structure relations in ASEAN.

References

Bell, S., & Feng, H. (2013). *The rise of the people's Bank of China: The politics of institutional change*. Harvard University.

Jones, L., & Hameiri, S. (2019). Southeast Asian region governance: Political economy, regulatory regionalism, and ASEAN integration. In T. Carroll, S. Hameiri, & L. Jones (Eds.), *The political economy of Southeast Asia, Vol. 4: Politics and uneven development under hyperglobalisation*. Palgrave.

Nesadurai, H. (2014). The political economy of Southeast Asia's foreign economic policies and relations. In R. Foot, S. Pekkanen, & J. Ravenhill (Eds.), *The Oxford handbook of the international relations of Asia*. Oxford University Press.

Index

A

accession, 89, 121, 155

actors, 22–24, 27–30, 33–36, 38, 39, 41, 42, 48, 49, 110, 168

adherence, 90, 107, 120, 123, 131, 146

adjustment, 40, 79, 85, 174

administration, 33, 66, 72, 85, 157, 159, 174

adoption, 7, 24, 29, 37, 63, 67, 69, 110, 144, 149, 151, 154–156, 159–161, 167, 168, 171

agency, 33, 42, 44, 46, 73, 79, 91

agents, 2, 3, 6, 7, 15, 17, 18, 21, 28, 35–39, 42–49, 55–57, 66, 71, 73–79, 84–86, 89–91, 99, 106, 107, 116, 117, 119–121, 136, 140, 143, 145, 146, 149–152, 154, 160, 168–171, 173–178

agents-in-context, 3, 7, 21, 46, 48, 49, 57, 90, 151, 173, 174

agreement, 16, 18, 40, 75, 77, 78, 92–94, 97, 102, 113–115, 119, 136, 149, 150, 153–161, 163–165, 167–171, 176, 178

amendment, 72, 76, 129, 131, 150, 151

analysis, 16, 17, 22, 26, 32, 34–36, 38, 47, 48, 91, 108, 131, 174, 175, 178

approach, 3, 5–7, 9, 15, 17, 21, 22, 24–29, 31, 36–38, 42, 45–49, 57, 90, 91, 94, 118, 129, 130, 146, 151, 154, 174, 175

approval, 8, 56, 72, 75, 93, 96, 105, 106, 108–110, 112, 149, 150, 154–158, 160, 163, 167, 171

association, 15, 16, 83, 160

B

background, 3, 7, 15, 18, 35, 44, 47, 56, 57, 68, 70, 78, 84, 90, 101, 114, 138, 150, 151, 174

banking, 8, 13, 33, 35, 44, 48, 62–64, 66–69, 71, 73–79, 81–84, 91, 94, 113–119, 122,

C. Kusuma, *The Rise of the Indonesian Financial Service Authority*,
https://doi.org/10.1007/978-981-19-3850-4

124, 126, 128, 131, 135, 137, 141, 143, 145, 165, 167
banks, 9, 30, 62, 63, 66, 68–71, 73, 75, 76, 94, 113, 114, 116, 117, 123, 135–137, 139, 140, 165
behaviour, 24, 28, 37, 38, 42, 46, 47, 143
benefit, 6, 9, 34, 39, 42, 100, 101, 107, 109, 152, 164
bidirectional, 21, 37, 43, 44, 46, 47, 49, 90, 174, 176
bilateral, 5, 113–115, 131, 136, 142, 149, 155, 156, 165, 166
Blueprint, 1, 113, 133
bond, 5, 25, 75, 143

C
campaign, 34, 111
capacity, 31, 34, 71, 166
capitalism, 31, 58
capitalist, 25, 26, 29
ceremonial, 45, 115
chairman, 68, 71, 74, 84, 95, 136, 141
coercion, 24
collective, 32, 42, 78, 91, 126
commitment, 1, 5, 9, 21, 108, 118, 120, 121, 123, 124, 127, 154, 160, 164–167, 169, 176
community, 16, 23, 166
compliance, 6, 22, 35, 36, 43, 120–123, 129, 131
conglomerates, 33, 66, 70, 71, 82, 84
connectivity, 97, 102–104
constitutional, 84
contemporary, 3, 14, 17, 21, 23, 29, 34, 36, 44, 45, 47, 64, 85, 132, 138, 146, 173–175
contestation, 23–25, 28, 29, 31, 36, 176, 177
convergence, 2, 24, 90, 120, 121, 124, 131
coordination, 80, 82, 92, 133–135, 140–144, 146, 176
country, 24, 32, 33, 97, 100, 105, 113, 122, 127, 140, 152, 155, 166
cross-border, 7, 8, 30, 31, 97, 98, 103–105, 108–111, 114, 122, 128, 131

D
debt, 5, 7, 8, 63, 98, 103, 104, 109, 110, 112
decision, 2, 14, 15, 23, 39, 46, 70, 78, 79, 84, 91, 95, 96, 111, 133, 134, 137–141, 145, 156, 160, 168, 173, 175
decline, 14, 56–62, 64–66, 102, 107
Decree, 18, 66, 93, 141, 150, 151, 153, 154, 156–158, 160–163, 171, 176
definition, 3, 5, 37, 40, 42, 43, 47, 70
deliberate, 9, 63, 105, 118, 127, 141, 146, 175
democracy, 30, 33, 168
dependence, 7, 40, 57, 58, 126
deregulation, 57, 58, 61–63, 65, 67, 101, 110, 116, 119
development, 14, 18, 26, 29, 33, 34, 40, 41, 43, 47–49, 66, 68, 82, 97, 102, 104, 107, 112–116, 119, 120, 122, 124, 129, 130, 133, 135, 136, 165, 166, 170, 176, 178
diffusion, 23, 24
disclosure, 8, 89, 90, 109–112, 146, 175
discretionary, 75, 160, 168
discursive, 37, 44–46
dispute, 101, 104, 110, 139

E

Echelon, 73, 74
economic, 9, 14, 25, 29, 39, 41, 45, 47–49, 56–61, 64, 80, 109, 112, 116, 139, 140, 152, 178
elites, 1, 5–9, 14, 26, 30, 34, 35, 48, 49, 97, 100, 104, 109, 118, 149, 154, 171, 173
elucidation, 68–70, 72, 91, 93, 151
emergence, 2, 3, 5, 7, 14, 17, 21, 22, 31, 33, 36, 38, 40, 41, 43, 44, 46–49, 55–57, 63, 70, 72, 75, 85, 173, 174, 177
emphasis, 22, 25, 26, 28, 32, 39, 41, 42, 46, 90, 108, 176
employees, 77, 80, 82, 84, 85, 175
enactment, 2, 3, 18, 68, 69, 72, 73, 77–79, 85, 126, 129–131, 141, 146, 149, 150, 152–157, 159, 161–165, 167, 168, 170, 171, 174, 176
equity/equities, 5, 7, 8, 17, 63, 98, 103, 104, 109, 110, 112
establishment, 4, 7, 17, 18, 39, 43, 49, 55–57, 62, 66, 68–72, 74, 77–82, 84, 85, 94, 95, 97, 116, 119, 122, 124, 126, 128, 130, 140, 141, 143, 160, 174, 175
exchange, 7, 9, 30, 34, 61, 75, 78, 92, 97, 101, 103, 118, 124, 131
ex-officio, 78, 91–93

F

facilitate, 1, 4, 8, 25, 26, 44, 61, 109, 140, 146, 176
fact, 26, 32, 38, 55, 77, 78, 83, 100, 101, 107, 111, 113–116, 129, 134, 139, 141, 163, 177
features, 7, 18, 37, 39, 46, 48, 49, 68, 74, 146, 149, 153, 170, 174
finance, 23, 25, 30, 35, 58, 62, 76, 78, 82, 94, 116, 132, 141, 169
financial, 2, 4–6, 9, 14, 15, 17, 18, 21, 24, 25, 27, 28, 30, 33, 35, 38, 40, 45, 47–49, 55–59, 61–63, 65–80, 83–85, 89–95, 99, 111–114, 116, 118–121, 123–125, 127–129, 132–134, 137–144, 146, 152, 161, 165, 166, 168, 170, 173–177
flows, 1, 4, 8, 14, 15, 22, 61, 63, 64, 74, 101, 103–105, 110–112, 118, 164
foreign, 9, 35, 36, 61, 63, 89, 107, 110, 118, 126
formal, 15, 16, 27, 30, 34, 35, 38, 43, 72, 77, 79, 83, 85, 97, 104, 126, 131, 132, 135, 136, 140, 146, 158, 160, 164, 165, 174, 178
framework, 4, 5, 7, 8, 15–17, 23, 26, 28, 31, 34, 36, 61, 67, 70, 82, 89, 90, 92, 98, 104–108, 110–116, 121, 125–127, 136, 137, 141, 146, 149, 154, 155, 159–161, 165, 167, 171, 173, 175, 176

G

gaps, 1–3, 7, 9, 10, 14, 16, 17, 21–29, 31, 32, 35, 36, 38, 39, 45, 46, 55, 89, 113, 118, 145, 173–175, 177, 178
general, 6, 9, 15, 16, 40, 44, 45, 63, 68, 89, 92, 94, 97, 99, 110, 118, 122–126, 132, 134, 137, 138, 152–154, 164, 166, 169, 173, 176, 177
global, 22, 25, 27–31, 56, 57, 59–61, 71, 77, 92, 104, 105, 124, 125, 128, 131, 144, 149, 155, 156
globalization, 25, 45, 152

governance, 3–5, 15, 21–23, 25–33, 46, 113–115, 118, 137, 138, 160, 174, 177, 178
government, 15, 23, 27, 33, 35, 56, 58–63, 66–70, 72–75, 77–80, 83, 85, 91–93, 101, 126, 127, 129, 139, 140, 143, 150, 153, 154, 156–161, 163–165, 167–170, 174, 175
governmentality, 22, 25–28
growth, 9, 17, 58–62, 64, 67, 133

H
Handbook, 104, 105
harmonization, 78, 92
historical, 3, 7, 14, 15, 17, 21, 32, 37, 40–44, 46–49, 55, 57, 64, 85, 90, 101, 119, 120, 173, 174, 176

I
ideas, 3, 26, 40, 42–46, 55–57, 68, 74, 75, 84, 85, 111, 168, 177
implementation, 1–7, 9, 14, 16–18, 21–39, 45–47, 49, 55, 70, 72, 73, 89, 90, 99, 103, 104, 106–108, 110–113, 118, 127, 139, 145, 146, 149, 151, 159, 161, 170, 173–178
independence, 2, 40, 70, 73, 78, 79, 85, 126, 151, 152
independent, 2, 3, 14, 17, 18, 21, 28, 30, 55, 63, 67, 69, 70, 73–75, 78–80, 85, 89, 91, 95, 126, 139, 145, 160, 173–175
Indonesia, 1–3, 5–9, 14–18, 21, 22, 24–27, 29, 30, 32–38, 40, 45, 47, 49, 55–74, 76–80, 82–86, 89–98, 100–102, 105–110, 114–118, 120, 121, 123–132, 134, 135, 139–143, 145, 146, 150, 151, 154, 156–158, 160, 161, 163–165, 173, 177, 178
industry, 6, 63, 67, 70, 71, 74, 79, 80, 83, 95, 104, 107, 112, 120, 122, 127–131, 143, 160, 165–168
inflows, 13, 14, 17, 62–65
information, 15–17, 30, 73, 78, 82, 92, 94, 124, 126, 131–133, 135, 137
initiatives, 1, 2, 4–6, 13–16, 18, 35, 75, 80, 89, 97, 98, 104, 107, 118, 119, 121, 126, 127, 131, 133–136, 145, 146, 171, 173, 175, 178
institutionalism, 3, 7, 15, 21, 36–49, 57, 174, 176
institutions, 2–4, 6, 7, 17, 21, 22, 25, 26, 28–31, 33, 34, 36–49, 55, 57, 62–64, 67, 69, 70, 73, 74, 76, 77, 80, 82, 84, 85, 89, 91, 93, 94, 96, 99, 123, 125, 128, 132–134, 137–141, 143, 158–160, 162, 164, 169, 174–176
insurance, 4, 67, 69, 74, 80, 91, 119, 120, 127–131, 167
integration, 2, 4, 6, 9, 14, 15, 18, 22, 23, 29, 31, 45, 71, 99, 101, 111, 113, 116, 119–121, 123–125, 128, 134, 138, 152, 165, 177, 178
interests, 6, 23, 25–29, 33–36, 39, 41, 78, 91–94, 124, 140, 146, 166
international, 1, 2, 6, 14, 15, 18, 23–30, 35, 40, 45, 59, 67, 75, 81, 90, 92, 93, 112, 119–125, 127, 129–131, 140, 142, 146, 153, 154, 156–158, 170, 173, 175, 176

investment, 1–7, 9, 14–16, 18, 21, 24, 25, 35, 36, 46, 55, 61, 63–65, 67, 75, 79, 80, 86, 89, 90, 95, 96, 99–101, 103–105, 107–112, 114–116, 118, 119, 121, 123–128, 132, 134–138, 140–146, 149, 152–157, 159–161, 164, 167, 168, 170, 171, 173, 175–178

J
juncture, 7, 40, 57
jurisdiction, 8, 104, 105, 109, 110, 125, 126

K
key, 3, 26, 28, 43, 48, 49, 55, 57, 67, 85, 97, 109, 131
knowledge, 15, 26, 74, 101, 136

L
law, 2, 3, 14, 18, 67–69, 71–73, 76, 77, 79, 80, 83–85, 91–95, 126, 129, 131, 140–142, 146, 149–157, 160, 163, 165, 166, 169, 170, 174, 178
leaders, 3–6, 33, 36, 70, 78, 115, 173
legal, 2, 5, 73, 76, 84, 85, 93, 120, 121, 123, 126, 132, 140, 141, 149–151, 154–156, 161–164, 167, 170, 171, 176
level, 1, 3–6, 13, 17, 22, 23, 27, 28, 31, 57, 60, 61, 63, 64, 73–75, 78, 79, 85, 91, 95–97, 99–101, 108, 113–115, 118, 122, 127, 130, 132, 137, 141–143, 160, 161, 165, 173, 177, 178
liberalization, 2–9, 13–16, 18, 21, 25, 35, 36, 45, 55–58, 61–65, 67, 75, 79, 80, 86, 89, 90, 95, 96, 99, 107, 114–119, 123–125, 127, 128, 131, 132, 134–138, 140–146, 149, 151, 153, 154, 156–161, 166–171, 173, 175–177
linkage, 43, 92, 97, 99, 101, 102

M
macroeconomic, 70, 108–110, 143
macro-prudential, 94
major, 6, 14–16, 18, 35, 41, 43, 46, 59, 64, 67, 70, 77, 78, 85, 91, 105, 122, 138, 162, 173–175, 177
market, 2, 4, 5, 7–9, 15, 16, 25, 27, 35, 36, 45, 58, 59, 62–65, 67, 74, 80, 82, 89–91, 97, 98, 100, 101, 104–114, 118, 119, 121, 124, 125, 128, 129, 131, 143, 160, 162, 165, 166, 178
measures, 15, 56–58, 61–63, 97, 113, 152
meeting, 15–17, 99, 102, 111, 115, 117, 132, 134, 135, 160, 163–165, 167–169
members, 45, 58, 76–78, 81, 85, 91–94, 101, 115, 121, 124–126, 128, 134, 139–141, 155, 164, 167, 175
micro-prudential, 94
Minister, 4, 68, 73–75, 78, 80, 95–97, 102, 109, 118, 132, 133, 135, 136, 139, 141, 143, 152, 153, 156, 157, 169
monetary, 48, 61, 69, 71, 76, 82, 92, 110, 118

N
national, 2, 5, 6, 18, 28, 31, 56, 62, 77, 78, 80, 90, 92, 93, 119, 124,

140, 146, 151, 153, 154, 166, 168, 175
need, 3, 7, 8, 15, 28, 32, 35–37, 39, 58–60, 62, 66, 70, 71, 74, 75, 78, 84, 92, 94, 97, 98, 103, 105, 106, 108, 109, 112, 115–117, 122, 126, 127, 129, 130, 133, 134, 137, 139–141, 149, 150, 154–160, 163, 164, 167, 168, 171, 173, 177
negotiations, 17, 96, 115, 154, 163
neo-functionalism, 22, 23
neo-Gramscian, 22, 24–26, 28
neoliberalism, 2, 22, 25, 26, 40, 89
non-bank, 62, 64, 67, 74, 80, 83, 116, 128, 145, 162
Non-Compliant, 122, 123
norms, 37–39, 42–44, 47, 84, 174

O

objectives, 38, 97, 119, 124, 129–131
obligation, 70, 96, 121, 127, 146
observance, 129, 130
offering, 8, 104, 105, 108–111, 115, 125–127, 131, 146, 175
officials, 5–7, 14, 16, 18, 45, 46, 73, 76, 78, 79, 91–93, 98, 100, 101, 103, 107–115, 118–120, 123, 124, 127, 131–133, 135, 138, 146, 165, 170, 175–178
oligarchy, 22, 29, 31–36
operational, 5, 7, 56, 83, 113, 151, 165
organization, 24, 25, 30, 37–39, 42–45, 73, 82, 83, 93, 104, 105, 112, 120, 162, 176, 177
overseas, 7, 8, 62, 77, 82, 98, 100, 101, 104, 109, 112, 175

P

package, 60–64, 66, 67, 150, 161, 165, 167
parliament, 2, 30, 67, 70, 72, 73, 76–78, 85, 150, 154, 156, 157, 159, 160, 167, 168, 170, 171, 175, 178
participation, 5, 97, 152, 159, 166, 168
parties, 16, 41, 42, 48, 49, 69, 70, 75, 78, 83, 91, 126, 133–135, 156, 158, 159, 168
path-dependent, 44
players, 16, 36, 57, 77, 85, 89, 95, 104, 106, 107, 109–112, 165, 168
policy, 1, 2, 5, 6, 8, 9, 15, 18, 21–26, 30, 32–36, 40, 42, 45, 61, 66, 69, 78, 85, 110, 132, 137, 138, 140, 141, 143, 146, 150, 152, 156, 164, 169, 175, 176
political, 1, 5, 9, 14, 15, 22–26, 28, 29, 31–37, 39–41, 47, 70, 78, 91, 150, 154, 158, 173, 178
portfolio, 1–7, 9, 14–18, 21, 25, 35, 36, 46, 55, 61, 63–65, 67, 75, 79, 80, 86, 89, 90, 96, 99–101, 103, 105, 108, 110, 111, 116, 118, 119, 121, 124, 127, 128, 132, 134–137, 140–143, 145, 146, 149, 151–157, 159–161, 167, 170, 171, 173, 175–178
postponement, 49, 56, 72, 73, 79
power, 2, 5, 14, 26–34, 36, 55–57, 60, 65, 68, 70, 72–76, 79–82, 84, 85, 89–96, 101, 104, 109, 112, 126, 139, 140, 143, 145, 146, 150, 154, 160, 168, 170, 175, 176
presidential, 18, 66, 72, 75, 150, 151, 153, 154, 156–158, 160–163, 176

principles, 2, 6, 105, 106, 121–123, 125, 127, 129, 130, 146
private, 24, 35, 36, 112, 168, 169
process, 2, 3, 6, 18, 21–25, 28, 29, 31–33, 36, 45, 66, 69, 72–74, 76, 79, 84, 86, 90, 93, 95, 96, 100, 103–106, 110, 111, 114, 126, 129, 132, 135, 138, 141, 145, 149–151, 153, 154, 156–164, 167–171, 175, 176, 178
products, 7, 8, 98, 103, 105, 108–110, 112, 116
protectionism, 3, 152
Protocol, 150, 151, 161–165, 168–170
public, 2, 6, 17, 26, 33, 34, 36, 45, 56, 66, 69, 72, 76, 92, 94, 101, 159

Q
qualitative, 16
quasi-autonomous, 30, 31, 36

R
ratification, 18, 94, 149, 150, 153–165, 167–171, 176
rational-choice, 37, 39, 43
reform, 33, 35, 47, 48, 55, 56, 58–64, 66–71, 73, 85, 130, 152, 162, 174, 175
regime, 1, 7–9, 14, 25, 26, 28, 36, 46, 57, 58, 62, 67, 91, 98, 100, 108–111, 113, 149, 173, 177
regional, 1–3, 6, 9, 14–18, 22, 23, 28–32, 45, 66, 82, 90, 95, 104, 109, 114, 115, 120, 121, 123, 125, 133, 138–140, 146, 149, 155, 166, 168, 170, 175, 177, 178
regionalism, 9, 15, 21, 22, 29, 31, 32, 49
regulatory, 2, 5, 7, 8, 14, 15, 22–24, 28–32, 47, 67, 70, 78, 81, 82, 90, 91, 98, 101, 105, 106, 108, 110–114, 119–125, 127, 129–131, 141, 143, 144, 146, 149, 150, 155, 159–161, 167, 171, 176
representatives, 17, 18, 72, 73, 76–78, 93, 135, 146, 149, 154, 158, 160, 161, 163–165, 167, 170
requirements, 24, 63, 72, 104, 106–108, 113, 126, 127, 154, 166
resolution, 101, 104, 129, 140
resources, 29, 30, 32, 80, 82, 93
restrictions, 8, 9, 59, 61, 62, 101, 110, 118, 126, 128, 132
review, 16, 17, 35, 49, 55, 83, 109, 110, 153
risk, 35, 67, 90, 101, 103, 104, 109, 111, 122, 123, 139, 143
rules, 30, 37–39, 43, 44, 47, 74, 109, 161

S
Secretariat, 16, 135, 141–143, 158, 164, 169
sector, 2, 4, 8, 14, 15, 17, 21, 27, 33–36, 38, 40, 55, 56, 60–63, 66–70, 72, 79, 80, 83, 85, 89–94, 113–119, 124, 130, 131, 135, 140, 146, 152, 165, 168, 169, 175, 176
securities, 5, 6, 30, 31, 69, 100, 101, 105, 109, 124–126
settlement, 5, 7, 75, 98, 101, 103, 110, 116, 133
sociological, 37, 38, 43

stability, 40, 71, 80, 90, 92, 94, 110, 114, 123, 125, 128, 133, 141–143, 178
stakeholders, 83, 92, 99
standards, 1, 2, 6, 8, 18, 24, 25, 30, 31, 35, 81, 89–91, 94, 105, 109–112, 119–125, 127, 129, 131, 146
state, 3–9, 15, 16, 22–31, 34–36, 43, 58, 59, 62, 69, 93, 109, 110, 113–115, 121, 163, 165, 167
strategic, 13, 14, 29, 97
structural, 3, 6, 7, 21, 26–29, 40, 42, 43, 46–49, 55, 56, 66, 67, 85, 90, 151, 174, 176
stymie, 2, 3, 6, 18, 21, 26, 36, 86, 89, 90, 96, 120, 145, 151, 170, 173, 175, 176, 178
supervision, 2, 4, 14, 17, 30, 35, 38, 44, 63, 68–80, 82, 83, 85, 91, 94, 95, 119, 128–131, 134, 143, 145, 160, 162, 175
supranational, 22, 23, 28, 29

T
technical, 97, 101, 104, 106, 108, 113, 114, 118, 127, 136, 137, 160, 161
term, 3, 5, 6, 26, 27, 38, 40, 46, 72, 91, 103, 107, 108, 114, 115, 118, 128, 138–140, 165, 174
trading, 3, 7, 8, 63, 75, 97, 98, 100, 101, 103–105, 108–110, 115, 127, 151–154
transactions, 5, 8, 9, 100, 103, 110, 116, 118, 128
transformation, 3, 22, 26, 28, 29, 31, 41, 48, 58
transition, 33, 49, 56, 68, 72, 79–85, 123, 174
transnational, 25, 26, 28, 30, 83

U
ultimate, 2, 3, 46, 82, 90, 95, 96, 99, 120, 121, 129, 133, 134, 137–139, 145, 158, 160, 164, 165, 173, 175, 178
unidirectional, 44
unified, 21, 23, 48, 69–71

V
variants, 37, 43, 46
venture, 62, 69
volatility, 64, 125
vulnerability, 58, 64

W
wealth, 32, 33, 35, 36

FSC
www.fsc.org
MIX
Papier | Fördert
gute Waldnutzung
FSC® C083411

Kolibri 360 GmbH
Ferdinand-Jühlke-Straße 7
99095 Erfurt, Deutschland
produktsicherheit@kolibri360.de